Lost & Found

Coming of Age
Coming Clean

J. Curtis Moran

Author's Note

You know this is a novel and therefore the characters are either pure fiction or a composite blend of real people no longer alive. No attempt is made to implicate or embarrass anyone.

Additionally, in order not to distract from the flow of the story, I have made every effort to accurately identify locations, travel times, and technologies. I had to revise some of the scenes when one of my characters reached for an iPhone before they existed!

I also invite you to look at the CREDITS at the conclusion of this story. As you read, maybe play some of the music I have referenced or enjoy a favorite beverage when my characters are thirsty or indulge. Along the way you will see an asterisk * when I have provided more information about that character or organization's background.

———□———

Contents

TERRI

————□————

————□————

RYAN

CHAPTER 1

The long summer twilight makes it difficult for 23-year-old Sean O'Brien to get his son settled into bed. After putting in a full week as an assistant carpenter at the University of Pennsylvania's Institute of Contemporary Art, he is tired. He tries to brush the irritating sawdust off his head and neck from the day's work, but the high humidity makes it stick. Freckle-faced and with reddish hair, father and son could enter a Philadelphia calendar contest for the Irish in America. Sean loves this bedtime ritual with his son. Terri, his partner of seven years, does not.

Where the Wild Things Are lies on Ryan's bed. A full-page illustration shows a "private boat for Max." Ryan asks, "Daddy, can I have a boat like his?" He springs out of bed and snuggles next to his dad on the frumpy, overstuffed chair in his room. Sean takes in a deep breath and smiles.

The next morning in their Kensington* rowhouse cellar, a power handsaw squeals as Sean makes a final angled cut on a scrap of two-by-four lumber. When Sean and Ryan leave the house a short time later, Terri is still upstairs. As she brushes her hair, she watches from the bedroom window. Seeing them holding hands, her face wells up with deep sorrow. Dropping the brush, she slaps herself to come back to the present. *Okay, Terri. Just cuz you didn't have a decent dad doesn't mean Ryan can't have one.*

Later that Saturday, father and son listen to the hissing, splashing sound of water falling on Wissahickon Creek as they walk beside it looking for a quieter place deeper in Fairmont

Park. When they find a spot, Sean gently grips the simple sailboat under his windbreaker, pulls it out, and attaches wood doweling and a white cloth sail. With his pant legs rolled up, he wades into the shallow creek and calls out, "Ready, Ry? Hold on."

Ryan holds the twine attached to the bobbling boat. The fluttering sail boasts a large, magic-marker R as the current and breeze pull the little boat across the creek. When a frog jumps on for a free ride, Sean exclaims, "Smart frog!"

Ryan adds, "Mom should see this."

Sean agrees thoughtfully. "Yes…that would be nice."

That same afternoon, Niko, a second-generation Greek American, has a guest in his tiny studio apartment. At 19, he might be too slim to be an Abercrombie model—handsome but more the boy next door with blue-green eyes and curly black hair. Naked, he dives onto his bed like a frog mating. His awaiting bed partner appreciates his prowess. Terri Gallagher, at 21, is experienced in these things. Her concealer doesn't quite hide her freckles and her blush doesn't give her youthful innocence. But her amber-hued eyes, Maybelline enhanced, are enticing and commanding, like a tigress.

She brushes Niko's chin with her long, bleached-blonde hair. Smirking with a secret laugh, she dominates him with more force than he expects. But he is happy to oblige. When he drifts asleep for a few moments, Terri studies him. Niko startles when he wakes up and sees her staring. Leaning over to see the clock (it's a little after four), he murmurs, "Work."

On the chair next to his bed are neatly folded black slacks, a white server's shirt, and a black bow tie. Before he squirms away to get dressed, Terri pinches him on the butt with a teasing smile. He winces but smiles back.

"You are really fun."

She answers, "Yep. You're not bad yourself. When can we do this again?"

Sean and Ryan walk from the trolley stop on Allegheny Avenue. The once-proud working-class neighborhood is now derelict, blighted with rundown businesses and abandoned manufacturing and warehouse buildings. Graffiti scars everything. Sean holds Ryan's free hand while his son clutches the little boat, his trophy.

They come around the corner to their street. A few of the red-brick rowhouses sport window boxes and scarlet-red geraniums. Some residents take pride in their neighborhood. So does Sean. His front door is painted a shade of red to match the flowers.

He sees Terri approaching from the opposite direction. Terri's eyes squint.

All three are silent as they enter their home together and walk through the front room toward the kitchen in the back.

Sean looks puzzled. "Work?"

Terri says tersely, "Change of schedule."

Hesitating, Sean takes a deep breath, pressing for a better answer. "You wore a dress—*that* dress—to work?"

The cut of the emerald-green dress shows off her natural endowments and is clearly more appropriate for evening, not the diner where she works. Terri mumbles something but gives no further explanation.

Ryan interrupts, "I'm hungry."

Sean is distracted but tries to stay cheerful in front of his son. "Can we talk later?" Turning to Ryan, he says, "How 'bout a pretzel, Sailor Boy?"

Ryan nods in approval but trudges out of the kitchen.

In their bedroom that evening, Terri is sullen, lost in thought, no longer wearing the dress and now in faded, ripped jeans and an old Philly Eagles sweatshirt. She stares out the window as if entranced by the glare of the streetlight. Sean wonders where her thoughts have gone. They certainly are not with him.

She avoids eye contact as she undresses for bed with her back to Sean. When she fumbles to unhook her bra, he reaches to assist her and notices a curl of black hair on the strap.

Terri snaps, "I don't need no help."

Sean grabs the curl and turns away, not letting her see what he found, holding it like a match in the wind. With a pained look on his face, he studies the evidence. When he looks up, Terri is watching him in the wall mirror.

Sean asks in earnest, "Is there something I needa know?" He shows her his hand.

Terri retorts, "Well, it's not yours…or mine. So?"

Sean shrugs his shoulders and attempts a brave smile. "Sometimes I think I can't be the man you really want. You used to tell me I was. Are you bored with me?" He approaches her with open arms but Terri tenses and barely tolerates his hug.

"What if I am? It used to be fun, like you were in charge, maybe trying to prove somethin'. Now I don't know."

"But I know you wanted to get away from your family. You never let me ask about what happened. It's always been off limits."

Terri backs away. "Lemme just say, my mother was a drunk and—and my fa—" She hesitates. "It doesn't matter now! Okay? We're tryin' to have this perfect little family. But you don't need me. You just keep him all ta yourself. It's Ryan, Ryan, Ryan. Well, fuck Ryan! Fuck you!" Looking away, she adds, "He's suppose ta be mine too, ya know."

Sean is speechless but the pain in his gut shows on his face.

CHAPTER 2

In the fenced play yard of Cramp's Grade School, Ryan's first-grade teacher checks off the names of arriving students. After giving Ryan a perfunctory hug, Terri adds a swat on his behind for good measure. He jumps but smiles at the attention.

The teacher's smile turns to a scowl but Terri couldn't care less about what she thinks and quickly leaves. Ryan clutches the iron fence. Like an innocent prisoner, he presses his face against the bars as he watches his mother walk up the street.

After school, Ryan waits in the schoolyard, trudging back and forth, looking through the fence for his dad, dispirited, until he sees Sean about half a block away. Ryan breaks into a run to greet him. Sean grabs Ryan's Air Jordan backpack, drapes it over his shoulder, and holds Ryan's hand as they begin to walk.

"Sorry I'm late. It took longer to wrap up today's job. But I have a project for you at Angelo's."

A short time later, they arrive at an old-style Italian neighborhood market that features imported pastas and sauces. Sean climbs a ladder and adjusts a light fixture for a display. Ryan fetches a spotlight bulb and proudly hands it up to his dad. That task complete, Sean steps down from the ladder and hugs Ryan like a junior partner, more man-to-man than affectionate, and hands him a dollar for his work.

Angelo is old enough to be Ryan's grandpa—if he were lucky enough to have one. Wearing a military-style twill cap with *ANGELO'S* embroidered over an Italian flag logo, and an American flag pin on the right side, Angelo's robust personality matches his bushy black eyebrows and radiant smile.

Ryan notices a large candy jar on the counter and points to one of the foil-wrapped Italian chocolates. They cost more than a dollar.

"That's-a just enough," Angelo says. "You come back, Ryan. There's-a more jobs for you."

Sean nods with respect. "Thanks, Angelo, for what you do for the neighborhood. For me. For Ryan."

Life is routine for Ryan—school, home, school, home. But months later, he gets to go to a basketball game with his dad and his dad's German friend from work. Heinrich Schneider, at 25, is slender and muscular in an athletic way. His thick, waist-length hair, held back with a scrap of leather, is the envy of any woman who wished she could have been a natural-born blonde.

In Philadelphia's Sports Arena, a cheering crowd introduces the Washington Wizards and even if Michael Jordan is playing against the Philadelphia 76ers in his last game, they are out-of-bounds crazy for him. Ryan bounces in delight to be at such an important event with his dad and Heinrich.

Heinrich has a real, old-style camera across his chest. "*Es ist eine Leica,*" he says with pride. When everyone cheers with a standing ovation for Michael's final free throw, Sean lifts Ryan onto his shoulders so he can see. Heinrich angles his camera to capture the perfect father-son photo.

That night, Sean tucks his son into bed and kisses him on the cheek. He takes off his red 76ers cap and gently crowns Ryan. Lost under the cap, Ryan's smile beams from under the bill. It is the perfect end to his day. Sean turns off the bedside lamp.

Terri, restless and unable to sleep, takes two Vicodin with a sip of water and hides the bottle under her side of the bed. Hearing Sean's footsteps as he approaches, she pretends to be asleep and lies facing away from him. Sean wears only a white T-shirt and slides into bed, gently reaching one arm over her. She shrugs away from him. He pauses, then kisses her on the head and moves to his side of the bed. Worry more than disappointment creases his brow.

The next Friday, Heinrich asks Sean to meet after work for happy hour at New Deck Tavern. Just a few minutes from the Institute, they sit across from each other in the back of the famous Irish pub. A poster proclaims, *Guinness is good for you—Gives You Strength.*

Heinrich holds his beer with both hands to take off the chill. "They serve it too cold," he says with authority. Sean looks into his own beer for an answer. Without a word, he glances up at Heinrich. When their eyes meet, Heinrich assures Sean, "*Du bist mein Freund.*" [You are my friend.] "You can tell me any— oh! I almost forgot. I have something for you."

From his vest pocket, he pulls out photos of Sean with Ryan on his shoulders, two of the same shot. Sean crumples. Heinrich is puzzled but lets him quietly sob while the tavern's patrons pay no attention.

The next Monday after school, at home with Ryan, Sean heats an iron frying pan to make melted cheese sandwiches. Ryan studies his every move, then, eyes crinkling, asks, "Are you mad at me?"

"Oh…no, Ry. It's just that I have a lot on my mind. Nana said we could come visit her. We can't dillydally."

Ryan smiles at the idea of a surprise visit to Grandma's.

After cleaning up the kitchen, Sean rushes upstairs. He hurries to unzip a canvas suitcase on Ryan's bed and crams his son's everyday clothes, underwear, and school supplies into it. Quickly testing the top of the now-bulging bag, he finds room to nestle in the sailboat as well. Anxiety flushes his face as he looks around the room for anything else. When Sean hears the front door creak open, he panics and glances at his own suitcase in the doorway.

Terri appears and towers over his suitcase, hands on her hips. "Leaving so soon?"

Sean rushes for the door with Ryan's bag, and grabbing his own, pushes Terri aside.

Ryan looks at his mother, confused.

Sean drops Ryan's bag and reaches for his son's hand. In a flash, Terri grabs the bag and storms back into the bedroom. Ryan's eyes are fixed on her as she unzips it and dumps its contents onto the bed. She tosses the sailboat to the floor, breaking off the doweling and sail, then snatches up the two-by-four hull and hurls it at Sean. He ducks and lets go of Ryan's hand.

Startled and with wide eyes, Ryan stands paralyzed as he watches his father turn and rush down the hallway. He winces as the front door slams.

Across the street, Wanda Kozlowski, wearing a dark polka-dotted headscarf, scrubs her already spotless porch steps. She looks like an immigrant from an Eastern Bloc country and another century. She sees Sean flee, suitcase in hand, and watches intently, shaking her head in disapproval. Then slowly, she blesses herself with the sign of the cross.

CHAPTER 3

Terri drops off Ryan at school the next day, giving him a heartfelt hug and his favorite fruit leather snack. Ryan is surprised by the extra treat and hugs her back. The schoolyard attendant nods to Terri as she checks off Ryan's name. Sean usually takes Ryan to school and Terri picks him up but it all depends on her changing work schedule.

Terri ambles homeward and passes a breakfast diner. She decides to go in and takes an open stool at the counter near the front.

The waitress greets her with coffee pot in hand. "Coffee fer ya, hon? Haven't seen you before."

"Nope. I'm usually asleep at this hour. I'm tryin' out this single parent thing. Dropped off the boy and I go to work later."

"Oh, yeah. I know about that. So do my two regalars here, Marcie and Josie."

Marcie, heavier than she might have been in her thirties and with solid streaks of gray, turns to greet Terri. She smiles like an older factory worker welcoming a newbie to the most boring job in the plant, but it is a genuine welcome nonetheless. Without interrupting the flow of a budding conversation, the waitress slides a menu over to Terri.

"So, he's been cheatin' on ya?" Marcie asks in such a matter-of-fact tone that Terri's mouth drops. "Or yer jis done with 'im?"

Josie jumps in to give Terri a chance to consider her friend's candid questions. Impulsively, swiping her very red hair over her right ear, she smirks a little as she leans in to listen better, hoping for some juicy gossip.

Terri is uncomfortable with an audience. She stalls, "Are we on a talk show?"

Josie snickers in delight.

"Yeah, kinda..." Marcie assures her. "But we're friends here. We've heard it all—"

Josie adds, "And done some of it too!"

Terri sits taller and considers just where to start. "I really didn't want to get a man in my life. I just figured having a kid would be the fastest way out of a shitty family situation. It worked. But my man is so boring. So, you'd say I'm done with 'im."

Josie solves her problem. "Well, drop 'im. Get child support. Then you have the best of both—you know, if he actually comes through with the money."

Terri's pupils focus. Looking into the mirror she hadn't noticed until now, she is surprised to see herself smile. She turns back to Marcie and Josie. "So, how does that work?"

The waitress comes back. "I see you've made it this far with our resident advisors. Did they tell you what the special of the day is?" Topping off the coffee, she waits for Terri.

"Yes. I'll have the dump-your-man deal with a kid on the side." With a wry smile, Terri adds, "And scrapple* with fried eggs. Sunnyside up." She sips her coffee and takes in a deep breath, then looks to her new companions. "I sure didn't expect my morning to turn out like this. Thanks."

That afternoon, Terri heads back to Ryan's school. He is waiting right where she left him that morning. "How'd yer day go?"

"Where's Dad?"

"Whaddya mean?"

"A lady today was asking me all kinds of questions about Dad. Where is he? Are you still mad at him?"

They stand against the torrent of kids rushing to meet their parents or older siblings. Terri grabs Ryan's hand but he doesn't budge.

"Where's Dad?"

Terri is losing patience. "Work, I 'spect. Now, let's get goin'."

———□———

That same afternoon at the Institute of Art, Sean sits on a sturdy plastic milk crate, thinking.

Heinrich leans over to him, and in a confidential voice asks, "Vhat's on your mind, buddy? You look kaput. You're keeping some secret to yourself. Should I ask?"

"I am kaput. I left Terri. And I don't know what to do about Ry. I stayed at my mom's. On her couch. Didn't sleep. Other than that," he chuckles, "I'm just fine."

Heinrich ignores the attempt at humor. "You can stay with me. Ryan too. For a while."

Barely breathing and closing his eyes for a moment, Sean answers, "That's very kind of you, Heinrich. Let me sort this out. Right now, I want to see my boy. It was pretty scary for him. And me. I can't leave my Ryan."

"Vell, take him; he's yours. And Terri—*Sie ist keine gute Mutter.*"

Sean looks puzzled.

"She's not a good mother," Heinrich clarifies. Trying to think of what to say next, Heinrich remains silent for a while. Finally, he adds, "If you need to talk to me, call. I don't think you have my home number, and I don't have a Nokia. Yet."

"A nooky?"

"Nooo… It's a portable phone from Finland. Anyvay, I'll give you my number." Using his utility knife, he cuts out a square of pasteboard, writes quickly, and gently slides it into Sean's chest pocket. "Otherwise, see you tomorrow."

Sean spends another night at his mother's. At work the next day with Heinrich, he keeps to himself and just listens to his own music from an old, duct-taped Sony Walkman on his belt, the earphone cord dangling. Heinrich respects his solitude. Late in the afternoon, Sean asks Heinrich if he can leave work a little early. It's clear he's a man on a mission.

After the familiar trip on the El and the trolley to his home—his *former* home—Sean resumes listening to his inspiration. He strides with purpose toward his street. He cranks up the volume, listening to Eminem's "Just The Two of Us," but when he turns his key in the lock, the extra deadbolt Terri installed keeps the door from budging. He bangs on the red door.

Ryan runs up to the window, stunned. Terri slides in beside their son and snuggles next to him.

Sean, trying not to yell, calls out loud enough to be heard down the street. "Hey! Open up!" He hesitates before adding spitefully, "You don't want him."

Terri retorts, "And you do? Don't worry, I'll get custody." Nudging Ryan away, she yanks down the window shade.

The music of Eminem takes over, takes control of Sean. Propping open the storm door, eyes squinting, and breathing like a bull, he takes a breath. Eminem continues in his headset and Sean yells, "He's all I have! Nobody's gonna—"

He smashes his shoulder against the door once, twice. Breaking the doorjamb, he charges through, then chases after

Terri as she runs into the kitchen. Ryan crouches in the corner and doesn't move or speak, terrified to see his father so angry.

Sean grabs Terri by the arm. She breaks away and slaps him across the face hard enough to leave a mark. He shoves her through the kitchen doorway but she slips and hits her face against the doorjamb. She is bleeding and Sean's face is flushed. He sweeps Ryan into his arms and bolts out the front door.

Wanda watches the disturbance from her doorstep. With resolve on her face, she runs inside. Within the hour, a police car turns onto Ryan's street and parks in front of Terri's house. The Crown Victoria's lights stop flashing and in a few moments, two cops get out. The lace curtains shift inside Wanda's front room as she watches the officers approach the address, glancing down the street as they walk toward the front door.

When the lead officer sees Terri's splintered doorjamb, he nods to his partner, Collins. "Forced entry, ya think?" In a reflexive, half-complete gesture, he puts his hand on his gun.

Terri tugs open the door. Despite her bruised face, she gives the officer a nervous but beguiling smile. He pauses. A question of recognition creases his forehead, followed by a facial twitch. He clears his throat and asks in a professional manner, "Are you okay?"

"Do youse guys needa come in?"

"Ah, yes, ma'am. That'd help." Stepping into the front room, he continues, "I'm Officer Brennan. This here is Officer Collins. You're Terri Gallagher?"

"Yep. Terri Gallagher. Terri with an *i*."

Brennan asks, "Is now a good time to talk to us?"

She nods. Then, suddenly impatient, she bursts out, "You needa keep him from coming here!" She nods to the damaged door and demands, "I want my son back!"

Taking a breath and gathering his thoughts, and not to be intimidated, Brennan measures out his words. "Okay. Is your son okay? Where is he right now?" Letting Terri take in what he's asking, he continues, "Ya know we're here to help, okay? You can tell us what happened…" In a calm, close-to-his-body gesture, Officer Brennan reaches for his pocket notebook. But Terri focuses on the Glock 22 while the younger officer studies her.

Looking at her facial bruises, Brennan states, "You've suffered injuries. What about your son? Is he safe?"

"I think so. He's with his father. He treats him like his little pet. It's weird. I'm guessing they're at his mother's. Margaret O'Brien."

"Do you have her phone number?" Brennan asks.

"Yeah. I'll get it."

When the officers begin to leave, Terri stands just inside her front door.

Officer Collins asks without it being a question, "You're gonna get that fixed…"

Terri, momentarily annoyed with the reminder of the intrusion, smiles in appreciation.

Officer Brennan looks away. Once in the cruiser and looking distracted, he turns on the ignition—until Collins points across the street to Wanda's. "Right. Thanks," Brennan says.

This time, Collins is the first to approach the home. Without delay, Wanda opens the front door and cautiously welcomes them in, as if they are distant family she hasn't seen in years but nonetheless expects them to come for dinner.

CHAPTER 4

Margaret O'Brien paces from her eating area to her living room to her bedroom and back again. She digs out a set of blankets from a chest in her bedroom, pulls a spare pillow off her bed, and plops them on the couch. The pillow brushes against her latest issue of *Maryknoll** magazine—"Stories of God's mission work across the globe." It falls from the sofa table to the floor. Margaret stoops to pick it up, then looks up to her collection of wall photos, her shrine for the men in her life. Declan O'Brien, her father at 47, was handsome in his lieutenant colonel uniform. The photo was taken several months before he accepted a consulting assignment with the CIA in Lebanon. It was his last before he was killed in the 1983 Beirut Embassy bombing.

Next to Declan's photo in a matching ebony frame is Margaret and Rowen's marriage photo, with Rowen also in uniform. Like his father, Rowen died doing undercover assignments, working with a Special Forces unit in El Salvador. His ambition was to become a Green Beret. In a second photo, however, he looks like a shaggy-haired American college student with his unmistakable red hair. Following the assassination of Archbishop Romero, he attended the funeral service in the village square where, along with over 40 others, he was massacred. The bishop's photo and a crucifix with the risen Christ complete Margaret's homage to her heroes.*

"Okay, men, what the hell am I supposed to do here? And you, Rowen O'Brien. May I still call you Row-B after all these years?" she says to the photographs.

Her cozy couch is perfect for an afternoon nap and okay for a soon-to-be-seven-year-old's sleepover at Grandma's. But the loveseat's length is not meant for a good night's rest. *Sean can have my bed again, and Ryan can sleep with him.* Thinking out loud, she adds, "I'll take the couch." *But what am I gonna feed 'em?*

Hoping maybe the refrigerator will speak to her, she walks to it and opens it just wide enough to confirm what she already knows: leftover steamed vegetables and rice, and lettuce in the crisper drawer. The freezer contains frozen vegetables, one Amy's General Tso's Bowl, and three little cups of Breyers Natural Vanilla ice cream. Laughing at her limited stock, she sputters, "What more do I need?"

The kitchen phone rings again. It's not Sean, it's not Terri.

"Good evening. Is this Margaret O'Brien?"

Margaret nods but fails to speak for several seconds.

"Hello?"

"Um, yes. I'm Margaret."

"I'm Miriam from Childhelp.* We're just checking in to make sure Ryan is okay. You're his grandmother, right?"

Her eyebrows pull together. "How do you know all this? Who are you?"

"Childhelp is part of Human Services here in Philly. Terri Gallagher was concerned and—"

Margaret's doorbell rings.

"Excuse me but my… I have to go now. Bye."

Margaret presses the button to release the lock on the main door of the building, then opens the door to her apartment with a scowl. Waiting with a withering glare, she hears Ryan stomping his way up the stairs, puts her hand over her lips, and shakes her head. Giving herself a quick pep talk, she whispers, "Come on, Marg," and gently goes down on one knee like she's genuflecting in church, waiting mere moments before Ryan comes running into her open arms.

"Nana! Daddy gets to stay with us too!" he enthuses, and as he announces his good news, Sean peeks around the landing, a sheepish smile trying to brighten his sad face.

Margaret hugs Ryan with a firm grip. She tries to pick him up but reconsiders. "You're getting to be a big boy now, a little too heavy for me to lift like a bag of groceries." Then to Sean, "Speaking of groceries...I don't have—"

He lifts a pizza box like a peace offering, "I brought dinner."

She smiles weakly. "You're so thoughtful."

But Sean turns his face away.

As they walk into Margaret's apartment, Sean says, "Thank you, Mom. This is difficult for me. And confusing for Ryan."

But right now, Ryan is happy to head over to his toy box in the corner of the living room. He digs through his just-at-gramma's toys. His current favorite: Geomag's multi-colored magnetic rods and steel spheres. After several minutes of quiet play, he assembles a triangle, then another one, then another, and interlocks all three. He takes his creation to his dad. Sean admires it with a smile and nods for him to return to his activities so he and Margaret can talk.

"Looks like he's made a little family," Margaret smiles. "Oh, I'm sorry."

Sean doesn't say anything for a few moments.

"Families aren't what they used to be—or at least what we like to believe they were," he finally says. "There weren't three of us."

"Yes, that's the problem with patriots. They feel compelled to serve a purpose greater than themselves, even willing—"

Cutting into his mother's staunch devotion, Sean says, "Willing to die for their country...even when it means leaving behind a wife to raise a kid by herself. A kid with no dad. I guess that really is patriotism. But it sucks."

Margaret, suddenly saddened, looks away from Sean and simply closes her mouth. Cocking her head, she suddenly remembers. "Childhelp—or something—Services called."

"Uh-oh."

"After dinner, we can talk."

Sean is distracted but sets the table while Margaret gently places an oversized salad bowl in the middle of the small table. She divides slices of the plain cheese pizza onto three plates and puts the remainder in the oven to keep warm.

"Okay, favorite grandson," Margaret calls to Ryan.

Sean teases, "You have another one I don't know about?"

Margaret offers a tight smile at Sean's effort at humor. "Okay, Sean. Grace."

He exhales with a quiet but reluctant, resigned look.

Again, Margaret calls over to Ryan.

He scampers to the table with a Geomag toy—this time, a triangle on a square. "It's your house."

"And since it's my house, we say grace before dinner, right Sean?"

It is not a question, of course.

After an uncomfortably quiet dinner, Sean tucks Ryan into Margaret's bed and tells him there's no story that night. It's late and he and Grandma need to talk. Ryan does not fuss and understands there is no negotiating. And he is tired.

Sean returns to the dining area and takes a seat across from his mom. With a sigh, he braces himself for the impending conversation and asks, "So, what about that call from children's whatever?"

"Child Protective Services." Changing the subject, she continues with her own thoughts. "It sure would be nice if

Ryan could go to a Catholic school. I think I failed you by letting you go to that public high school."

Sean looks puzzled. *What is she talking about?*

Reluctant to return to the present, Margaret reflects, "All I know is that Terri must have called them. Or a neighbor, maybe?"

"Yeah. I get along so well with Ryan, I think Terri's jealous."

"She's kinda distant. Not very warm. I don't think she had a good family life herself. She's trying to figure it out and is way too proud—I hope you don't mind my sayin'—way too proud to admit she doesn't know what to do. May I ask…" Clearing her throat, she hesitates. "Why did you marry? I mean…"

"Okay. Basically, I was totally taken by her. I was 16 and…well, it was the way she paid attention to me. And her sexuality. And I thought she needed me. I wasn't counting on a kid. We weren't even out of high school! But she saw pregnancy as an escape from her…what do they call it? *Dysfunctional family.* She told me I was different from the other men in her life. Of course, she was only 14. But now, I don't… Now I don't think I'm…" Sean stops in mid-thought. *I'm not enough fun.*

Margaret leaves the silence alone so he can unburden himself if he needs to. After a minute of quiet, she recalls, "Well, when you and Terri were here at Christmas, I could see she was kind of stiff with Ryan, like he was not really hers. Or maybe she was just uncomfortable around me. Anyway, you should know that I think you are a great dad." She takes in a small breath to add something more but stops.

"Thanks. What I'm really concerned about is how she and I, living apart, are going to deal with Ryan's day-to-day school. And I don't even know where I'm going to live. I know you don't have room here."

Margaret does not interrupt or protest. She waits, then

adds, "Sooo, if Child Protective calls me again, what should I say?"

"Tell them the truth," he says, and adding a sly smile, "You're good at that." Suddenly, her forehead shows a question. Was that a compliment or an insult?

"So…tell them I'm a good dad and Terri and I are just working it out? Actually, I don't know how single parents do it… Wait. You did it." Sean drops his head into his hands for several moments.

Margaret reaches over and strokes his head like she used to when he was a boy.

Just as he looks like he's about to cry, Sean stops himself with a few deep breaths. Slowly rising, he says, "I'd better get to bed. Thanks again, Mom."

Sean takes Ryan to school, which is more of a trek than he anticipated—over an hour with half of that time lugging Ryan's school things from the subway-surface trolley, then to the El and another trolley to his school in Kensington.

In the schoolyard, Sean hugs his son for an extra-long time, to the point that Ryan squirms. "Now, Nana is going to pick you up right here after school, like we talked about. Okay?"

Ryan nods.

At the appointed time, Margaret does indeed wait for Ryan at the exact spot. And Ryan greets her with a big smile. Not seeing Terri, who is half a block away, Margaret holds Ryan's hand as they head for the K&A trolley, Ryan springing up and down as they walk.

Terri sees them and frowns, her eyes squinting. Frustrated and disappointed, she stops in her tracks to decide what she should do.

Margaret and Ryan make the last leg of their journey home. His earlier enthusiasm diminishes with each step up Gramma's stairs.

"You need a good snack, my boy. I've made you your favorite—blueberry-walnut muffins."

Once settled in at the table, and with a glass of milk and blueberry juice staining his face, Ryan lunges into another bite. The phone rings. Margaret winces and hesitates, but gets up and answers it. "Okay, we'll be ready," she says. She hangs up and turns to Ryan. "That was your dad. Tonight, you get to stay at his friend's house. He says you know him. The man with the camera. Heinrich, I think."

"Yes, he's very nice. He likes my dad. We even went to Michael Jordan's last game."

"Well, you'll get your own bed. We'd better get all your things together. And wipe up your face. You look like you crashed into a giant blueberry."

Sean arrives in a few minutes, retrieves his suitcase, and grabs Ryan's bag in his other hand. Margaret hugs both of them like they're in a huddle. Looking at Ryan but speaking to both of them, she says, "You come back soon." To Sean, she gives an encouraging wink. "I assume Heinrich is circling the neighborhood."

"Yep. Thank you for your understanding."

With a faint smile and a nearly silent shushing sound, she accepts his gratitude.

Once Ryan and Sean are gone, Margaret goes back inside and collapses onto her couch, only to see Ryan's school things. Grabbing his Jordan backpack, she dashes out the door and down the hall, leaps down the stairs, and catches them just in time as they're getting into Heinrich's car. As they pull away, she waves goodbye.

Margaret heads back to her apartment and realizes that she is locked out of her building. "Damn! No good deed goes unpunished." She waits for a few minutes. *One of my neighbors is sure to arrive home soon.*

Within five or six minutes, her upstairs neighbor, Mr. Girard, approaches carrying a bag of groceries from Di Bruno Bros. He greets her with a smile.

"Margaret. Good evening. You're waiting for your ride?"

"Nooo. I left my keys in my apartment when I made a mad dash to give my grandson his schoolbag."

"Well then, please join me for a sip of wine. I've been meaning to ask you up for ages."

"Oh, no. But thank you, Mr. Girard."

His face falls and he looks down, but he recovers quickly and carefully extracts his prize wine of the day from a bag within his grocery bag. He proclaims like he's telling a secret, "It's a *Vietti Barbera D'Asti Tre Vigne.*"

Margaret looks puzzled, hearing what might be an Italian wine pronounced with a vaguely French accent. But she smiles. "What am I saying? Of course, I should try that one." And she adds, "I have no idea what that wine is, but I do believe you are a gentleman."

He leads the way and unlocks the front door but with his arms full of groceries, lets Margaret pull it open for him.

She goes into her apartment and grabs her keys, not noticing the answering machine's flashing red message light. Rejoining her neighbor, who is heading up the stairs, a wave of anxiety briefly flushes her face. Drawing in a silent, deep breath, she smiles as she enters Mr. Girard's place.

Their conversation is as light and refreshing as the wine itself. Yes, his name is the same as the bank—but without the money, he says. Yes, she is Catholic and yes, she was married to an Army man, Margaret says. Both lie about being happy as singles and they agree to meet again another time.

Feeling a bit tipsy after a single glass, Margaret holds the railing as she goes back down the stairs to her apartment. Now she can relax—until she notices the answering machine in the hallway by the bedroom. Clicking the playback key, she hears the simple message: "Margaret O'Brien? This is Miriam of Childhelp. Please call us immediately at 1-800-4-A-CHILD."

Margaret goes over to the couch and sinks slowly into the cushions. Gathering her strength, she returns the call.

"Kidnapped? Oh, no, no, no. He's with his father... No, they're not here. They are with a friend—actually, his boss. He has more space for my son and Ryan to stay. Sean is a very caring father... Oh, no, I don't actually have a phone number for them. Damn! I shoulda thoughta that. I'm sorry... I didn't think this was going to get so messy."

Margaret listens. Then she jots down Miriam's local phone and a case number next to that. She volunteers, "These parents should be communicating better, don't you think?" *Should I call Terri?* she thinks. "Well, thank you, Miriam... And you have a good evening too."

Walking to the living area, then back to the hallway, she encourages herself out loud, "Brace yourself, Marg..." *On second thought, I shouldn't call. I don't want to complicate things.* "I am the mother-in-law after all... And to think I said no to a second glass. And an Alfredo dinner!"

CHAPTER 5

Terri waits, pacing in the schoolyard. The first morning bell has already rung and there is no sign of Ryan. *He's late again…* she worries. *Or has Sean kidnapped my Ryan?*

Finally, Sean and Ryan come running up the sidewalk in a father-son race. Terri does not cheer the winning boy when they screech to a halt in front of her. She glares at Sean. Neither wishes to speak, but Terri stoops down to give Ryan a hug. Sean then hands Ryan's backpack to her.

She asserts, "I'll pick him up after school. You can leave your mother out of this."

"But I have plans with Ryan for the weekend."

"Well, do something with Kraut-Rick."

The bell rings again.

"It's Heinrich," Sean mumbles.

Terri wastes no time getting Ryan to the door. Sean just stands there looking like he's been hit on the head and needs to recover. He trudges off toward the trolley.

When he arrives late at his job at the ICA, Heinrich greets him with a wary smile and a warning wink. "They're here to talk to you," he says, nodding toward a waiting area. He tries to reassure Sean, "I told them you are a kind and loving dad. And somehow, they know you and Ryan are staying with me. Vhat you think of that? The *Stasi* is back."

"What are you talking about? Who's back?"

"It's a yoke: East German Secret Police. Anyvay, the two women asked me about you. And Ryan. And me too. They think you might hurt Terri some more—that you're violent, you beat her! I said 'No, no, if anything he is too kind.' I also said you were the better parent. But I got the feeling they don't trust me because I'm your boss—and I'm a man. They are vaiting for you. Don't worry. Take your time."

"I'm so sorry for the interrogation." Slumping away, Sean adds, "Thanks, Heinrich."

Half an hour later, Sean returns to clock in and Heinrich gives him the look of "tell me, dude." But Sean doesn't want to talk. "It's just what you said," is all he can muster at the moment.

———▢———

Terri heats up macaroni and cheese and tries to get Ryan to tell her about his day.

Ryan says, "Ben Franklin has a heart you can see inside."

Looking puzzled, Terri thinks, then counters, "Um…you mean the museum? The Franklin Institute? It's expensive but that would be nice. I never got to go there. Let's do that for your birthday."

With a quiet whine, Ryan calculates, "But that's a long time from now—that's a whole month away."

The microwave beeps and Terri turns to her dinner duties.

A few minutes later, at the table with Ryan, who is now gulping down his first bites, Terri again leads the conversation. "I didn't get to ask you how it worked out at Nana's house last night."

"We didn't sleep there last night," Ryan replies. "There wasn't room at her house. She had to sleep on the couch and Dad and I slept in her bed. That's why we moved to Heinrich's. It was very nice. They slept in his bed and I got the couch."

Terri furrows her brow, puzzled, then thinks for a moment and finally reassures Ryan with a smile, "Well, you have your own bed here. And your own room."

"So, for my birthday, do we get to go to the big heart?"

"We'll see. If you're good."

His nose wrinkles like he smells something off.

The next morning, Sean shows up a little after 8:00 and suspecting Terri may still be asleep, gently knocks on the door. Ryan comes to the front room and peeks out the window. He looks happy but puzzled to see his father with a soccer ball. Not sure whether he should open the door this time, he dashes upstairs to ask Terri for permission. Within a minute she appears in the window, glaring.

"Go away. I'm filing a PFA," she sneers.

Sean jerks his head like he's dodging a ball whizzing by. "A what?"

Terri yells through the closed window, "Protection from abuse!"

He shakes his head, stunned and confused. "Would Ryan like to go to Lighthouse Field?" He holds up the soccer ball as proof of his intentions but Terri just scoffs and pulls the shade down.

Sean backs down the steps and starts to head toward his bus, then stops midstride. Turning back, he notices his geraniums are wilted. He slowly lumbers toward Angelo's Market. It is two days past garbage pick-up day but the bin is still on the narrow sidewalk. Going out of his way, he gives the can a solid kick as he passes by. Across the street, Wanda's curtain ruffles. Sean gives a sad shrug.

At Angelo's, there are only a few Saturday morning shoppers. They either know exactly what they need or wander around, shopping baskets in hand or pushing compact carts, trying to plan a dinner menu. Angelo is at the register finishing a transaction. Seeing Sean, his face momentarily brightens even more than it was for his customer. He glances at the soccer ball and speculates, "Lose the game? Something's gone kerflooey!"

Sean looks blank. Angelo studies him but is interrupted by another customer ready to check out. He reassures Sean, "My guy will be here in just a few minutes."

Sean nods and takes to meandering through the tidied-up store. He checks the light that he and Ryan replaced just a few weeks ago. A short time later, Angelo finds Sean in the oil-and-vinegar aisle.

"So, tell me, my man, what's-a up?" he says, but he doesn't stop walking toward his backroom office. He motions to Sean. "It's-a more private."

Sean follows him and once inside, Angelo closes the door. He picks up his earlier question, "Soccer? I didn't know you played."

"I don't. I mean, I want to play with my son. My boss—well, actually, he's my friend—he plays a couple times a week. He loaned me his ball so I could take Ryan, to see if maybe he would like it." He is short of breath and stops.

Angelo takes a breath as if for both of them. "There's-a more to all this, right? Take a seat." Angelo drops his head into his hands, thinking, but then looks up from his desk without an answer. "What's going on with Ryan?"

"I think I'm losing him. Both Terri and him. I don't know what I did wrong. I thought I was a good dad. But Terri wants to keep him all to herself. It's like she's jealous. And…and…and she's telling me she's calling for protection from abuse. I think it's like a restraining order." His mouth drops open. He's not sure what more to say.

Angelo covers his mouth, thinking, letting Sean's words sink in. Finally, he says, "You know, Sean, I could only wish for a man like you to be my own son. And I wish Ryan could be my grandson. I'm concerned for you both."

Sean settles back a little into the chair and whispers, "I know."

"But it looks like your Terri wants her own way and you-a be damned. The biggest trouble with parents splitting up..." He shakes his head. "...is what happens to the kids—like bocce balls getting banged around. I see it with some of my customers playing games against their exes—their kids bounce from one house to another. Or worse, it's like a hostage exchange." Pausing again, he adds, "I dunno what-a tell you..."

"I think Terri wants to fight—like to get even. I just don't want to hurt Ryan in her warfare with me. If I go for custody, who wins anyway, really?"

Angelo nods in vague understanding as a devoted fan might assure an athlete after losing a match. Then, trying to make the best of things, he asks, "What about visitation rights?"

"I don't know. If it goes like this morning..." Trying to keep himself from crying, Sean chokes, "I'd best...be...going..."

But before he can leave, Angelo jumps up, crouches next to Sean, looks up at him, and silently clutches Sean's knee.

Sean takes a few breaths. "Thank you, Angelo."

At the bottom of the stairs, barely controlling her irritation, Terri calls again, "Ryan! Come out now. Enough-a this." But there is no answer.

Ryan sits in the big chair in his room turning the pages of a well-worn copy of *Grimm's Tales for Young and Old*. He's in the "Hansel and Gretel" chapter and although he can recognize only a few words, he isn't really trying to read anyway. Reluctantly, and taking his time as if he only just heard his mother, he closes his book and climbs off the chair. He shuffles to the kitchen, where he casually asks, "What's for lunch, Mom?"

Terri squints, giving him more of a jeer reminiscent of her glares at Sean, then lightens the mood by saying, "Hunger brings 'em out every time."

"Can you make a melted cheese?"

"A cheese sandwich?"

"Dad knows how. He even showed me."

Terri's mood turns gloomy again. "Let's see what we got." Checking the refrigerator, she finds Velveeta slices. "So, are you making this? Or do you think I can?" Her sarcastic humor escapes him.

"Well, um…would you?"

"I think so."

———□———

Monday at noon, Sean and Heinrich are having their lunch together when Sean is served the restraining order Terri had promised.

Sean fumes, "It's a PFA—a fucking protection from abuse." His eyes swirl as he glances through the 30-plus pages containing bullet points of do's and don'ts, legal threats, expectations, and demands. He hands the bundle over to Heinrich, so he can see what he has to deal with.

When Heinrich obliges, likewise scanning the monster document, he notes with sarcasm, "Did you see those all-capitalized words yelling out at you? It looks like a software agreement!"

Sean only concedes with, "Yeah."

As he continues to peruse the document, Heinrich observes, "Looks like you have a court date. And you need a lawyer too.

And turn in your firearms... I didn't know you had weapons at home."

Sean grabs the document. "You're not helping me with this! I'll deal with it tonight." He gets up from his crate. "We need to get back to our project. Sorry, Boss. I shouldn't treat you this way, should I?"

"Ya...I mean no." Confused by the question, Heinrich jumps up to embrace his friend.

Nine long days after being served, and after reading over the document several times, Sean decides he will represent himself. He shows up at the historic Philadelphia City Hall and remembers as a seventh grader, his mom taking him to the top of the building for an amazing view of the city. But today is no day for a field trip. He just needs to get to the Court of Common Pleas and deal with Terri.

The judge grants Terri only part of what she wants. She gets a year of protection and Sean is allowed to see Ryan. That privilege, however, comes with a hefty price. It is only under supervision and he must personally pay out of pocket for an approved supervisor, which turns out to be three times his hourly wage. Additionally, Sean must enroll in a year-long domestic abuse anger-management program. And he must pay Terri for Ryan's support without getting to live in the home he continues to pay for.

Fortunately for Sean, Heinrich is a good sport about his living with him. Sean feels awkward, even embarrassed sharing his space. And his bed. But he appreciates Heinrich. One day, Sean catches himself staring at his roommate's physique and well-developed legs. Heinrich is wearing his soccer gear and preparing for his Saturday morning practice.

"So...how long have you played soccer?"

"Since I was a kid. In Hamburg. It seemed we all did. Almost 10 percent of Germans play football, what you—sorry, *ve*—call soccer here in the U.S."

"Maybe you could join me and Ryan at the Lighthouse Field and show us both some of your techniques. The supervising counselor might agree to play along—though she was uncomfortable with the idea at first. I told her it should feel more natural for Ryan. I told her you are a good coach and clearly know the sport."

When Terri picks up Ryan after soccer at Lighthouse Field, she makes it clear that she does not approve of this kind of meeting, especially when she notices Ryan walking with a slight limp.

Heinrich asserts, "He vas very enthusiastic. He twisted his ankle vhen he missed the last ball."

Ignoring Heinrich but addressing Sean, she says, "So, this is how your fuck buddy treats little boys? Kinda rough, wouldn't ya say?"

Heinrich, surprised, looks to Sean for support. Sean, stunned, looks at the supervisor.

Without further comment, Terri dismisses the men with a glance and kisses Ryan on the head. The supervisor slowly walks with Terri to the side of the field and holds a brief discussion with her before checking back with Ryan. Terri has him put a little weight on his right foot. Ryan shrugs his shoulders, dismissing all the fuss.

CHAPTER 6

A few days later at school, Ryan stands at an easel painting something resembling the letter *R* inside a triangle. When he starts slapping and smashing black paint over his artwork, the teacher looks concerned. Her face softens, then tightens, and she jots down a few words on a nearby notepad.

Sean does not see Ryan for several weeks. More court-appointed sessions with a mediator and Sean's weekly anger-management meetings bring no change in visitation privileges. And no soccer.

The Institute of Contemporary Art is a labyrinth of avant-garde paintings. No patrons yet browse the galleries but the music of Enya's "Orinoco Flow" echoes from a boom box somewhere in the museum. In the workshop, Sean works by himself. His eyes, like an overcast sky, blur over. He is distracted as he grips an I-beam and tries to steady his Milwaukee drill. He hears, "Sail Away" But the noise of the drilling drowns out the music. Heinrich, coming from behind, wraps both arms around Sean as if Sean had asked for help. Sean looks confused and he weakens in his arms—but only for a long moment. "What are you doing?"

Heinrich winces. "You needed help. I don't know vhat to say. So much going on with Terri and Ryan. But I think I have some good news. After work, before we go home, okay?"

Heinrich and Sean find a table in the same Irish pub where several weeks ago, Heinrich gave Sean his Ryan photo.

After ordering beers, Heinrich clears his throat. "I know you are dealing with lots of problems. So, I didn't want to trouble you."

Sean suddenly looks worried. *He wants me to move out.* He says nothing but looks intently at Heinrich, eyes wide, listening.

"Don't tell anyone..." Heinrich takes a sip of his beer and a deep breath. "I've accepted an offer from the Boeing Company."

Sean stutters, "You—you'd move to Seattle?"

"No, Chicago." Then, letting that thought settle for almost a minute, he adds, "You come with me. Ve could—"

"Could what? Leave Ryan here?"

"I've already told you vhat I think of Terri as a mother. I think you should have custody—not her."

"You got that right. She made it look like I'm a criminal and should pay her to raise my son—like I'm a danger to him... So, how soon?"

"A few veeks. You can stay for a little longer at my place but—"

"I understand."

"Actually, Sean, there's a lot you don't understand."

And without asking, Heinrich stands and offers, "Let me take you to dinner."

Sean obliges, takes a few generous gulps of his beer, and notices Heinrich's only half-finished pint. Hesitating for a moment, he thinks, *It's not right to leave behind a fresh beer.* But, realizing that he should not distract Heinrich, Sean gets up with him.

Taking the same bus toward home but getting off near Washington Square West, Heinrich leads the way through a visibly gay-friendly neighborhood. Sean and Heinrich follow a short distance behind two men in their early twenties who are conspicuously holding hands.

They must need to show off, Sean thinks. Aloud, he asks, "Why do they have to do that?"

Heinrich gently ignores the question with a slight shrug but nods to Sean a few moments later for him to enter the upscale Tavern on Camac. Sean hesitates but follows along.

"They have good food. My treat. No one's going to bite you. *Aber ich möchte vielleicht bei dir knabbern.*" [But I might want to nibble on you.]

Sean, mildly annoyed at being taken to a neighborhood like this, shrugs—actually, it is more like a shiver. Greeting them at the door is a handsome host in his mid 50s with a salt-and-pepper mustache and sideburns—a style he has not changed from the '70s. He leads the way to a comfortable booth, then hands them menus.

Sean takes furtive peeks away from the menu to look around at the other patrons. He looks puzzled, hesitates, and finally asks, "So, you're actually gay? And all of them too? They look so…*normal.* I mean, you know, like regular guys…"

"Vhat you mean *they?* I see the way you stare at other men—and me."

Sean's mouth drops. Confused, he feels he must explain himself but is not sure just what to say in his own defense.

Heinrich, however, is undaunted in his opinion. He scoots closer to whisper into Sean's ear, "It's okay. Sometimes the man himself is the last one to know it. Or admit it."

After dinner, Heinrich shows Sean the near-empty dance area upstairs. Sean stays in the shadows. Heinrich, standing close, puts one arm around his guest and gives him a supportive, understanding hug. Sean leans hesitantly into Heinrich's embrace. Across his face, relief alternates with anxiety. Sean's mind dishes up dozens of questions without time for him to attempt an answer to any one of them. *The man himself is the last to know? Does Terri know? How could I have not known? But am I really? Heinrich isn't gay…is he? What about Ryan? What will he think?* Exhausted by his own barrage of questions, he turns to Heinrich, giving him a tentative, then too-intense hug. And then he asks simply, "Can we go home now?"

In the days following, Heinrich tries to convince Sean to move to Chicago with him. While he is wrapping trophies and medals, Heinrich suggests, "Ve could work together maybe. And ve would have each other. Ve could—"

But Sean stops him in mid-sentence. "No, I need to fight for my son. I can't take Ryan without Terri's approval. And I don't have a job there. I will need to look for a more affordable place right here in Philly. I do understand your wanting to advance in your work. I probably should be looking too."

Heinrich approaches Sean with an affectionate hug but clearly wants more. Sean tries to laugh. "Not right now. I'm still working on this stuff."

"Vhat stuff? Okay, I'm back to sorting through *my* stuff."

In the next couple of weeks, Sean tries to be supportive of his friend's departure. But when he is by himself, he looks pensive, disappointed at losing so many of the things he assumed were part of his life. Even seeing Ryan now feels like visiting a distant nephew, someone you have to think about what to say when you're together.

Ryan asks him during one of their Saturday meetings, "You look sad, Daddy. Did I do something wrong?"

"No, son. It's my work and where I live. And my friend, Heinrich, is moving far away."

Ryan says, looking away from Sean, as if just to himself, "I miss you reading to me at night. And doing things."

A week later, Heinrich asks Sean again, "Come with me. You've told me that even seeing Ryan is painful. You're still going to have to pay child support. But ve can have a new life together." Pausing only long enough to catch his breath, he continues his proposal. "There are more openings at the Boeing Company—I checked." Then making very direct eye contact, he states emphatically, "And...I love you."

Sean stoically takes all this in—until the *I love you.* Holding back nothing, he replies, "I know. And I love you too... I just need to take care of things if I'm going with you. It seems like a crazy adventure."

Sean pretends to tackle Heinrich between the packed boxes and the entrance hallway. Pulling Heinrich to the floor, Sean willingly lets him take charge. The German is confident, yet considerate, in what a man who has never had sex with another man might want done for him.

Afterward, Sean confides, "I didn't know sex could be so much fun. It's not like I have to prove something."

"Prove something?"

"Well, Terri was more interested—and better at it—than me. I thought it was... I thought it was my...*responsibility.* Maybe that's what was wrong."

A few days later at work, Sean receives a document asserting Terri's claim that Sean *and* Heinrich are a danger to Ryan, and that Sean should have no contact at all with him. Sean exclaims to Heinrich, "This does it! She just piles on more accusations. And it can't be good for Ryan. Maybe Angelo was right."

After work, Sean calls Margaret. "May I come over after dinner?" is all he asks and all he needs is a simple answer.

"Sure."

She doesn't quiz him or qualify him. After she hangs up, he can't hear her say, "Okay, Row-B, I need your help tonight."

That evening, while sitting at her dining table, he hesitates when Margaret asks, "So, tell me what's heavy on your heart. Terri? Ryan? Work?"

"It's mainly Ryan. I need to pay child support but I'm not allowed to see him except under weird restrictions. I'm worried that it puts too much strain on him with Terri competing against me at every turn. I'm thinking I should let her be the mom she wants to be and not interfere. I can't afford an attorney." He leans back, shoulders drooping, forcing a brave smile.

Margaret slowly considers what to say. "I'm reminded of the famous story of wise King Solomon when he was asked to decide which of two women should keep a child they both claimed was theirs. It's a thousand-year BC version of a child custody dispute. They didn't have DNA testing, so he tested the resolve of the competitors. And as you may remember from your grade-school Old Testament stories, he sees that the *real* mother is willing to give her son to the impostor. Today, however, our courts are corrupt, and God's loving justice is dismissed with clever negotiations. They're willing to cut the baby in half. I'm afraid you will lose if you fight."

Sean wasn't expecting this. He hesitates, his mouth slightly open, then finally blurts, "Well, I'm also thinking of a move to Chicago. It's better pay and since I'm out of the picture with Ryan…"

"Move? Chicago? So that means losing you *and* Ryan? That woman isn't going to let me see him either. I just might talk to him about Jesus."

Lowering his head for a moment, then making eye contact once again, Sean says, "I'm sorry, Mom. I know when Dad went off to El Salvador…"

"Yes…"

"Well, I was just a baby. How did you do it all by yourself?

Emotionally."

"I prayed for strength and guidance. And insights from the scriptures. I also kept a souvenir of his in my pocket for many, many months." She stands and walks over to her shrine above the sofa table. From under a votive candle, she picks up a little laminated shamrock the size of a communion wafer. "Here," she says with loving resolve. "This was your dad's. He told me it reminded him to believe in the luck of the Irish—the good luck that comes from perseverance. It was in his personal things..." Looking distant, then slowly turning back to her living room memorials, she bows her head.

Sean keeps a respectful silence.

Ryan walks home, absently kicking a Coke can, and does not see his father waiting around the corner. Startled when he sees Sean, he exclaims, "Daddy? Um...are you gonna hurt me? Mom says you want to take me away."

Sean's puzzlement at his son's words turns to sorrow, then anger. "Of course not, son. I just..." He clears his throat. "I just want...I *need* to say goodbye." Stooping down to Ryan's level, he says nothing for a long while, trying to remember what he has rehearsed. "I'm going to move away. My friend, Heinrich, is going to help me get a job with him. That way, I can send you money. That way you can stay here in Philadelphia with Mom."

Ryan is confused and his little face shows disbelief. He doesn't know what to say or even ask. Eyes wide, he just stares. He waits. Sean reaches into his jacket pocket. He pulls out the little shamrock and thrusts his hand forward. "This belonged to my dad—Nana gave it to me. It's from him, your grandfather. She says he kept it to give him the luck of the

Irish. Like the Irish who make their bad luck turn into good luck. I want you to have it. It's probably not a good idea to show your mom. I'm not supposed to be seeing you."

Ryan nods without really understanding. He hesitantly plucks the memento from Sean's hand.

Slowly turning his head away from Ryan so his son won't see his tears forming, Sean moves backward, as if avoiding a cliff, step by step. Then he spins on his heels and begins to run.

Ryan sees his father shrink into the distance. Looking again at the shamrock, he turns it over. Not sure whether to keep it or toss it, he slips it into his jacket pocket.

That night, Ryan tosses and turns, finally finds a rhythm, and rocks himself to sleep.

———□———

The next day, Sean visits Angelo. "I've thought a lot about this."

Angelo listens intently.

"I hope I'm making the right decision. I'm moving to Chicago with my friend, Heinrich."

"Oh, boy. What about Ryan? You getta take him?"

"No. That's the problem. Terri doesn't want me to have any contact with him. And even if the courts say it's my right, she is making it nearly impossible—even accusing me of being a threat. Like a sexual predator."

"Because you're gay?"

Sean gapes at him. "What? But I'm not...I mean—how did you know?"

"Sean, it's okay. Really. It's not something you get to decide. You have to accept it or hide it. You think it's like choosing between Alfredo or puttanesca?"

Sean fidgets, wanting to change the subject.

But Angelo presses, "This Heinrich. Do you trust him?"

"Yes."

"Good-a, then."

"I want to do the right thing. Even if I can't see Ryan, I will send him child support. And since she's prohibiting me from contacting him, maybe…" His voice trails off and he sits there like an actor who has forgotten his lines until he finally comes up with a question. "Maybe you could let me know how he's doing? But we can't let her know you're actually on my side."

Angelo's mouth softens, his eyes not looking at Sean, staring instead at the calendar as if into the future. "I'll think of something. I know your address—sorry, your *old* address. When's his birthday?"

Sean breathes a deep sigh. "Soon, actually. The ninth, coming up. He'll be seven. I'd better go. But I'll keep in touch with you."

Reluctantly, and with a shrug of his shoulders, Angelo says, "I will miss you. You're a good man." They hug like father and son. Angelo doesn't want to look at Sean as he leaves.

CHAPTER 7

Ten Years Later

Ryan's reddish-blond, fuzzy mustache is convincing evidence that he is Irish American, while the freckles from his childhood have given way to a teenager's acne-afflicted, ruddy complexion—like his dad's. He has not seen or heard from his dad in all that time. Terri has made sure of that. His black-framed glasses and long-sleeve shirt suggest a serious geekiness for a high school student.

As he approaches Angelo's grocery store, he crushes a littered Coke can, then places it into the recycling bin next to the store's front door. His phone rings. It's his friend, Daniel, from Central High School. *Stuck again, I'm sure.* "What's up, buddy? I'm just clocking in at work." Listening for a moment, he answers, "Sure. Of course, I don't have my textbook with me. Let me call you later." He smiles to himself, confident he can help. *Does he really need my help? Or does he just like to talk to me?*

At home that evening, he's in his back bedroom, his hideaway. He now has a small desk, big enough for a grade-school boy, but cramped for a seventeen-year-old. A secondhand Compaq computer from Daniel, with its TV-style monitor taking up most of the desktop, and the tower on the floor squeezing his legs against one side of the desk, don't give him much room. He smiles as he remembers Daniel setting up the system and hovering over it like a proud parent gently handing over an infant to the uncle. Ryan didn't see Daniel's look of concern that this funky little room was his best friend's bedroom.

Ryan is happy to have a way to email Daniel and research the internet for his school assignments. He is required to contribute to the cable service each month. When he needs to study a school text or workbook on a flat surface, he moves the keyboard onto the top of the monitor. For most reading, he likes his overstuffed chair—and this is where he cuddles up for an occasional call with Daniel. He has a seven-year-old Samsung flip phone he bought used with his earnings from Angelo's Market.

Okay, Buddy. Pressing the *Dan* button, he waits only moments, and without so much as a hello or greeting, Ryan jumps in, "Let me guess. You're wondering which to use: t-score, z-score, or percentile rank. At work, I was thinking about our case and wondering which would be best." Ryan just hears Daniel laugh.

"You do read minds. No wonder you want to go into psych,"

Ryan settles back in his chair and lets Daniel unload his frustration with statistical analysis. Concluding his call, Ryan agrees to come over to Daniel's house on Friday after school.

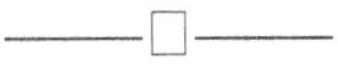

In the lunchroom that Friday, a young man with a messy head of dark-brown hair isn't messy at all. It's just the look. Daniel is a little young to be a *GQ* model and his eyes aren't sultry or the eyebrows pampered, but the sculpted lips could tempt someone to kiss them. He is saving a seat for Ryan. Glad to see him, he announces, "Mom will pick us up—my car's power steering decided it didn't want to do all the steering."

"What? I don't understand."

"It's back at the dealership. That's why I was late this morning—it's one of the Mini Cooper's little quirks. Yesterday, without warning, the power steering stopped assisting, like a tired little dog on a walk just stopping and refusing to take another step. Anyway, I'm carless."

"That makes two of us!" Ryan laughs.

Daniel scrunches his forehead. "I didn't know you had a car."

Ryan only glances back with a sardonic smile.

After school, Mrs. Allen is late, but only 10 minutes, apologizing with polite but rudimentary concern for her son's wait, and more concern for Ryan, giving him a wince. "You know traffic…"

Daniel interrupts with a quick introduction of Ryan to his mother.

"I've heard so much about you," she says to Ryan. "It's nice to finally meet you. Daniel respects and appreciates you—even if you do like walnuts in your cookies."

Ryan isn't sure what to make of this.

Daniel comes to the rescue, "At school once, I brought some cookies. You asked if there were walnuts in 'em too. I don't like the taste or the texture, but you actually like them with their high arginine and hydrolysable tannins. I'm just guessing."

Ryan puzzles over this discussion about nuts but lets Daniel carry on.

"I think it's best to let the chocolate speak for itself without interference from walnuts. Mom agrees with me. Dad is undecided."

Ryan feels like a foreigner. *What are they talking about? It might be better to relax in the back seat and just listen. And watch.* Mrs. Allen turns right from West Upsal Street, where a stately home dominates the corner. *And that's just one home?* Ryan grows a bit uncomfortable as the homes become more like statements of social importance.

Indeed, Daniel's home fits neatly into the historic Pelham neighborhood of West Mt. Airy. It's a three-story feldspar stone Victorian with gothic arched windows, and has the mystery of a castle. Ryan fidgets as if he's come to a party not dressed for the occasion. He stays silent.

Mrs. Allen asserts that they love the neighborhood's charm. "So many lovely shops and restaurants nearby—not too close, you know? Did Daniel tell you he auditioned last year for Chekov's *Seagull?* He did a great audition—"

"Mom!"

"—but they were looking for an older man for the part. Anyway, the Sedgwick Theater has nice productions. It's nearby. Have you ever auditioned?"

Ryan is surprised by the question. "Uh, no. It never occurred to me."

The evening's darkening sky seen through the wooden shutters of the room doesn't provide enough light. Daniel closes them and turns on a halogen desk lamp. The queen-size bed and dark wood bookshelves all have the designer look of a Restoration Hardware showroom. And like a professional salesman, Daniel offers Ryan his desk chair as he pulls up a small, armless side chair for himself.

Ryan does not look comfortable in the deep-burgundy cordovan leather desk chair in his friend's room. But he can focus on Daniel's psychology textbook, which is open to the section on statistical graphs. Daniel tilts his head, sticks his tongue out the side of his mouth, and to finish the look, crosses his eyes.

Ryan messes up Daniel's hair. Then, feeling his own fingers, asks, "How much product do you use anyway?" Wiping his hand on his jeans, he returns his focus to the laptop on the desk and brings Daniel back to the task at hand. "Yes, it is kind of mind-numbing, but with Excel, we can make it all work out great."

"Of course. My dad says Excel is the answer to whatever the problem might be. He says it's duct tape for bankers."

They work through the questions with Ryan clearly adept at Excel functions and even enjoying the process—to Daniel's chagrin. "You're so good at this," he says.

Ryan smiles at the compliment but barely shows his emotions and keeps his head down.

"Look at me, Ryan. I'm commending you. I think you are awesome."

Ryan glances up now but he looks like he just might cry. "Sorry…" he says. "Maybe we need a break. How 'bout a peek at Facebook?"

"Yes, sir. BRB," Daniel replies.

"What?"

"Be right back."

"Oh, yeah."

Thoughts elsewhere, Ryan saves his work, closes Excel, and opens his own Facebook account. He admires the main photo of his online friend, Cynthia. It's portfolio quality; her blonde hair with perfect lighting and perfect teeth, good enough for an orthodontic ad. Her headshot would stop anyone searching for an attractive eighteen-year-old woman in the St. Louis area.

Daniel returns to his bedroom, interrupting his friend's gaze. Waving one hand in front of the screen, he gets Ryan's attention by weaving a Wedgwood china plate of freshly made cookies in front of his friend's face. Their warm fragrance wafts up to greet Ryan's nostrils. "Mom made these just now. She calls them hunk-a-chunk chocolate. And just for you, she added walnuts to some of them." Daniel sits on the edge of his bed and takes one of the walnut-free cookies.

Savoring his custom cookie, Ryan mumbles, mouth full, "You sure have a cool mom." Turning back to Daniel's latest laptop, the MacBook Air, he commends him, "Your new computer is faster than your old one—which I totally appreciate. I'm trying to find the right words to answer Cynthia."

In his native Bostonian accent, Daniel says, *"Woods…"* then springs to his feet.

More interested in composing his thoughts, Ryan tries to ignore him. But like a drama coach to his listless actors, Daniel expects full attention.

"Ah, yes! *'Woods are the clothes thoughts weah.'"*

And Ryan counters with his own version of street talk, "What the fuck you say'n? Is that Shakespeare?"

"No. It's Samuel Beckett." Daniel is not sure whether or not Ryan deserves an explanation. Looking frustrated with Ryan, he waits.

Ryan gives a meager level of attention. Sarcastic and pleased with himself, he teases, "Oh, yeah, Mr. Go-Dot. *Let's go… We can't… Why not?… We're waiting for Godot."*

Taking facetious offense, Daniel adds, "Hey, he's one of my heroes—Irish too, don't ya know."

Ryan, staying focused on his online efforts, dismisses, "Whadever ya say, dude. Sometimes I don't know what yer sayin' an' it's not yer *Baston* accent."

Daniel pouts until he notices a friend request pop up on Ryan's page. Ryan repositions his glasses to improve his focus.

Daniel snickers, "Now who's hitting on you?"

Ryan clicks on it absently, annoyed by his broken concentration in composing his response to Cynthia. "Maybe one of Cynthia's friends… No. It's a guy. Sean… I don't know any Sean. Except my dad. His name was Sean O'Brien—unless he changed his name. Like changing addresses so we couldn't track him down. I haven't seen or heard from the bastard in—in like 10 years when he left me and my mom." Repulsed, Ryan pushes himself back in Daniel's chair, almost tipping over.

Daniel tries to lighten the mood. "Hey. You know how many Irish have polluted the planet—sorry, *populated* the planet? Maybe he's a stalker and not your dad at all—you're a Gallagher."

"That's my mother's name. She didn't wanna get married. And you'd think if she wanted to get away from her family, a new name would be to her liking. But she won't tell me anything about 'em."

"So why'd he leave?

"I dunno. She's only said he wasn't her kind of man. And that he was a danger to us. But from what I see, she likes 'em kinda rough."

Daniel squirms, needing to come up with something to say. He just inhales slowly.

Ryan adds, "I don't know how many men there've been. I stopped keepin' track. I'm in the way. So, I jus' stay outta the way. Library or work. Or holed up in my room."

Daniel continues looking at Ryan, uneasy hearing about his friend's family life and not sure he should ask anything else. But he does. "You can tell me about your family. It sounds like it's not a bedtime story. But it is yours and I think you are amazing. You are very inspiring. I want to understand what makes you *you*. I care about you."

"So, how 'bout the time when my dad tried to kidnap me, but my mother stopped him. She said he abused her. She even went to court over me, so she could have custody… If he loved me, why'd he leave me? Just kinda sailed off into the sunset. She's tried being a good mom—I guess…" Ryan takes his right hand off the keyboard and turns it palm up. "Unless…you want to know how I got this?"

Daniel stares at his friend's right palm, which has a very old scar. "I've wondered what happened."

"I was seven or eight. It was after my dad left. I was trying to make myself scrambled eggs at the stove. My dad used to make me breakfast. Sometimes we'd even have eggs for dinner or supper. Anyway, the kitchen was a disaster with my production. When my mom came in, she shoved the iron frying pan to the side, grabbed my hand, and pressed it onto the hot burner. In a weird voice, like a man's voice, like she was repeating something she heard once said to her, 'This'll teach ya.'"

Daniel's mouth is agape and his lips quiver when he tries to speak. So, he doesn't.

"There's more," Ryan says. "But for now, I need to get going. We both have homework."

"Um… What about your mystery dad? Wouldn't you like to find out what happened to him, if this is actually him trying to reach you?" He nods at the Facebook page.

"My mom says he's violent and I am better off without 'im."

Daniel presses, "Well, what about the child support?"

"Support? Like money? We never—I never—"

Daniel asserts, "It's state law, buddy. Married or not, fair or not, fathers have to pay to play."

Ryan looks like a kid being told that Santa is make-believe. "You're sayin' my runaway dad might not be a…what do they call 'em…a deadbeat dad, and sent money to my mom and me?" Distracted and distraught, Ryan stands, "I gotta go."

"I'm sorry, Ryan."

Ryan quickly grabs his red Michael Jordan varsity jacket and turns to leave. Daniel gathers the remaining cookies and quickly wraps them in a paper napkin.

Ryan says with sincerity, "Yer so thoughtful." Quickly adding in mock sentimentality, "Thanks for being my fwend."

Daniel tucks the pouch of cookies into Ryan's jacket pocket like a mother seeing her son off to school.

As they head out from the bedroom, Daniel offers, "I can drive you home—Mom's car. She's not using it tonight."

"No, that's okay. I'll get the 23. Thanks though."

After Ryan has left, and hearing the front door gently close, Daniel goes back to his desk and looks at the screen. Slowly dragging the curser, he pauses, then clicks *ACCEPT*. Wincing at his actions, he now looks pensive.

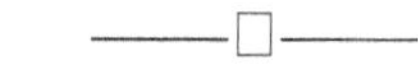

It's Saturday morning and Ryan marches into Angelo's Market, annoyance on his face and walking with the determination of a man ready to give notice. But hearing the frazzled owner with his Italian-accented, generic-but-friendly greeting, Ryan softens.

With a smile and genuine look of relief, Angelo says, "Good-a, you're here, my scholar. Orders stacked up crazy."

Chagrined, Ryan quietly skulks into the back room. Barely squeezing through the dingy space to the check-in counter, he puts on his apron and store cap, and clips his box cutter onto his belt. Now he is almost ready for work. He shakes his shoulders and shivers, trying to focus on his chores instead of confronting Angelo. *What do you know about my dad?* But only blurting out loud to himself, "That's what I wanna know." He takes a few deep breaths, signs his timecard, and launches into his duties.

Ryan appears unperturbed with Saturday morning chores, making short work of the massive mounds of merchandise for the cramped space. Boxes are unpacked, grocery items shelved, and customers greeted. He smiles and keeps up his pace, his private worries kept to himself. Ordinarily, he might have winked or at least smiled at the attractive customer his own age in the pasta aisle—after all, she was paying more attention to him than the pastas. But not this morning. There was too much work to do that day and Angelo needed to make a delivery later in the afternoon. So, Ryan keeps his big inquiry to himself. For now.

Later, his shift complete, Ryan slogs home.

CHAPTER 8

Terri, now *33*, does not look 10 years older but much, much more. With her hair pulled back and *35* pounds heavier, she slouches in her chair at a small table that is shoved up against the wall and barely big enough to seat three. Missing now are two upper-left teeth—due to a fall, she claims. She doesn't smile in front of strangers. But Mike doesn't care.

Mike Simonelli would have been considered ruggedly handsome in his high school days—if he had gone for more than a couple of years. His jet-black hair and shadowed brown eyes can't quite distract from the severe scar across his neck and throat. He is impulsive and quick to anger.

Finished eating, they enjoy their cigarettes in the quiet of Terri's kitchen. Several cans of Pabst Blue Ribbon sit empty, one crumpled next to Mike. Terri's security guard jacket hangs on the back of the empty chair. When they hear Ryan enter the house, they say nothing.

As he walks into the kitchen, Ryan sees no plate awaiting him. He gets only the slightest nod of recognition from Mike and a weary smile from Terri. Ryan peers into an empty box of Rice-A-Roni sitting on the counter. He returns Terri's smile with a look of wary disgust.

Like he's trying to pick a friendly fight, Mike asks, "Hey, Ryan. Did'ja bring smokes home for the man of the house?" He pauses, "Oh, that's right. You ain't 18 yet. Won't your good buddy Angelo let you bring 'em home for your daddy?"

Terri glares at Mike.

Ryan ignores the taunt and looks in the refrigerator. Not

seeing anything but half a carton of milk, he leaves the kitchen and heads upstairs.

"Needa get 'em myself then," Mike mumbles, talking to himself but turning to Terri. "Do ya got a 10? I'm a little short till Friday."

"But *yesterday* was Friday," Terri asserts, knowing it doesn't matter.

Mike reaches over to Terri's wallet. She doesn't protest.

When the front door closes behind Mike, Ryan storms downstairs. "Mom! How can you put up with him? He must be one hell of a fuck."

Terri objects, "Don't you talk to your mother that way."

"Well, maybe if you acted more like a mother..." Shoving her chair, he adds, "Why'd you make my real dad go away? He wanted me."

"Who told ya that? He said, 'Do you want to keep it?' when I found out I was pregnant. All you needa know is, I stayed an' he didn't."

Ryan bolts out of the room. He grabs his jacket, stuffs his phone into his pocket, and leaves the house.

Heading toward Allegheny Avenue, Ryan trudges on, hungry, tired, and now with even more unpleasant things to think about. *My own father wanted me aborted?* He stops and takes out his phone, scrolls down to *Dan* on its little screen, and presses the *CALL* button. Several seconds later, Daniel's voicemail greeting comes on. Ryan's face contorts in disappointment. Resuming his slow walk, his mind swirls with questions.

Ryan does not see the five guys coming up behind him, all wearing jackets in shades of light gray, dark gray, and black—a striking contrast to their white faces. Tallboy, second in command, calls out to Ryan, "Yo!"

Ryan does not want to respond and doesn't stop.

The shortest one is the leader. Not of legal age or legal conduct, Stunt gets Ryan's attention with a voice of authority. His shaved head as well as his posturing in front of his boys make him look older. Maybe 22. "Hey, deef Boy."

Trying not to look surprised, Ryan is more annoyed than threatened.

"We're talk'n to ya," Tallboy says.

Then Stunt challenges Ryan. "Whatcha doin' in our neighborhood? Or you jis lost?"

Ryan retorts, "I don't have anything you want."

"We'll decide that," Stunt says.

Tallboy chimes in, "You live around here?"

A third member, Repeat, overweight and snickering, echoes Tallboy's words like he has missed his cue. Behind these three boy-men are another two—one hooded, the other baseball-capped and obviously nervous.

Ryan forces a scornful smile and slowly folds up his phone in his left hand. They have his attention. He squares his shoulders and faces then directly. "So, what youse guys look'n for?"

Stunt responds, "Jus' a good place for cheesesteaks and hoagies. How 'bout you treat us?" As he says this, he pulls out a Ruger LC9. It glistens blue-black in the flickering streetlight.

Eyes popping, Ryan lifts his arms. Stunt smiles as he keeps the gun close to his waist but aimed at Ryan. "We jis needa lil' cash. Relax."

Tallboy frisks Ryan, taking his wallet and phone. And his stash of cookies. After pulling out all the cash—a 20 and three ones—in mock politeness, he hands Ryan his wallet with deliberate ceremony, then purposely drops the phone on the sidewalk.

Ryan flinches but resists moving. "Don't drop the cookies," he admonishes. "They're too good to waste."

Everyone stands like statues, frozen for a moment in the dim light of dusk.

Stunt smiles. "I like yer attitude, buddy. Looks like—"

Someone coming around the corner behind Ryan makes Stunt discreetly tuck away his gun. It's Mike. And the moment he sees the mugging, sees Ryan, he crosses to the other side of the street, pretending not to notice.

Stunt continues, "Looks like it's jis hoagies after all. Next time, bring more cash so we can invite ya along."

With seething anger, eyes squinting, Ryan watches the five head toward Allegheny Station. As he stoops down to pick up his phone, he notices Mike, six-pack in hand, turning the corner, not looking back. Ryan coughs out quietly, "Man of the house."

He picks up the main body of his phone and is relieved to see it light up. Searching the sidewalk for its back panel, he finds it several feet away. He leans up against a graffiti-covered brick wall and on his phone, scrolls down to Daniel's button. He tries calling again and, only getting voicemail. Ryan gazes up into the dusk-darkened sky.

The Facebook notification on Ryan's personal page waits for input. Daniel types almost as fast as he thinks. *So why did you leave me?* He mutters out loud, "Why didn't you take me with you?" His eyes show worry as he looks around the room. Seeing his iPhone charging next to his pillow, he picks it up out of habit, just to see if he's gotten any calls. He turns the phone on its edge, sees the ringer is off, and glances at the time—8:15. *Damn. I missed 'im.*

Daniel looks back at his computer and sees another message on Ryan's Facebook page: *May I call you?* He quickly closes the Mac display. *Oh, no,* he thinks. *Now what?* Bracing himself against the back of his chair and taking a breath, Daniel touches the phone screen to call Ryan.

Still standing against the brick wall, Ryan answers with a look of relief and blurts out, "I've just been robbed. I've been ripped off, and not just my money."

Eyes wide and blank, Daniel looks guilty. He doesn't know what to say. He waits.

Ryan, annoyed with the connection but relieved to have gotten through, needs assurance. "Are we still connected?"

"Yes, I'm here."

"Five wannabe thugs. They took all I had. Well, not my phone."

Gasping to take in what he's hearing, Daniel stammers, "I'm…I'm so sorry. Are you okay? Are you hurt?"

"I wish I coulda stood up to the sons a bitches. But there were five of 'em!"

There was silence on the phone.

"No," Ryan continues, "I'm not hurt. Physically. They even took the cookies."

Daniel exhales in sympathy.

Ryan mumbles, "I don't wanna talk anymore. I'm just a couple blocks from home. See ya tomorrow, okay?" Ryan ends the call. Still leaning against the wall, he gives himself a few more moments to recuperate.

A short time later, Daniel slowly lifts open his Mac screen. It awakens from sleep mode and Ryan's Facebook page reappears with another message: *Hey, Ryan. I'd love to reconnect.* Daniel quickly logs out of Facebook and closes his computer again.

Ryan returns home. As he enters the house, he hears bits of conversation coming from the kitchen. Once upstairs, he quickly slips down the hallway and into Terri's bedroom. Bed unmade, his mother's room is only lit from the hallway but is bright enough that he can see inside her nightstand drawer. He is reassured to find the handgun—larger than Stunt's little gun he saw earlier. Ryan leaves the gun there and darts to his room.

CHAPTER 9

Daniel watches the door to his homeroom. He glances at his iPhone that displays the wallpaper of himself in an Elizabethan costume and the time, then looks up to see Ryan making his way into the classroom. He takes his seat and Daniel heaves a sigh of relief. They exchange glances.

They meet after class in a calmer, less congested walkway, shadowed from the morning's sunlight and with fewer students shuffling to their next classes.

Daniel confides, "I was thinking about you all last night."

But Ryan blurts out, "Can I come over after school?"

"Yes, you *may*."

Ryan retorts, "Ya don' needa correct me. I know fuckin' English."

Daniel, ignoring his insult, replies, "I need to talk with you."

"What about?

"Um… He wants you to call him."

"Who?"

"Your dad."

"How's he know I'm the right one—that I'm his only begotten son?"

Daniel hems and haws. "I…uhh… You left your Facebook open and…"

Ryan wrinkles his forehead as he puts this together. "You mean you…"

In an instant, Ryan shoves Daniel hard enough that he falls. When Daniel tries to get away, Ryan tackles him.

"When did it become okay for you—"

Daniel cuts him off. "Leave me alone. I was just trying—"

As Daniel hits the ground again, his glasses fly. They tussle and a crowd forms around them. Several in the crowd chant, "Fight! Fight! Fight!" Another guy in the crowd taunts, "Hey, gay boys can fight too!"

Ryan and Daniel stop. Each looks around and they quickly get up, trying to regain their composure. Daniel looks for his glasses. Ryan finds them first and hands them to his friend with a mix of resentment and hurt. Daniel tries to straighten Ryan's shirt but Ryan lands another punch to Daniel's gut. Daniel doubles over and falls again.

The same guy taunts, "A lover's quarrel! Come on, now. Kiss and make up."

A burly, self-important security guard shows up. The crowd steps aside and the guard grabs Ryan in a chokehold. Ryan dissolves and the guard lets go.

"Whatever it is, both of you, save your story for the office."

Looking ashamed in front of their classmates, Ryan and Daniel are ushered by the security guard. Several of the kids snicker and some whisper but most have lost interest in the morning's entertainment and go their separate ways.

The school bell rings while Ryan and Daniel seat themselves in the dean's office.

The dean looks back and forth at the offending students with a look of incredulity. Shaking his head, he finally asks rhetorically, and with barely suppressed exasperation, "Ryan? Daniel? Why now? You're both good students. And graduating in just days... And if you didn't already know, you, Ryan Gallagher, have a scholarship to Temple. I was going to tell you later today. So why don't you two smart young men talk this out in private? ... Do either of you want to see our nurse?"

They shake their heads in unison. After a brief pause, the dean shoos them out of his office with a private smile.

After classes that day, instead of going home with Daniel, Ryan goes to the Barnwell Library's research area. Finding an available terminal, he opens his Facebook account and scrolls through several messages, including Cynthia's, until he sees the message Daniel claims is from his father. He sees the phone number and enters it into his phone. *Now I can block the bastard.* Noting another student hovering, waiting to use the terminal, he logs out.

On the bus ride to work, surrounded by other passengers but ignoring all of them, Ryan fidgets in his seat. He takes out his phone. Scrolling down to *Dan*, he deletes the entry. When the message displays *Are you sure?* He presses *No.*

After Ryan has worked several hours, Angelo snaps a couple of photos of him standing next to a display of imported cheese. "Stand proud, Ryan. Another day's work well done." When he pats him on the back with a little too much enthusiasm, Ryan's phone falls out of his pocket and crashes to the floor, breaking apart again. He scrambles to pick it up and Angelo motions him to the backroom.

Laughing, Angelo says, "Duct tape is the answer. So what-a is the question?"

Angelo reaches for a roll of the silver-gray tape and hands it over to Ryan. Quite dexterous with his box cutter, and needing no explanation, Ryan secures the broken back.

Angelo looks away, sad. He steps over to his desk and pulls out Ryan's paycheck. "I'm-a looking for you full-time but my bum of a nephew thinks I needa hire *him*. My brother Mario loaned me money… So, you gonna go to college anyhow."

Ryan answers, "I'd like to. I have a scholarship from Temple… But I don't know."

Raising his voice, Angelo booms, "Whaddya mean, ya don' know? That's-a why you been goin' ta the top school in town for smart kids like-a you. And you been gettin' good marks." Angelo thrusts him a wrapped chunk of Parmesan cheese as if it were a piece of his advice.

As he walks out the swinging doors of Angelo's store, Ryan unfolds the handwritten paycheck, smiles, and carefully returns it to his jacket pocket. On the walk home, Ryan casually takes out his phone but suddenly stops. He looks back and flinches. The memory of his recent mugging causes him to lean against another graffiti-covered wall and look around. He opens the phone. Three missed calls, one message: *Dan*. He presses the *LISTEN* key. The message is so brief he can barely hear it on the tiny speaker so he plays it again.

"I'm sorry. Call me."

It's as if Daniel were there in person, giving Ryan a reassuring hug. Ryan turns and faces the bricks. Snapping the phone closed, he smashes his fist against the wall.

Ryan makes it home without incident and quietly enters the dark house. He shuffles into the kitchen and switches on the ceiling light, which is harsh and hard on the eyes—like an interrogation room. He checks the refrigerator, sees nothing he wants, then looks in an overhead cabinet for crackers. Once seated at the table, Ryan notices a single-edge razor behind the salt and pepper. *Mike's, of course*. He turns away, trying to block out distractions.

Ryan unwraps Angelo's Parmesan gift and eats it like an apple. He can hear Terri and Mike upstairs, arguing. With a look of weary loathing, he takes out his phone, swallows hard, and touches the *Dan* button. Prepared to leave a confidential voicemail, he jumps when Daniel answers before the second ring. Without introduction, Ryan rushes, "No. I'm the one who should say I'm sorry. I just feel I've been exploited. I'm at home, so now isn't a good time to talk. *May* I see you tomorrow after school? We needa talk about—about your…discoveries."

"I'm…I'm—" Daniel's sobs are muffled.

"Okay, man. I didn't mean to hurt you. You're still my friend. Right? After school?"

Daniel makes a noise that Ryan interprets as yes.

"Okay, my friend." He ends his call and sighs with relief. *At least I didn't say you're my ONLY friend.*

He quietly enters his upstairs bedroom at the back of the house and closes the door behind him. It's completely dark until Ryan switches on his bedside lamp. Like a nearly forgotten ritual, he pulls out from under the bed a kids' 2003 retro-release shoebox containing a pair of original Nike Air Jordan sneakers, his first, and other souvenirs of his youth. After opening the lid for the first time in years, he touches each one—a report card from third grade, the laminated shamrock, and a photo near the bottom of Ryan on his father's shoulders. *Who took the photo?* Thinking back, he recalls, *My father's friend. They liked having me with them… And soccer was fun. I can't believe my dad didn't take me with him.* Just as he's about to switch off the bedside lamp, he hears moans coming from Terri's bedroom.

"No, Daddy…" And more muffled, "Daddy, no…" A thunk, then silence.

Ryan slams his eyes shut. *Not again!* Grimacing, he switches the lamp off and throws his head into his pillow.

Early the next morning, Ryan readies himself for school and is eating peanut butter on toast. Mike enters the kitchen. Ryan gets up to leave but Mike blocks his path.

"So, when's faggot-boy moving out? How 'bout trackin' down yer deadbeat dad? Then mooch off him."

Ryan snaps, "Shut the fuck up."

Mike sees a butcher knife lying on the cutting board, grabs it, and lunges toward Ryan.

Dodging through the doorway, Ryan shouts, "You son of a bitch!"

Suddenly realizing what might have happened, Mike freezes for a moment, staring at Ryan, then at the knife, which is stuck in the door trim. "Best you don't snitch to your mommy."

Ryan briefly deliberates, defiant. "Or your parole officer? You don't think I know you're in the candy business? And more? So, yes, I needa find a different place."

Mike glares at Ryan, distrusting him to keep silent. He slowly mutters, "Okay."

———□———

The Central High School bell announces the first period, but Ryan isn't there to hear it. From half a block away, there's too much street noise. When he finally slides into his seat, as if that will make his tardiness less obvious, no one notices except Daniel. Ryan glances at him sideways with an apologetic grimace to acknowledge his friend. Whatever was discussed in class, Ryan is not the one to ask. His thoughts keep going back to earlier that morning, his memory replaying the scene with the butcher knife—on the counter, in Mike's grip, thrusting, embedded in the door trim, Mike's fearful expression…

After first period, Ryan is still not quite present. He walks with Daniel from their classroom out to Daniel's car.

"Are you okay? Let's get outta here," Daniel says, not really expecting an argument or even an answer. "Fairmont Park?"

Ryan nods but doesn't say anything for the few minutes it takes to get to Daniel's car. It is excruciating for Daniel to be silent but he knows to keep quiet. Daniel's 10-month-old blue

Mini Cooper convertible waits at the end of the student parking lot.

Ryan thinks, *No cars around it to ding or dent his precious baby. Oh no!*

When Daniel turns on the ignition, his CD blares Carly Rae Jepsen's "Call Me Maybe." Daniel looks at Ryan and he gives a faint smile.

"I love the video," Daniel says as he dials it down to a modest volume. "It's so cool the way she's charmed by a neighbor boy, but he..."

Daniel notices Ryan is not paying attention so he drops the topic.

The 10 minutes it takes to get to Fairmont Park's Wissahickon Creek are quiet except for the Jepsen hit song playing on repeat. The music stops when Daniel turns off the ignition. They walk without a word from the parking area to a calm section of the creek. Daniel is attentive to Ryan, waiting for him to speak his mind, but only hears the murmur of the flowing water and the argument of springtime birds.

Finally, Daniel can't keep quiet. "So, Ry, tell me what's on your mind."

Ryan is startled by the question. He remembers when he was a boy with his father. Pant legs rolled up, standing in the shallow creek, setting his 2x4 sailboat and white paper sail and adjusting the sail with the big letter *R* on it. "You called me Ry. Only my dad ever called me that."

They continue along the edge of the creek. When a small frog jumps onto the path, Ryan tries to crush it.

Daniel demands, "What are you doing?" Waiting for an answer and not getting any, Daniel walks faster ahead, then suddenly stops and turns to confront Ryan. "What's wrong with you?"

Ryan tries to organize his thoughts. *Okay, I have to tell him.* "My mother's boyfriend tried to kill me... He grabbed a butcher knife, lunged at me—really coulda hurt me. But I moved fast and it stuck in the door trim." Embarrassed, Ryan attempts a joke. "Maybe he was just trying to make a point."

"It's not funny." Daniel's glare melts into deep concern.

"Jealous of my drama?"

"I don't like how they treat you."

Again, the two continue in silence for a while.

When they pass the spot where Ryan and Sean first set sail, Ryan gasps a deep breath and begins to sob. Daniel doesn't know what to do, so he hugs his friend gently like an older brother—or dad—might do.

Later that day, Daniel parks in front of his home. While he retrieves his backpack from the trunk, Ryan secures his side of the cloth top to the Mini, then steps back. "Why didn't you get a flamboyant red one?" he teases.

Daniel opens his mouth to respond but words are not needed. He merely rolls his eyes.

The boys enter Daniel's castle and Mrs. Allen calls out from the kitchen, "Danny? That you?"

Ryan, mimicking Daniel before he can answer, and wanting to shift to an upbeat mood, says, "Yes, Mom. And Hunk-a-Chunk."

Mrs. Allen appears in the hallway with a quizzical smile. "Well, I'm glad to see you two have made up. Can you stay for dinner?"

Ryan hesitates and looks over at Daniel.

She adds, "It's just mac-and-cheese tonight."

"Sure. Thank you, Mrs. Allen."

"Ryan dear, you may call me Kim."

Daniel heads up to his room, followed by Ryan. His room is perfectly organized and clean enough for a photo shoot. He pulls his laptop out of his backpack and sets it up on the desk. When Ryan comes in, Daniel, in a mocking tone, says, "Ryan, dear, you may call me Kim."

Ryan ignores Daniel, surprising him with a trick question. "Do you know where area code 510 is?"

"Berkeley, I think."

"And how would you know that?"

Daniel takes a breath, "Um…"

"I know, I checked. It's far enough away. I can't just go beat the crap out of 'im for being a deadbeat dad. Maybe I should track him down and kill him. Anyway, I've blocked his number."

Daniel, with some uncertainty in his voice, says, "But he's been sending support—like how many years?"

"If he did, I never saw it. Or my mom never let me know."

"You gonna write him back?" Leaning away from Ryan and making a mock blocking gesture with his right hand, Daniel teases, "Or should I?"

Ryan instantly responds with a fisted right hand—just playing along. "Okay, wise guy, what should I say? You're making me out to be a pathetic little kid."

"I just thought…" Daniel sighs. "It doesn't matter. If you want to respond, just call or write him yourself. Tell him what a bastard you think he is. And be done with him."

Ryan sits silent and still, his hands hovering above the keyboard.

Daniel, pensive, cautiously suggests, "Maybe you could find out what really happened—you know, from *his* point of view."

Ryan types in the message window *ok call me*, followed by

his own phone number. Closing out of Facebook, Ryan hesitates and looks at Daniel. "Or do you want me to leave it open?" *Oh, I'd better unblock him…*

The Allen house phone rings downstairs. Part of a beautifully appointed home with an eclectic combination of art deco, mid-century modern, and Federalist-era furnishings, the dining table setting gives Ryan pause for its formality. Mrs. Allen hands Daniel another setting of dishes and silverware, offering an explanation.

"Your dad wasn't coming home for dinner. But now he is." And then to Ryan, she adds, "Intern orientation at the school got canceled for tonight. At least Wharton isn't like the big, bad-boy banks."

Ryan feels like he has stepped into someone else's conversation again and yet is expected to say something. So he does. "Mrs. Allen, um, I mean, Kim, so you like living in Philly?"

"It was a wonderful opportunity for Neil. And what's not to like about Philadelphia? And I love teaching here with such wicked museums…"

Ryan controls his urge to laugh. He does not want to scoff but questions to himself, *Wicked? Museums can be wicked?*

"…and cultural and historic venues—well, everything. And your orchestra. Did you catch the lovely James Earl Jones tribute back in November? It was awesome."

My orchestra? Ryan tries to smile but the effort gets choked up with a grimace as he thinks of what to say. He looks to Daniel, hoping he'll give him a line or shift the topic, but his phone rings and comes to the rescue. Ryan looks relieved—until he sees the number on the screen. "Excuse me. I think I should take this call."

Daniel tenses.

Ryan walks briskly into the adjacent living room. Answering hesitantly, he speaks in a confidential tone, "Hello..." Apprehensive and attentive, he listens as he paces back and forth.

"Ryan?"

"Yeah..."

"Your dad here. You've asked some really difficult questions."

Ryan looks back into the dining room.

"But I'm glad—really glad—you did."

From the entry vestibule, Ryan hears the front door open and Neil Allen calling out, "The master of the house is now home!"

"I'm in the scullery like a good wench," replies Kim.

Ryan tries to block the background repartee.

Sean asks, "What? Is this a good time to call?"

On Sean's side of the call, Ryan hears a girl's voice. "Daddy, Daddy."

"Yeah, I guess this isn't a good time. Maybe tomorrow. No, Sunday." Ryan looks up, takes a breath, closes his phone, and returns to the dining area just in time to see Neil and Kim kiss a cheery peck on each other's cheeks. Noticing Ryan, Mrs. Allen nods her head to Neil that they have an audience.

Turning to Ryan with his hand extended in welcome, Neil says, "Nice seeing you again, Ryan. Looking forward to graduation? Of course." He answers his own question, but still waits for Ryan to respond and puzzles over Ryan's hesitancy. "It's just that Dan thinks so highly of you and says you'd be good in law or business—you're so competitive. In an edgy, good way. Well, most of the time."

Ryan is again at a loss for words. *Is he playing with me or what?* Without Daniel in the room at the moment, he offers,

"Well, I'm not sure what comes next for me."

"Of course, lots of choices for your life. Then again, some things aren't choices, are they?"

Another rhetorical question?

Looking back to his wife for acknowledgment or validation, Neil sees that she did not hear him. He shrugs and smiles. From the kitchen, she announces that dinner will be ready in minutes.

After dinner, Daniel and Ryan bring the dishes to the kitchen and Kim thanks Ryan, only smiling at Daniel. *Of course, he is supposed to do that*, Ryan thinks. They head upstairs.

Ryan notices for the first time a framed photo of Daniel with friends, posing extra-friendly with one another. There is a dramatic ribbon-like sculpture with a spider in the background.

"Where was that?" Ryan asks more out of politeness than curiosity.

"The Guggenheim, in Spain. The one designed by Frank Gehry. My friend in the middle there wants to be an architect. What a sweetheart. That was last summer." Daniel sighs with wistful satisfaction. Changing the subject, he asks, "Are you gonna let your mom know you're here for the night?"

"Right. Like she cares… But where am I supposed to sleep? I don't want to be any trouble to you." He facetiously adds, "You must have a guest room, like the maid's room on the next floor up?" He turns serious and pulls out his phone to call Terri. The phone rings, no answer…rings, then voicemail. Ryan muffles the speaker so Daniel does not hear his mother's gruff greeting. "Mom, I'm staying at a friend's house tonight," he says, then hangs up.

"That's it?"

Dismissing Daniel's surprise, Ryan waits a moment for the Mac to boot up and for Daniel to log on. Daniel makes no effort to hide his password. Nevertheless, Ryan leans away so he does not see it. Daniel gets up and gives his chair to Ryan so he can log in to his own Facebook account.

"Now, let's see what my babe in St. Louis is up to." A photo of her with a couple of friends—much younger-looking girls—at the Gateway Arch accompanies her earlier one.

Daniel looks skeptical. "Is that the same girl? Look at her main headshot. I think she's done a Photoshop number on that one. She can't be 18."

"But she said... " After studying the photos more closely, Ryan pushes back from the desk. "Damn! You're right. She's been playing me. So, do you have any better websites?"

Daniel moves from the edge of his bed and takes off his glasses. "Um, not really."

A *Boy Next Door 2013* wall calendar with April's model showing off his defined abs, catches Ryan's eye. Looking annoyed, he keeps his focus on Daniel's laptop. Ryan is keyboarding when Daniel, noticing Ryan's hunched shoulders, gets up from his bed, stands behind him, places his hands squarely on Ryan's upper back, and begins a gentle but firm massage.

"Ah... That feels good."

"You're so tense." Daniel's touch is confident and effective in relaxing Ryan's shoulder muscles. "You are a handsome hunk—better 'n a cookie."   And without words to explain himself, Daniel kisses Ryan, first on the shoulder, then the neck.

"No, Billy!" Springing to his feet, Ryan demands, "What are you doing?"

"Billy?" Daniel puzzles, stepping back, stunned and

embarrassed.

Ryan retorts, "I'm afraid you're too queer for me." Wasting no time, he gathers up his backpack and jacket.

"You're right. You're afraid."

"I thought you were just rich—and that's why you talk and act the way you do. But you're gay."

"I'm sorry. I didn't mean to scare you. I just really appreciate you. You're my friend."

Ryan is at a complete loss for words.

Daniel continues, "You have such potential. I hope you see that. And college. You've even got a scholarship. Don't push your opportunities aside."

This is too much for Ryan. He rushes out of Daniel's room and pulls the door closed with more force than necessary. He quickly and quietly leaves the house, then walks fast, retracing the route Kim drove from Germantown Avenue.

On the bus, sitting sullen, Ryan passes his open phone from his right to left hand, back and forth. He closes the phone and slips it into his coat pocket. Closing his eyes, he exhales like he's shedding a distant memory. *Did I overreact?* He mumbles to himself. *Some people think I'm queer. But I'm not.*

Philadelphia's oldest and most prestigious public high school uses its own numbering system for their graduating seniors. Central is also the only high school authorized to grant Bachelor of Arts degrees in addition to the usual diploma for graduates who did not wish or did not qualify for college-level work.

A large banner over the auditorium entrance proclaims "Congratulations 272!" As the throng of students streams out, Daniel keeps his distance but observes Ryan, avoiding eye contact in case he should look for him. Ryan moves through the crowd without looking at anyone. He slips out a side door and heads for the library. In the expansive Research and Reference room, Ryan sees plenty of computer stations available—all of them, in fact. He checks into his Facebook account, where he sees a message from Sean: *Ryan. Minor emergency last night. You've got my cell. Sure would like to talk.*

Ryan looks up, staring into the upper level of the library as if his memories are stored there. Waiting for inspiration, he just sits there, looking at the screen, then again at the upper level.

Days later and still in a daze, Ryan has not called or responded to his father's message. At Angelo's, with customers making routine purchases, Ryan glides in on schedule as always, and after heading into the backroom, takes command of his workspace, clearing, organizing, and checking in that afternoon's deliveries.

Angelo approaches respectfully. "Ryan? You know I told you about Mario. I owe my brother..."

"I know. It's okay. Really."

"There's-a something else."

Ryan is suddenly unprepared.

"I'm proud-a you. You are a son to me. I wanna give you this." He holds up a windowed business envelope plump with 20s, then pauses. "I knew your dad—know your dad. He could fix almost anything. He asked me to keep an eye out for you— but not let you or your mother know."

Ryan stares at Angelo. "That's why you had me do things around here—when he skipped?"

"Um... Things are not always what they look. He's been sending you—well, Terri—child support every month."

Ryan listens with annoyance and disbelief: *Does everyone*

know this but me?

"You were too young. I couldn't hire you official like."

Ryan flushes.

Angelo's eyes swell with tears as he hugs Ryan. Finally loosening his grip, he pushes himself to arm's length and hands Ryan the envelope. "My graduation present for you."

"I don't know what to say. Did you know my father was trying to reach me?"

"What? He knows he's not s'posed to contact you till you're old enough."

Looking around, Ryan pauses, then confirms, "He's trying to get back to me. I don't know what to think." A brief shiver makes Ryan change the subject. "Thank you." He hugs Angelo. "You've taught me a lot."

"Well, you wanted to learn. Now, you might wanna take a-vantage of summer for a little travel, maybe go see him… Send me a postcard."

Ryan gives Angelo an affectionate hug. He passes by the small wall-mounted mirror with a handwritten question above it: *How you look?* Ryan surprises himself with his own smile.

A week later, in the Gallagher backroom kitchen, the sunlight barely makes its way inside. All that is heard is the sound of Ryan upstairs, rummaging from room to room, including his mother's room. He comes downstairs with a backpack and gym bag in hand. In the dreary kitchen, he takes inventory of his memories: the sink's dirty dishes and the countertop with a peanut butter jar next to the toaster, the cutting board with the butcher knife, the table, cigarette butts overflowing an ashtray, and a partially crumpled beer can. He heads for the refrigerator and grabs a nearly empty carton of milk and a clean-enough glass, pours himself what's left, and sits down.

At the center of the cluttered table is a Hallmark card. Ryan picks it up and reads it out loud as if it were a question, *Happy Birthday, Son...* He glances inside at the sentimental copy with only Terri's signature. After setting it back on the table, he reaches into his backpack for the *Central High School Outlook Calendar for June 2013.* With a sigh of satisfaction, he circles graduation day and slashes it with an exclamation mark. He turns over the calendar and writes:

> *Thanks for the card.*
> *Going to travel while I can.*
> *Take care of yourself.*
> *Dump Mike. You deserve better.*
> *R.*

Pensive, he stares at the gash in the door trim for a second. Ryan gets up from the table, takes Terri's Glock 17 from his waistband, and tucks it into the backpack, deep on the bottom. *I don't want Mike using it. And I might need it.* Almost an afterthought, he retrieves his birthday card and slips it into the gym bag.

When he leaves, Ryan takes the house key—his only key—out of his wallet and slips it into the mail slot. It drops to the floor with a definitive *clunk.*

CHAPTER 10

The sound of a Greyhound bus door opening to let passengers on board is Ryan's only welcoming greeting. He finds an open seat that is more or less clean. He sits next to the window and unzips his backpack, feels for his phone, and hesitates. He finally calls *Mom*. It rings with no answer but her voicemail message: "Yo! You know the routine. Speak up." He hits the phone's *OFF* button, folds it closed, then slips it into one of the backpack's side pockets. Sighing, he pulls out a much-read paperback, *The Sea-Wolf*, by Jack London. He begins to read but is too fidgety to make much progress. Once the bus is on the Schuylkill Expressway, Ryan looks anxious as he leaves the only city he has ever known.

The throbbing of the tires at high speed creates a rhythm for Ryan's semi-conscious dream images. The Philadelphia skyline dissolves into a vintage postcard version of the sun setting behind the Golden Gate Bridge. In the Gallagher kitchen, he sees Terri and Mike drinking beer at the table, and himself storming into the kitchen and confronting his mother about Mike. In the Allen dining room, Ryan sees Neil and Kim kissing in a gently passionate and mutually loving embrace. Ryan sees himself resisting Daniel's kiss and earlier, him taking another punch into Daniel's gut, and Daniel trying to straighten Ryan's shirt. A momentary deceleration of the bus jars Ryan back to the present.

After hours of riding, Ryan just stares out the window at the seemingly endless open space. Eight hours of soybean fields and more soybean fields and cornfields and dairy farms, and he's still not out of Ohio.

If I go to sleep and wake up the next day, will I know I've actually traveled anywhere?

———☐———

The iconic Gateway Arch of St. Louis is now only a recent memory and does not soothe the passengers in their various stages of discomfort. They just sit, read, or talk in quiet tones. Or doze. Ryan sleeps, then stirs and gets up. He sets his backpack on his seat and goes to the restroom at the back of the bus. After locking the restroom door, expressing his repugnance, Ryan's eyes cross. Suddenly, the bus lurches to one side, then the other. Ryan hurries to make his way back to his seat. His backpack is now on the floor, lying on its side. He retrieves it and sits down. He does not see his phone under the seat in front of him.

It is nighttime in Kansas City, Missouri, and there is a change of buses. The tired, disgruntled passengers transfer to another coach like reluctant livestock being herded. Ryan crams his gym bag into the bus's outside luggage compartment and trudges with his backpack onto the bus along with the rest of the sleepwalkers.

A few new passengers, more than before, crowd into the bus. Most try to sleep. Ryan's bleary eyes are barely open. He tries to sleep until a brilliant flash of morning sunlight startles him into a state of uneasy wakefulness.

The driver, more cheerful than necessary, announces, "Okay, Bronco fans. Ready or not." Experienced and friendly, he pulls out a gold pocket watch, glances at the time, and nods with satisfaction as he pulls up to the Denver depot. "We've got just about an hour—55 minutes, to be precise—for that Denver omelet. Eleven straight up."

Ryan looks inside his backpack for his wallet and phone. Not finding the phone, he panics. He drops to his hands and knees in the aisle to look under his seat and the surrounding seats but sees only candy wrappers and a newspaper. No phone.

Minutes later, in the depot's restaurant, Ryan is distraught and distracted. Passengers and locals line up for a cafeteria breakfast. When it's his turn, he points to scrambled eggs and toast. He sits alone, disheartened. Within moments, two punkish and tattooed teenagers sit at the same table. The boyfriend, who has turquoise-dyed hair, takes a seat next to Ryan. The other, an attractive younger woman, streetwise with exotic face tattoos and a nose ring, sits across from them. Comfortable and friendly toward each other, they chat while the male guzzles his coffee.

The young woman leans forward to Ryan. "So, where you headed?

"San Francisco."

The turquoise male assures, "Very cool."

"You've been there?" Ryan asks in an effort to be pleasant.

"Not yet. We live here in the Mile High City… Know what I mean?"

Ryan looks puzzled, then uneasy.

"So," the boyfriend says, "you have everything you need to enjoy Frisco?" Then to his girlfriend, "More coffee?"

She shakes her head in a polite *no* as she continues in hushed tones to Ryan. "Well, we're pretty friendly here. Jus' wanna welcome folks to Denver."

Turquoise gets up to fetch more coffee and just as smoothly snatches Ryan's wallet out of his open backpack.

Ryan smiles at her sincerity, "I've been days on the bus."

"So, where'd you say you were from?"

"Philly. This is the farthest out West I've been."

"Don't want your eggs to get cold."

She quickly gets up and excuses herself with a little nod. Ryan acknowledges her as he looks around for her boyfriend. Only slightly puzzled, he peels open a small plastic container of Smucker's strawberry jam.

When he finishes his toast, Ryan reaches into his pack's side pocket where his phone had been. Still annoyed with himself for losing his phone, he now discovers something else. His wallet is not there. *Now, where did I put it?* Throwing himself back in his chair, his eyes squint in serious thought. *Turquoise!* Springing to his feet and grabbing his backpack, he dashes for the door. Just outside the Greyhound depot, he looks both ways, not sure which way to run. There are only a few people on the street, none who look like the duo. Dejected, he drags himself back inside.

In the main waiting room, Ryan drops his backpack onto an empty chair. He takes out his gear, placing each item one by one with deliberation in the seat next to it. Startled at seeing the Glock at the bottom, he leaves it alone. In another pocket, he feels something. He pulls out the envelope Angelo had given him, and finds his Greyhound receipt, a 20-dollar bill, and two ones. With a sigh, he leans over his backpack and clutches it. He appears to be praying. Or retching.

A new thought crosses his mind. He gasps. Looking around, he stuffs his bag with his belongings. Jamming his free hand into his pocket, he pulls out a couple of quarters and other loose change. *Where are the phones?* Lined up against one wall are what used to be real phone booths, now only empty stalls, one of which is occupied by a man on his cell phone.

Panicking, Ryan goes to the ticket counter. The several people ahead of him seem bored, anxious, or annoyed. An African American* mother and two young children are the most annoyed and most willing to let everyone know. At the ticket counter, the agent, a woman in her early 50s with ultra-blonde hair done up enough to compete with Dolly Parton, tries to be friendly unless pushed too far.

Biting his lip, Ryan turns his head to see the digital clock, which reads *10:46 AM*. Seconds later, he turns his head again. An elderly lady, not overweight but with a sturdy build, smiles. Her silvery hair and pageboy haircut give her a youthful advantage. She makes cheery conversation, "Time and tide—and the bus—wait for no man. Especially when you're in a hurry."

Caught up in his own worries, Ryan barely turns to see if she is talking to him. When he realizes she was, he forces a smile but says nothing.

Finally, it is his turn. The ticket agent only points to the other sign: *CUSTOMER SERVICE*. He protests, "There's no one there. I need to make a call to my bank AND be on the bus in five fucking minutes. I'm sorry, four fuck'n—"

Ryan charges out to the bus bays. There, another line of passengers awaits the driver. Eventually, at 11:10 AM according to the digital display, a new driver saunters out to his coach. The once-cheerful lady gets in line behind the rest of those in a hurry.

Ryan reclaims his former seat. With everyone on board, he sees he still has a vacant seat next to his own—until the lady makes her way, reluctantly, to it. She says, "Sorry." Ryan looks uneasy and says nothing for a few moments. He moves his backpack to the floor. Cautiously, she takes the open seat.

Frustrated, Ryan explains himself. "My money. My wallet. My debit card. Stolen right before my fuck'n eyes… Sorry."

"I know. I saw—kind of. After it happened. At first, I thought they were your friends. But you're too clean-cut.

Except for your rough language."

Ryan heaves a sigh of exhaustion. "I'm on this stupid quest to meet my father… Now I don't even have his phone number."

Taking her time, the woman assures him, "The Lord will provide."

Oh, no…not one of those! Ryan braces himself, holds his breath, and fixes his gaze straight ahead, saying nothing. The woman leans back in her seat and just smiles to herself, closing her eyes peacefully.

Ryan closes his eyes too, but forcefully. "And my phone!" he adds. "If I can't call my bank, my savings could get hijacked too—you know, overdraft protection."

Opening her eyes as though stirring from a pleasant afternoon nap, the woman looks over at Ryan. "Would you like to use mine?" Not waiting for him to answer, she digs into her purse and pulls out a new iPhone. "My grandkids said I need it to stay in touch. Or out of trouble." Seeing Ryan's surprise, she adds, "You do know how to use one, don't you?"

"You're *awesome.* Thanks."

Within less than a minute he has contacted his bank and is listening to music-on-hold.

Out of the corner of her eye, she notices him fidgeting. "Don't worry about the time."

Ryan smirks, "Yes, I know. Time and tide…" He leans back with suppressed impatience, waiting his turn. When he looks out the window, he notices the magnificent Colorado Rocky Mountains for the first time. His mouth drops and his eyes widen. "I need to report a stolen card…"

Hours later, and although weary from the day's ride, the passengers are more alert now. Ryan's travel companion asks, "Do you have enough cash to tide you over?"

Extracting a single 20 and two one-dollar bills, he shrugs.

"This is it."

"Hmm. Let's double that. I bet you have at least one person who's waiting for a call—maybe someone who didn't get a proper goodbye?"

She again hands him her phone. He turns his face away from her, as if an answer will come if he just listens to the strumming sound of the bus's wheels speeding toward Salt Lake City. The setting sun, red-orange, is turning the sky into copper and indigo.

"So, make the call, Ryan."

Looking away from Ryan to the other side of the bus in a polite attempt to give him his privacy, she reflects on recent events, smiling.

The phone rings, then voicemail: "Your digital Daniel here. Talk to me."

"Dan, Ryan here, reporting in to tell you I'm on my way to California. Oh, I'm on a borrowed phone. I hope it's okay to call you…to thank you for your friendship. And to tell you I'm sorry…sorry about how I ran out on you. At another time, if you want, I'll tell you about my adventures."

A short time later, at the Salt Lake City Greyhound depot, Ryan hugs the lady goodbye. "What is your name?"

She does not answer. She simply smiles and nods farewell.*

Back on the bus, Ryan silently bemoans, *One more day!* With the seat next to him empty, he pulls up his backpack and rests against it. Almost comfortable, he drifts into a dream state of impossible images: the sun rising in the west over the Golden Gate Bridge, and red-brick rowhouses—like in Philadelphia—in a tree-lined lane. A handsome forest-green front door with a classic brass knocker opens. His father with his blonde wife and an even more blonde child greet him as he approaches.

CHAPTER 11

Zooming along with light traffic, the bus is citybound on the San Francisco-Oakland Bay Bridge.

The driver calls out, "Final stop. It's Sunday in The City by the Bay. Thanks for ridin' da hound!"

San Francisco's Temporary Transbay Terminal is not classic, not important looking—just functional. The building ejects its contents in heaves. Ryan is part of that chum cast to The City's vultures.

Outside, Ryan looks both ways, then returns inside, visibly tired and scratching himself as if his shirt were made of sackcloth or scrap wool. He enters the men's room and stands in front of one of the sinks, unbuttons and removes his long-sleeve shirt, then strips off his plain white T-shirt. Out of habit and without deliberation, he smells the underarms of the shirt and his eyes peel wide open. Focused on his bathing efforts, he shoves his pack and gym bag under the sink. Ryan does not notice the guy in the corner.

The hunky and handsome African American man, who appears to be in his early 30s, takes an extra-long time to dry his hands. Shorter than Ryan, with a slight smile and an unthreatening, younger look—especially owing to his box haircut—Lloyd watches Ryan intently without blinking.

Ryan puts his head down close to the sink to wash his hair, face, and neck. And using several paper towels and a squirt of hand soap, he washes his underarms and repeats the soap-and-towel routine along with a rinse towel. When he's finished, he pulls his gear into an extra-wide handicap stall. He begins to undo his belt as he closes the commode door and notices his admirer.

Lloyd approaches the stall. "Hey. I'll hand over a few towels."

"Um…thanks."

In a few moments, Lloyd hands over additional warm-water rinse towels. "Dry ones coming up."

Ryan finishes wiping himself down. Feeling more refreshed, he leaves the stall and looks at himself in the mirror. He pats his hair dry, then squints at his sleep-deprived eyes and moves closer to make a cursory examination of his fuzzy chin and poor excuse for a mustache. He complains to himself but loud enough for Lloyd to hear. "Skip a whole week shaving and no one would notice."

Hushed but direct, Lloyd says, "I would."

"Um…thanks for the help. But I still need a shower."

"You can have one at my place."

Ryan's face brightens for a second, then nearly as fast, sobers. "What the…"

Lloyd's eyes make it obvious as he gazes at Ryan's crotch. "I know how to make a man happy."

With scorn in his eyes, Ryan glares at him and retorts, "Not *every* man."

With that, he leaves the bathroom.

Outside the terminal, Ryan shakes his head and shakes himself like a dog doused in water. Clutching his backpack and gym bag, he walks against the flow of commuters. He scrunches his forehead. "So…where the hell am I going?"

No one notices him talking to himself. He keeps walking toward San Francisco's Market Street and slogs his way along the long, long blocks until he sees a Chinese corner grocery. Picking up his pace, he enters as if he expects to find a friend awaiting his arrival, and taking in a deep, satisfying breath, he smiles at the elderly store owner.

Mr. Chan acknowledges him with reserved politeness. At the same time, another patron enters. A burned-out hippie with waist-length dreadlocks, his gait is a bit wobbly. Ryan assumes he must be a regular because Mr. Chan, without being asked, reaches for a pint of Southern Comfort and a pack of Marlboros.

Ryan steps back and waits for Mr. Chan to complete his transaction with his patron. Ryan gives a nod of acknowledgment to the aging hippie and looks over the groceries and sundries. *Sure different from Angelo's…* When he notices Mr. Chan looking at him, Ryan nods again. "Good morning. Oh, it's afternoon. Nice store, very orderly… What do you recommend for a hungry guy fresh from Philly?"

Mr. Chan, with a hint of a smile for guessing what might be the right answer, says, "Bagel and Philadelphia cream cheese."

Dreadlocks, who is still hanging out, overhears this exchange and chimes in, "Whiskey Bill's the name."*

Mr. Chan is trying to serve Ryan. He grimaces at the interruption and nods in apology to Ryan. "Something else, Bill?"

"Yeah. Hell, yeah. I'll have what he's having…. Or was it, 'I'll have what *she's* having'…" He laughs at his own joke.

Ryan and Mr. Chan have no idea what he finds so amusing.

"Damn right! For both of us. I'm payin' too," Bill adds.

"Bill, you want a bagel and cream cheese?" Mr. Chan says.

To Ryan, Whiskey Bill adds, "Southern hospitality. Since you're new to town. Right?"

"Um. Yes, I just arrived in Frisco—"

Whiskey Bill leans forward like a professor wishing to make an important point to an errant college student. "Hold 'r right there! You get your first lesson right now. You tell 'im, Mr. Chin."

Mr. Chan, addressing Ryan, says, "*Chan. Mister Chan.*" And ignoring Bill's request for endorsement, Mr. Chan glances over to the door when the electronic buzzer announces another customer.

Continuing his lesson in etiquette, Whiskey Bill proceeds, "Like I waz sayin'. No sayin' *Frisco* in this fine city—not that I mind, mind ya. But proper folks will think yer ig-NOR-ant."

Ryan looks to the store owner for assurance. Mr. Chan wants no part of this and simply rings up the complete order and goes over to the deli area to prepare the bagels.

A few minutes later, bagels in hand, Ryan and Whiskey Bill walk toward the door.

Ryan says, "Thank you for the bagel. And the advice too. I'm just a little wary about accepting—"

"—about accepting the *kindness of strangers?*"

Ryan wonders out loud, trying now to guess the reference his host has in mind. "American Analog Set...*Kindness of Strangers.*" Smiling that he remembers, Ryan waits.

"What? Nooo! It's Tennessee Williams! *Streetcar.* Oh, you're too young."

"No, I'm not. I remember. Marlon Brando. *Streetcar Named Desire.*"

"Now we're talkin'... We're outta here. Thank you, Mr. Chin."

In front of the store a small, uninviting bench to accommodate squatters sits baking in the early afternoon sun. Ryan arranges his gear underneath and scoots himself as far to one side as possible to allow Whiskey Bill room.

"So, Bill, how long have you lived here?"

"It's Whiskey Bill. Since nine...teen...sixteee...seven. Yep.

That's when 10,000 of us, right here in San-Fran-cis-co, protested. And no, not everyone wore flowers in their hair."

Ryan is savoring every bite of his bagel. Whiskey pauses with obvious pride.

"Muhammad Ali had refused military service. And The Beatles released *Sgt. Pepper.* What a year!" Leaning back against the store's window, and basking in the memory, he sums it all up. "It just doesn't get any better. I was here for it all!"

All Ryan can say is, "Wow."

Bill is in no hurry but Ryan's right leg, fidgeting in a fast idle, makes it obvious he wants to get going. "That's really interesting. In school, I loved history. But right now, I need to find a place to stay. And have a real shower. I needa find my dad, I haven't seen him in like—over 10 years."

"I know where you can stay. Cheap."

Ryan springs up, grabs his packs, and begins walking—but in the wrong direction. He looks back and sees Bill heading the other way. Noting his limp, Ryan turns and catches up to him, then slows to match Bill's gimpy pace. Ryan opens his mouth to ask a question but resists.

In the Tenderloin District, in broad daylight right on the sidewalk, two guys—an African American and a Hispanic— offer two different colored cell phones to a skateboarding white teenager. Two men who appear to be in their mid-30s cook crack between a black Mercedes and a parking meter. At a bus stop, a hooker waits for two other men to settle up their agreement. On the nearby corner, a police car idles.

Ryan, like a horse held back and champing at the bit, plods along with Bill while the veteran of city living gestures for him to stay calm and just keep an easy pace.

Ryan complains, "This is like home. Same illegal shit goin'

on here… Where are you taking me?"

Nearby, a youth hostel is a refreshing contrast to the neighborhood—a sanctuary of cleanliness with front-desk staff as gracious as those at a nice hotel. Foreign languages, the din of lobby conversation, and the indiscernible conversation between Whiskey Bill and the desk clerk begin to jumble Ryan's frazzled brain. But then he blurts out. "I can't afford this. It's all the cash I have."

Bill smiles an apology to the clerk and takes Ryan by the arm like an uncle about to confide a family secret. But saying nothing, they walk out. Bill takes a swig of Southern Comfort.

"Okay. There's another place. It might have better rates. So…how much can you spend? You didn't come here thinking San-Fran was still The City of free love, did ya?"

"Whiskey, I have 40 bucks. I was robbed in Denver. I have money in my bank in Philly, but—"

They plod into another hostel lobby that is several rating points down in ambience, cleanliness, and courtesy. Ryan now leads the way into the lobby. A clerk with a name badge, *Vihaan*, looks up from his textbook.

Ryan, trying to sound confident, states, "I'd like to have a bed for one night. And a shower, for sure."

Vihaan answers with a lilting Hindi accent, "Certainly. Just yourself or both you and your friend?"

"Just me."

"That will be $22 even. We just need to see your ID, please."

"What? ID? I'm paying with cash."

Vihaan responds as if reading a text. "It is the law, my friend. No guests to be admitted without documentation. I would lose my job before your head touches the pillow."

"But it was stolen."

Vihaan looks at Ryan with the sympathy of a weary nurse about to give his one-thousandth vaccination. "I am so sorry."

Stating the obvious, Whiskey implores, "You mean your money and your ID too?" He pauses, then adds, "You are FUBAR!"

Ryan looks lost, now wary of yet another Whiskey-ism or movie reference. He turns to leave with minimal enthusiasm and plenty of annoyance. "FUBAR? I think I've heard of it. But…"

Whiskey Bill feels compelled to enlighten his new friend. "An Army term. I learned it in Nam."

But Ryan is not interested in movies or a history lesson. Dejected, the two of them trudge out into the afternoon. Bill nips again and offers some to Ryan. Ryan shudders.

On a different block but still in the Tenderloin, a leathery-faced derelict, weary from too many years fending for himself on the streets, is talking in animated conversation with no one and stops to urinate on a stick of a tree. Held in place with tall stakes, the tree's green plastic tag proudly proclaims, *Friends of the Urban Forest.*

Whiskey scoffs, "No respect!"

"I'm back in Filth-a-delphia," Ryan moans.

"Okay. Plan B. I sneak you into my hotel so you can get a shower."

Ryan gives him a shrug of acceptance.

"Then I'll show ya my favorite place to stay. And it's sure as shoot'n not my hotel."

"So, couldn't I just shower at their place?"

Whiskey just shakes his head.

———□———

Maybe in the 1930s, the Seneca was a fine enough hotel, popular with Chinese and Filipino dockworkers. Then. But now, it might be last on the list of historic buildings awaiting rehab. It is a city-owned single-resident occupancy (SRO) housing facility for the homeless. Tourists and workers scurry quickly past its controlled access doors while three handcuffed men in their 20s are shoved into a black-and-white San Francisco Police SUV. It is late afternoon.

The door opens for Bill as if he were a celebrity and a hefty, wafting dose of marijuana greets anyone close by. A husky African American guard approves Whiskey with an upward nod of the head, but grimaces at Ryan, indicating for him to stop. The guard gets up from his stool to question Bill about this unexpected follower.

"Jesse," Bill explains, "he's my friend from Philadelphia. Here for a few minutes before we head out."

Jesse is satisfied with Bill's confident answer.

Ryan smiles more sheepishly than he would care to admit. He straightens himself up and presses forward. Embarrassed at seeing his reflection in the faded mirror next to the elevator, he turns away to see a woman wearing a pastel, floral-print housedress and a mismatched bright-orange scarf. She smiles. With most of her teeth missing, she has a kind of jack-o'-lantern look about her.

Ryan stands closer to Bill. When the elevator doesn't arrive, Bill turns to the staircase and complains, "It's busted again, have ta walk. Four floors up. Sorry."

The chipped woodwork and worn, splotchy-blue carpet combined with odors of cigarettes, marijuana, and the musty smell of mold from bathrooms compete with each other to offend. The battered door of Bill's private room must have had a crowbar break-in at some point. Bill unlocks it and steps in first. The full-size, unmade bed takes up most of the tiny room. Only a chair by the open window and a corner sink jam the remaining space.

"The City makes me stay here. They don't want me living on the street." The noise of a police car siren emphasizes his point. "After you shower, I'll show you where my friends live."

A short time later, with Ryan freshly showered and shaved (save his attempt at a mustache), they leave the Seneca. He carries his gear and does not ask about the bulging grocery bag Whiskey Bill lugs. Whiskey takes another dose of Comfort.

On Market Street, only moderately busy for a Sunday, Ryan sees a pizza-by-the-slice vendor, nodding to Bill to ask if he wants one as well. Not interested in food, Bill shakes his head.

Ryan breaks one of his two $20 bills. A wave of worry crosses his forehead. After wolfing down his pizza, and looking like he could eat several more slices, he picks up his gym bag and follows his guide to the nearest bus stop. As they pass by a Bank of America entranceway, Ryan sees a man younger than Whiskey sleeping on a piece of folded cardboard. The single blanket draped over him isn't big enough to cover his bare feet. Simultaneously, two women in their mid-40s pass by. Their designer outfits of dazzling white shorts and halter tops in vibrant colors are perfect for a Southern California resort. At the sight of the homeless man, one objects with a grunt of disdain and the other counters with optimism.

"But what a great place to be homeless; it's not that cold."

Ryan shoots the women an incredulous glance. Ryan looks toward the downtown Ferry Building, then Twin Peaks. He notices the rainbow-colored banners celebrating June as Gay Pride Month and tells Whiskey Bill, "Philly's got a pride thing too, but I've never seen so many of these flags. Does the whole city go all out to be queer?"

"Best not say 'queer' unless you are one," Bill says, his Southern origins sounding through. "Where have ya been, boy?"

"Obviously, not from here. And I don't want to join their camp."

"So, you think they still recruit?" Chuckling at his own humor, Bill adds, "But around here you'd swear they're kinda protected—like an endangered species. And it's good for tourism. We're not goin' ta the Castro. So relax. Instead, we'll be goin' through the famous Haight-Ashbury. But you won't become a hippie."

Upon seeing the 6 Parnassus bus approaching, Bill motions to Ryan that he can board the bus via the back door. Looking slightly puzzled and definitely tired, Ryan follows along without protest. In the back of the crowded bus, an over-enthusiastic tourist plays "White Rabbit" on his Android for a few too many of his friends, probably children of former hippies. A work-weary passenger looks mildly annoyed but says nothing. Other passengers pay no attention at all—until these "Friends of Alice" chime in singing bits of Jefferson Airplane's most famous song.

With passengers now glaring at the jubilant visitors, their singing subsides until the final lines, and they break out again in a chorus, almost as a reprimand to the bored and homeward-bound passengers. Ryan admits to Whiskey, "I never understood that feed your head thing."

Ignoring that comment, Bill asserts, "I knew her. Grace Slick. We were close." He pauses to see if any of that registers with Ryan. "What a fox. She lived next door to me."

Fidgeting in his seat, Ryan cannot keep his anxiety from showing. "Whiskey? Where are we going?"

"Don't worry, my boy."

"Right. The Lord will provide."

"Hey! Show some respect."

"Whatever," Ryan huffs.

Many of the tourists, including the Friends of Alice, get off at the famous Haight and Ashbury stop. The bus is now almost solemn. Several stops later, Ryan notices the street numbers progressing higher, now in the teens, and a park on the right. Bill rises with a flourish.

The density of trees and bushes is at once attractive and defensive against pedestrian invasion. But Bill knows his way into the woods away from the heavily trafficked Lincoln Way. The lengthening days of June are beautiful with their long shadows and golden light. In the cooling hours of the day, the tall trees send out an intoxicating fragrance, and as they enter the park, Ryan exclaims, "What is that smell? It's awesome."

"Eucalyptus. They were brought from Australia."

"So, where do your friends live? Near this park?"

"Actually, *in* the park. Golden Gate Park. It's where you can sleep tonight. Free of charge. I'll introduce you to my friends. You'll be okay. Just be cool. Okay?"

Ryan's mounting anxiety makes him hyperventilate. This makes Bill stop.

"Are you all right, man?"

Ryan looks around at the trees. "You mean I'm supposed to sleep...in the woods? Couldn't I sleep with you?" Surprised at himself that he would ask such a question, panic shows in his eyes.

"You'll be fine. I wish I could stay in the park. The songs of the crickets and frogs, and fog horns from the Bay...the fresh breeze... But I have to be *a-ccount-ed for* at the Seneca. Or I get *other* city accommodations."

What the hell have I gotten into? Ryan worries.

As they progress further into the park, Bill assures Ryan that he knows where he is going. "They're near Stow Lake."

"Well, that's reassuring. So, your friends…where are they?"

"They'll be here soon. They've been here awhile, so they know their way around."

Ryan, slowing down but still following behind Bill, plods deeper into the park, his apprehension growing. They approach a cluster of rhododendron bushes in full bloom but shadowed enough by the towering trees that their color is indeterminate. Ryan's color is also indeterminate but his exhaustion is obvious as he lets out an unmistakable yawn.

Bill pulls something out of the grocery bag and Ryan sees that it is an Army Surplus overcoat.

Bill offers it to him. "You'll be comfortable. The ground is soft and this will be just fine this time of year."

Ryan's mouth drops open but he is not ready to say thank you.

Hushed conversation coming from somewhere in the surrounding bushes does not surprise Ryan as they stand there.

Bill talks into the closest bush, "Hey, Ronnie. Whiskey, reporting in. I have a friend for you to meet."

The odor of high-performance cannabis boldly invites all to enjoy. Bill approaches with enthusiasm while Ryan reluctantly lags behind several steps. Stoned and unsteady from too much hard apple cider, two men come out of the shrubbery. They might be too old to be considered punks, but the tattoos on their faces and necks, and the chrome nose ring and wood earlobe ornamentation on Ronnie make Ryan uneasy, sending flashes of Denver through his mind.

"We've been waitin' fer ya. Kinda."

A woman named Frida, presumably Ronnie's girlfriend, follows along with a wholesome-looking 18- or 19-year-old with earnest, dark eyes, wearing a U.S. Army camouflage fatigue cap and an oversized black sweatshirt. Bill takes Ronnie aside and whispers to him. Frida then introduces her friend, Rob. Ryan tries to be polite, but he's exhausted.

Whiskey Bill makes a formal introduction. "My good friend here has survived three long days on the bus and is really ready to zone out."

All three look at Ryan, hardly keeping secret their blend of curiosity and suspicion. Their looks give away their wary thoughts.

Bill continues, "Ryan, you're in good hands here with my friends. They'll let you stay with them for the night. I, however, have to report back to my cell."

Ronnie nods with disinterested understanding. The other two study Ryan while he watches Ronnie hand over a stash of something to Bill.

After flashing a victory sign and with a nod to Ryan, Whiskey leaves. Ryan carries his backpack, his gym bag and the overcoat, as he follows his new hosts into their hideaway. Enormous bushes and eucalyptus trees silhouette a sky that is still blue after sunset. The breeze creates ripples on the moonlit Stow Lake as conversation wafts from the rhododendron bushes.

Rob asks, "So, where do you come from?"

"Philly. How 'bout you?"

"Portland. Not Maine. Oregon."

"I'm sorry. I'm so wiped."

Frida redirects the banter. "But you won't mind if we get wiped. You're welcome to join us."

Hesitating, Ryan shrugs. "I'm okay. You go 'head." Yawning, he adds, "If…I… could…just…lie down."

In the early morning, Ryan stirs from his sleep on the ground only inches away from Rob. Ryan tries to focus his eyes to make sense of his surroundings. He mumbles, "Daniel?"

Rob's eyes are fixed on him, penetrating, dilated, and unblinking. Rob gives Ryan a reassuring smile and asks, "Daniel?"

Suddenly realizing that he is face to face with someone he doesn't know, Ryan freezes. Rob laughs lightly and lets him focus his thoughts and adjust to his surroundings. Slowly and with grimaces of pain, Ryan sits up, looking much like an Army recruit roused from a drunken stupor.

"Where am I? Who are you?" He looks around. "Weren't there others?"

"Yeah. Frida works at night. Well, Ronnie too. Whiskey Bill brought you. Quite a storyteller, isn't he?"

"Uh-huh... Frida?"

"Yeah. Like Frida Kahlo, the painter. It's her nickname. People like nicknames. I'm Rob."

"Like Robin Hood? Like I've fallen into a band of outlaws?"

"Right."

Ryan blinks and twitches his head while Rob pulls out an iPhone. "It's 5:15—in the morning, in case you're not sure. Our nearest Starbucks isn't open yet."

Ryan throws himself back onto the ground, disengaged and unsettled. "Starbucks? Now?"

"Of course. But we can go a little later this morning."

Ryan looks up at the canopy of leaves, the earliest light of dawn filtering into the hideaway and his eyes. He blinks again, as if it will make things more clear. Not convinced that he wants to go anywhere, he mutters, "Okay."

Closing his eyes again, Ryan shifts himself to relax and maybe get more sleep. Almost immediately, he begins to snore softly. Rob smiles and lies down next to him.

CHAPTER 12

ater that morning, Rob saunters into a busy neighborhood Starbucks on Irving Street with Ryan following behind and taking in the fresh coffee aromas.

"Allow me," Rob says. "What'll you have?"

"A coffee. Regular."

Rob chortles. "Okay. What to eat?"

"That's all right. Something later, maybe."

"Don't be shy. You have to be hungry. You can treat another time."

Ryan smiles.

After getting their drinks and food, they sit at one of the sidewalk tables. Rob sips on a luscious-looking latte, then reaches into a canvas bag and slips out an iPad, setting it on the table next to the drink.

Ryan's interest is piqued as he takes a bite out of his muffin. "I don't get it. I thought you were—um, like...homeless. Where do you come from? Why are you living with—with strange people? Aren't they illegal?" Picking up momentum for questions, he continues, "Do you always buy the coffee?"

Rob gives Ryan a Cheshire-Cat grin that suddenly turns pensive. Coming back to the topic, Rob asks rhetorically, "You don't have homeless people back home? Not everyone is privileged—like some of us."

Ryan is not sure if he is being reprimanded or included in the *some of us*. "Privileged?" He pauses. "You should see Kensington, where I grew up. Like in the *Rocky* movies, but worse. However, I did manage to get into a good high school."

Rob squirms and looks beyond Ryan, seemingly distant, taking time to answer, thinking. Peering directly into Ryan's eyes, Rob confides, "I'm beginning school in the fall. UC Berkeley. But before that, well, I think of it as investigative work. Others might call it slumming. But I have been doing research on the criminal forces exploiting the homeless. Even cartels."

Ryan stops sipping his coffee and cocks his head, not relieved to hear this, but more engaged.

Rob continues, "I'm only a freshman and will be studying sociology. Deviant behavior, is my special interest. Law enforcement, ultimately."

"Ya wanna be a cop? You mean, this is kind of undercover work?" Ryan is not sure what to say next. He looks at Rob's hands. Then he blurts out, "You're pretty wholesome looking to be a cop. Sorry. I just expect cops to be more, you know, macho." Now not sure he should have said that, but still curious, he adds, "What do your parents think of all this?"

Rob stiffens in self-defense. "They just know that I'm here. My father is an Episcopal bishop and a couple of parishioners—*former* parishioners—live here. I'm house-sitting. That's why I'm here for the summer. You?"

"I'm trying to meet up with my dad. But my money and ID were stolen in Denver. And my phone is in some godforsaken place between here and home—or what used to be home."

"So you're on a quest—an odyssey, like, uh, Homer's..."

"Odysseus."

Rob looks surprised at Ryan's matter-of-fact, fast response. Shifting back to the seriousness of Ryan's mood, Rob keeps from speaking too soon. Then, thinking out loud continues, "You did have a bank back home, didn't you? You could have them wire you your money. Right?"

"Yeah, but to where?"

"Western Union. A few people I've met here get money that way. And they don't have regular IDs."

"So, I'm an undocumented white boy from Philly. Not Odysseus?" Ryan chokes on a muffin crumb and coughs. "You remind me of a friend in Philly. He knows the classics too. He wants to act."

Again, Rob asks, "So, your dad's expecting you, right?"

"Nope. I was going to surprise him with a call when I got to Berkeley. But that's the problem. His number was in my phone."

"You mean..." Rob leans back, thinking. "Does he have a landline?"

"I don't know. Probably."

"So what's his name, and we'll look it up right here."

Ryan brightens with a jolt of excitement as Rob opens up a phone directory app. "Sean O'Brien. Berkeley," he says.

Rob types in his name. Within a few seconds the app flashes back its results: *Sorry, no results found. Please try again.*

"Humm... *S-E-A-N, O apostrophe, B-R-I-E-N.*" Rob's eyes rove the protective overhang of Starbucks as if an answer might float down. Finally, they come back to Ryan, who is glum once again. "Before the internet!" Rob says.

"Sooo?"

"Before the internet, there was paper—as in printed on paper. In phonebooks. Where data doesn't disappear in a blink of an eye or the plink of a keystroke. Remember, a long time ago—"

"Yes. *Star Wars,*" Ryan interrupts. "I loved Luke Skywalker's quest. Sorry, you were saying?"

"Well, what seems like a long time ago, grade school teachers would bring their students to libraries. And there we just might find printed phone directories. Then you can continue your hero's journey to find your father."

Ryan questions, "Even if he is Darth Vader?"

Rob tries to brighten his mood. "Do you have your lightsaber? … You've got your backpack. I can carry your gym bag."

The Presidio Library is an updated classic providing the perfect answer for those who enjoy old-fashioned reading and reference material not subject to digital disappearing acts. They look through phone directories and in short order write down Sean's phone number and address on a library-provided scrap of paper.

Rob asks, "You're sure you want to just show up instead of calling first?"

"Yeah, Why not? I've come this far. Surprise 'im!"

"Okay… BART can get us over there. Let me go with you."

"Who's Bart?"

Rob doesn't hold back a laugh. "BART—Bay Area Rapid Transit."

They leave like church bad boys sneaking out of Sunday service. The Greco-Roman columns and the cascading steps of the library are almost grand, not like the Philadelphia Museum of Art, but impressive for a neighborhood library. They descend the steps together.

At the downtown Embarcadero BART station, Rob pays Ryan's fare. As they pass through the turnstile with many passersby weaving around them, the two friends appear to be on a different schedule from the others.

Moving at a slower pace, Rob assures Ryan, "I won't interfere or anything. I'll go to the campus and hang. When you're ready, we'll meet up."

They have to raise their voices to talk above the live jazz

echoing from the tiled walls. Almost yelling, Ryan says, "You're so thoughtful. Like my friend, Dan."

"Your boyfriend, right?"

Ryan swings around, shoves Rob on the shoulder, and blurts out, "Fuck no!"

Just as quickly, Rob drops the gym bag, grabs his arm and bends it straight back, taking Ryan smoothly down to the platform and into a shoulder lock. Stunned, Ryan lies there for a moment while the late-morning commuters move out of the way without much thought of what looks like a fight.

"I'm no queer—or whatever you call them out here," Ryan mumbles.

Rob notices two BART security guards approaching and states calmly to them, "He slipped," and to Ryan says, "Let me help you up."

Ryan, seeing the guards, looks back to Rob and springs up.

The BART police continue on their way. As they pass by, one of them tosses out to Rob, "Nice takedown."

Without further comment, Rob directs Ryan to a wall-mounted BART route map.

Ryan, still puzzled, finally asks, "Why'd you—*how'd* you do that?"

"You shoved me like you wanted to fight. It was just my natural reflex. You were talking about your friend Dan."

"You said I was—"

"So? What if you are? What if I told you I was a girl?"

Ryan stops. "What? I dunno… I just wanna meet up with my dad, say I love you for leaving me when I was little. And here's a bullet as a souvenir."

Rob's eyes narrow. "What…are…you…saying?"

"If he loved me, why'd he leave me with a drug-addict mother?" Ryan huffs. He stops to let Rob take that in.

After a few awkward moments, Rob says, "Obviously, you've had a lot on your mind. And you don't know what to expect from your dad."

"From him or anyone else out here… Let me go by myself."

"Okay. I'll stay here in The City. You deal with your dad. Call me if you want." Rob turns and walks away, but within a few paces, stops. "You don't have my number."

Ryan, still annoyed, says, "No, I don't… I'm sorry. I'm tired and it's hard to know whom to trust."

He pulls a pen out of his backpack and hands it to Rob. But Rob is already poised to write down the number on a small notepad.

Ryan tries to shift the mood, "Your detective pad?"

"Yeah, like *Harriet the Spy*, one of my favorite books as a kid."

Trying to remember if he ever saw that one, Ryan simply says, "Okay. Thanks again. I really do appreciate your help. I'll call."

CHAPTER 13

It is now late afternoon and Ryan finds himself in Berkeley's charming Elmwood District. Built in the 1920s with craftsman-style bungalows being the dominant style, it feels like a college-town neighborhood. Barking dogs in backyards compete with one another for bragging rights about their families. Ryan, feigning confidence, strides halfway up the block. He consults his note, comparing the address with the house numbers, and begins to slow as he approaches the home.

In the front yard, a pink bicycle with purple tassel streamers flowing from its handlebars is evidence that a princess might live there. Taking an extra-deep breath, Ryan rings the doorbell. A triple-tone chime heralds him. Within a minute, an eight-year-old girl opens the door. African American, with definite Asian eyes, she is exotic and delicate. Smiling at Ryan with the confident demeanor of a hotel concierge, she makes her announcement with a slight lisp, "Papa, dares a man at the door."

Wearing a chef's apron and a naturally welcoming smile, a man appears and defends the entrance.

"I'm looking for Sean O'Brien," Ryan states. "I'm his son."

"Ryan? I'm Giovanni Innocenti." At age 38, he looks like a younger version of the talented Italian tenor, Andrea Bocelli. With silver threads interlacing his black hair, he warmly welcomes Ryan.

Ryan flushes with embarrassment. "Oh, I'm sorry. I must have the wrong house."

"You have the right house. And this is Aida. Come in."

Taking in a breath and exhaling as if he had just completed a run, Ryan opens his mouth to speak. But Giovanni answers his own question with his unmistakably Italian accent. "So, you're Ryan. *Benvenuto.*" Extending his right hand, he waves Ryan into the inviting but eclectically furnished living room.

Ryan reaches out to shake Giovanni's hand and cautiously moves through the living room. Trying not to gawk as Giovanni leads him toward the dining room, Ryan notices some of its unique decor: A modern red sectional couch configured in a conversation-friendly nook with Aida's iPad mini; a control panel for lighting and high-tech media devices sitting next to an Italian vintage rotary telephone; a massive Italian Baroque Rococo mirror on the wall; children's books everywhere; and on a column presides a marble bust of Virgil with the inscription *Amor Vincit Omnia.*

Ryan reads it. "Love conquers all." Then adds rhetorically, "Really?"

"That's right, you studied Latin," Giovanni affirms.

"How would you know that?"

Ignoring his question, Giovanni continues toward the dining area, gesturing for Ryan to have a seat. "Your dad's at a conference. An end-of-the-year retreat for his people. Berkeley Art Museum. He'll be back Wednesday."

Ryan sets his gym bag and backpack down. He does not notice at first when Aida glides over to his backpack and looks like she's about to open it as if it had a present inside for her. Reflexively, Ryan swats at Aida like a mosquito.

Giovanni snaps, "Aida, no!"

Ryan looks at Aida with contempt, then back to Giovanni in apology. Aida runs to Giovanni and clutches his leg, pouting.

Giovanni admonishes, "She's only eight. You don't have to hit her."

"I'm sorry. I, ah..."

Giovanni strokes Aida's head as he examines Ryan. "Well. Aren't we off to a good start? May I get you something to drink? Or would a punching bag be better?"

Seeing Giovanni's slight smile, Ryan realizes the intended humor and meekly answers, "Um...water'd be great."

"Sean didn't know you were coming out, did he?"

"I thought I'd surprise him. But...who are you?"

"I'm Sean's husband."

Ryan's face shatters. He starts to stand but like a seatbelt is holding him down, he freezes, then sits silently for a moment.

"Not in front of our daughter," Giovanni warns.

"Like...you're both—"

Giovanni gives Ryan a moment of silence, gestures to Aida to leave the room, then reassures Ryan, "You've come a long way. And he really wants to see you. I didn't mean to spoil anything."

"My dad is gay?"

"He didn't tell you?"

Giovanni's cell phone rings with an Italian aria ringtone. He glances at the phone but doesn't answer it.

Ryan mutters to himself, "Fuck, fuck, fuck," and gets up to leave.

Giovanni commands, "Sit down. Your father and I have waited too many years for you to show up, only to just walk out!"

But Ryan bolts from his chair, knocking it over.

"Show a little restraint, son."

Upon hearing the word *son*, Ryan turns to face Giovanni, fuming. His hidden gun has shifted and its outline is visible on the side of the backpack. He pauses and grabs his other bag almost as an afterthought, then dashes out the door.

As the front door slams, Giovanni calls out, "*Tu sei un vero bastardo!*" [You are a real bastard!] Giovanni collapses onto a dining chair as Aida cautiously returns to his side.

"What happened to the berry mad man?"

As Ryan wanders among the walkways between the buildings of the Berkeley campus, looking disoriented, he consults Rob's note. He goes into one of the libraries only to return in moments, then stops a student with an implied plea, "No phones anywhere?"

"You don't have one?"

Without stopping, the guy continues walking. Ryan follows.

"I'm supposed to meet a friend. I have his number."

But the student only states, "Sorry."

Ryan looks for another student to ask but it's the same response. It is now early evening on Shattuck Avenue. Ryan discovers a T-Mobile store, goes inside, and approaches the salesclerk. In a few moments, the clerk obliges with a new phone to try out. He hovers within arm's reach next to Ryan.

Ryan pulls out his scrap of paper and calls Rob's number. Tense and irritated, he tries to be polite when Rob answers. "Where are you? You're house-sitting, right?" He digs for his pen. "Let me write it down… No, my dad wasn't home."

The salesclerk hands him a business card and Ryan politely accepts with a nod.

"I'll tell you later…got it." And to the clerk, while looking at the card, Ryan again says thanks.

CHAPTER 14

Ryan steps off the #71 bus at Haight and Buena Vista East, looks at his hastily scribbled address, and sees he has quite a hike yet ahead. Resigned to the task, he trudges up the steep hill ahead of him. Surrounded by restored Victorian and Edwardian homes and art deco apartments on his left, and Buena Vista Park on his right, he plods onward and upward. Near the summit, Ryan scans the San Francisco skyline, which is lit golden from the lingering light of the late sunset.

He stops for a moment to lean against an iron fence and catch his breath. An uncountable number of steps lead high up into the park. With a sigh, he continues his trek, looking at the address as he walks, until he stops at a three-story Edwardian with a commanding turret. *Could this be it?* he wonders. The home sits confident on the corner, understated in clean white with light taupe trim and a professionally maintained yard. He closes his eyes, just to relax for a moment.

Standing inside the iron-fenced yard is Rob, wearing a Giants baseball cap, a heather-colored hoodie, and Levi's. "Ryan!"

Ryan opens his eyes and stares. "Here?"

Without waiting for an answer, Rob walks back to the open door of the stately home, turns to face Ryan, and waits for him. Ryan straightens and grabs his backpack and crumpled bag, then steps forward slowly. Travel-worn and weary but willing to follow Rob's directives, Ryan approaches the open door but just stands there, waiting for permission to enter.

"Well, come in."

Ryan shakes his head. "One day it's bunking in the bushes with drug dealers…" He steps forward into the parlor and takes in its sweeping view of silver and golden high-rise buildings downtown at dusk and lights decorating the skyline. "The next day it's staying with a guy I barely know in a mansion overlooking The City."

"Friends of my father's—the parishioners I told you about—they inherited this place. Anyway, they're on vacation in France." Motioning for him to sit, Rob smiles sympathetically as Ryan tries to come to terms with everything, adding agreement, "Yes, it boggles my mind to go from here and then pretend to be one of them. Not for the faint of heart."

Ryan can only take in so much. He tries suppressing a yawn and turns to the window as he continues to listen to his host.

"So many reasons for ending up homeless—often beyond their control. Predators and criminals mixed in. It can be a cover for them too. It's wild." Rob, standing behind him, takes off the hoodie as Ryan gazes out the window. In the window's reflection, Ryan notices Rob's chest.

Turning, he exclaims, "You really *are* a girl!"

She is in a white-ribbed tank top, and Ryan's jaw drops.

"My dad's queer and married to a man. You're a *her* and not a *him*. I'm mind-fucked. So…you're not Robert?"

"Rob is short for Robin," she says, choosing her words carefully. "Maybe you should think of getting a good night's rest. There's a guest room for you and an actual bed."

Ryan nods, befuddled. Faintly smiling and not knowing what to say, he squints to read the tattoo on her right arm.

Rob shows him the classic typeface spiraling around her arm. "The LORD is my light and my salvation; whom shall I fear?" Turning to show off her other tattoo, she flexes her left arm, which has a tattoo of a raven with a golden orb in its beak and crossed arrows in one claw. "I designed it myself. Well, a friend helped too. It's part Native American, part Christian. I'll explain it another time."

"I just hoped we could be friends."

"But because I'm a woman…" Rob raises her eyebrows. Not waiting for an answer, she saves him from saying anything he might regret. "You'll feel a whole lot better tomorrow."

———□———

She was right. I do feel a lot better. I wonder if she's up yet… Ryan wonders early the next morning as he stretches and thinks about getting up. He gets his answer with the sound of coffee grinding. Quickly dressing, then poking his head into the hallway, Ryan has to think about which way to go. He turns left and sees a staircase—not the main one, but the back stairs for use by servants of a bygone era. *A secret passageway?* Ryan muses. Taking that one, he heads down to the main floor. The welcome-to-a-new-day aroma of freshly ground coffee wafts up the back staircase to greet him.

Skillfully remodeled while maintaining some of the look and feel of the original, but equipped with the finest gourmet appliances, the Edwardian kitchen includes a breakfast counter and an impressive commercial espresso machine.

"I didn't want to wake you too early. I hope you slept okay," Robin says.

"Yes. Thank you. My first good night's rest in…days. So, is it Rob or Robin that you prefer?"

"I do go by Robin. But my dad would sometimes call me Rob or Robbie. So, a latte to start your day?"

Ryan shakes his head in bemused appreciation. He studies her coordinated command of the twin-head La Marzocco Linea. *She's amazing! And her eyes… I never really noticed them before.*

With an effort at seriousness, Robin announces, "Barista training is essential in Portland—you know, like Seattle. A good friend taught me." Suddenly looking away from Ryan, she seems distant and sad.

After giving her time to come back to the moment, Ryan says, "You were going to tell me about your tattoos."

But the hissing of the espresso machine steaming keeps Robin's answer waiting.

———□———

A cell phone ringing in a pile of other lost-and-found items calls out for attention. A young woman's tattooed hand snatches up a duct-taped orphan. The Greyhound worker, with a mischievous smile, waits while the phone rings. It displays *Mom.*

Terri, wearing her security guard uniform, sees her phone ring. A scowl crosses her face and she answers with a snarl, "Where the hell are ya, ya good-fer-nothin' runaway?"

The Greyhound woman, repulsed, throws the phone back into the bin. After a few moments though, she reconsiders. With a look of scheming curiosity, she picks up the phone again and scrolls to an earlier number with a different area code.

———□———

The La Marzocco, having performed its duties, sits quiet but ready. Robin blinks, dabbing her eyes. "Excuse me. You asked me something... Yes, tattoos. Oh, another time. I'm wondering how you slept—if you're okay after your venture to Berkeley." She hands him her latte creation in a clear, double-walled cappuccino mug, showing off its three layers of light and dark espresso and a foam top with a star signature.

What a creation! Ryan thinks as he takes the mug. He nods his appreciation, then blurts out, "Actually, I need to apologize. I'm sorry for hitting you. And yes, I had a rough day and a night of weird dreams, but at least I did sleep."

"I'm sorry. Were they about your dad?"

"Um…sort of." But Ryan falls silent, thinking, *I was at my high school. You were there. On the ground. And I kissed you.*

Robin waits.

Ryan finally says, "I was at my high school. It didn't make sense. You know how dreams are. Maybe this surprise visit to my dad's wasn't a good idea. I don't know whether I can love him again or if I should kill him. I don't get why he left me. Turns out, I'm the one who is most surprised. Like, um…like I'm being played the fool. I feel I don't belong here."

Prioritizing her thoughts from that onslaught of disclosure, Rob replies, "Well, I'm glad you're here. And you don't have to tell me your dreams for us to be friends—after all, we have just met. We have some great discoveries ahead. All good, I think."

Maybe I told her too much… Robin worries silently. "By the way, what happened to me at the BART station? How did you do that?"

Relieved to shift to a new topic, Robin answers, "I studied Brazilian Jiu-Jitsu for several years. I'm a purple belt. It's great self-defense, especially for women. And it's great life training as well. I'm sorry if I hurt you at all." She grins. "Other than your pride."

With a faint smile, he assures her, "No, I'm fine. But my pride has taken a few falls lately."

Smiling again to shift the topic, Robin asks, "You like your latte—even if it's in a cappuccino cup?"

"Well, I was wondering about that," Ryan teases, but he

puzzles, *What's the difference between a cappuccino and a latte?*

Later that morning, Ryan and Robin go into a blinding-bright but rundown Western Union storefront in the Fillmore District. Robin hands her phone to Ryan so he can talk to his bank. After negotiating with them for authorizing a transfer and sending him a replacement card, the African American clerk with gorgeous braids (Robin later says they are extensions) hands over $300.

"Thank you for letting me use your address," Ryan tells Rob.

"I appreciate that you trust me."

They walk several blocks from the Fillmore District, up the hill toward the Castro, and past the famous Painted Ladies Victorian homes across from Alamo Square. Robin tells Ryan that some neighborhoods may not look dangerous but are, depending on the time of day.

They enter a lively neighborhood restaurant on Duboce Park full of San Francisco's urban mix of patrons—gym-fit mothers and their children in jogging strollers, gay couples having lunch together, techies at their Apple laptops, and old men with their white-muzzled old dogs at the door, greeting all who enter.

Ryan sneaks a glance, then another. This is clearly his first time in a café with this assortment of people. He notices two young women at another table, one affectionately kissing her sweetheart on the neck. Ryan shrugs his shoulders and sits back in his chair, mildly surprised at his own calm reaction.

Robin shows Ryan a selfie of herself with long hair. Her thumb slips and the next photo shows another selfie of Robin and a handsome Latino guy in front of a massive espresso machine.

Ryan studies it and looks at her with a genuine smile.

"Boyfriend?"

"Yes. Kinda. He taught me the difference between a tryst and a treasure… Let's catch the next streetcar."

The N Judah stops at Duboce Park before it tunnels through Buena Vista Hill—the same hill that gives Robin's temporary home its amazing views. They sit together without much conversation, only Robin's brief comments about the ride out to Sunset and Ocean Beach.

"They didn't try too hard to come up with something more original, did they—I mean, the street numbers…"

Ryan nods absently.

At the very end of the line, Robin leads Ryan to the beach. "Well, here it is. This is as west as you can get and still be on land."

The fog is lifting as dogs and their owners run along the surf-soaked sand. Waves crash in the distance.

"I thought you might like to air out your thoughts in the fresh breeze and when you're ready, you can call your dad," Robin adds as Ryan stares at the ocean.

After walking for about 10 minutes, Ryan looks to Robin. She hands over her phone. "I think we should have reception."

He calls.

A receptionist answers. "Good afternoon, Berkeley Art Museum. How may I direct your call?"

Ryan shivers and hesitates.

"Hello?"

Ryan, clearing his throat, struggles to say his father's name. "Sean O'Brien, please."

"I'm sorry, he's out."

Ryan looks defeated, then the receptionist amends her announcement, "No, wait. I'll connect you. He was away but now he's back."

A half a minute of mutilated classical music-on-hold seems like forever to Ryan as he waits. Calming himself with deep breaths and looking out over the ocean, he watches the seagulls fly overhead and paces.

"Where are you, son? I'm so excited to see you. I came back from the retreat early... What's that noise in the background?"

"I'm here. Um, at the ocean, here in San Francisco."

"I will come meet you. Ocean Beach? Or...where are you staying?"

"I'm staying at—" Thinking out loud, he speaks away from the phone to Robin, "What do I tell my dad?" Then he blurts out, "I'm staying at Robin's."

"Okay. Who's Robin?"

"Just tell him I'm your girlfriend," Robin whispers.

Chagrinned at her claim on him, Ryan is not sure he wants to accept an alibi not of his own making. Nevertheless, daring to let Robin take over the call to provide directions, he steps aside, disgruntled. Smiling, Robin accepts the challenge.

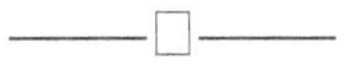

Later that afternoon, back at the house, Ryan admits his anxiety again. "I really don't know if I want to see him. Why'd he leave me? Why'd he send support all those years but never told me? I never saw the money. Didn't he know my mother was an addict?"

"Good questions. I think I understand."

But can she—with her privileged life and loving parents? Ryan paces between the entryway and parlor, looking out the beveled window next to the front door, then into a mirror in the hallway, back and forth like a dog in a kennel. He notices sweat on his forehead and wipes his brow with his sleeve. He then realizes that Robin is standing silently in the next room.

From a safe distance, she pulls out from under a napkin Terri's Glock 17. Leaving the magazine on the napkin, she steps forward to Ryan. Pointing it to the ceiling, she pulls the slide back and the chambered bullet ejects into her left hand. "So, I've cleared the weapon." She pulls the slide twice more, then demands, "Were you really expecting to use this?"

"What the fuck! You took my gun?" *How can I trust someone who goes through my stuff?*

"You left it loaded. In your backpack. With a bullet in its chamber! … And with you holding grudges—"

"You went through my personal stuff!"

"Just taking precautions, kiddo."

Kiddo? "Who the hell do you think you are?"

"Don't get defensive, sweetheart. Actually, I have training in firearms. This is a good one. But my favorite is the Glock 19."

Ryan stands there, unsure what to say. *Now I'm a sweetheart?*

A sudden knock on the door makes him jump. He goes to the front door and braces himself. Ryan reaches for the door handle, testing it as if it were too hot to touch without gloves. Robin discreetly leaves the room with the weapon.

Standing outside the solid midnight-blue door, Sean likewise braces himself as he steps back slightly. He is handsome in his Levi's and a green-and-black plaid hunter's shirt, and he's focused.

Ryan pulls the door open, his face tense as he lets his father in. Sean steps forward and opens his arms to hug Ryan. Ryan freezes as his father embraces him.

Sean exhales in relief. "Finally," he whispers. He steps back to look at his son, then hugs Ryan again. He can barely hold back his tears.

Robin comes into the entryway, cautiously waiting for Sean to acknowledge her, while keeping a polite distance.

Sean apologizes, "You know us Irish." He straightens and extends his hand, noticing her buzz cut and looking at her longer than he should.

Robin steps forward and grips Sean's hand more forcefully than he expects.

"You must be Robin."

She is respectful with the, "How do you do?" But when Sean holds her hand—locking eyes as if he should recognize her—she is the first to withdraw.

Sean smiles. "It's very nice to meet you. You have a lovely home, so tastefully updated without losing the charm of that wonderfully ornate period."

"Why, that's just what your son was saying."

Still brooding, and now irritated that he is the butt of some inside joke, Ryan interjects, "What're youse talking about?"

Robin cocks her head, puzzled, while Sean interprets for her.

"*Youse* is Philly for *you*, more than one."

Now Ryan is even more irritated with his accidental lapse into Philly lingo.

"Anyway," Robin explains, "I'm just house-sitting for parishioner friends of my father, an older couple who'd rather spend their summers in France—or anywhere but here in cold and foggy San Francisco."

"Right about that," Sean agrees. "So, are either of you hungry? We can talk over lunch."

Robin smiles with the graciousness of a diplomat. Ryan squirms in discomfort.

"When I'm over here in The City, I like to check out the competition. Colleagues, of course, at the de Young Museum.

They have a café. It's in Golden Gate Park. Have you been there yet?"

Ryan looks over to Robin but only says, "Um, sort of."

Glancing at each of them, Sean asks, "So, how did you meet, if I may ask?"

Ryan surprises himself. "In the bushes."

Sean looks chagrined.

Robin squints her eyes in disapproval. "Maybe you two should meet without me tagging along."

But Sean gives her emphatic reassurance. "No, I'd like you to come along."

Ryan looks impatient to just get going. *Let's get this over with.*

They leave the house and get into Sean's spotless Pathfinder SUV. Sean switches on the ignition and a CD of Gershwin's "It Ain't Necessarily So" comes on—too loud.

Sean reaches to turn the CD off but Robin, in the front seat, interrupts. Sean lets her take command of the audio system. She hits the back-arrow button so Ryan can hear the song from the beginning. Turning to Ryan in the back seat, she says, "I love that song. Ryan, what do you think of these lyrics? From the Gershwin brothers' *Porgy and Bess.*"

"I've heard them before but..."

Robin paraphrases, "The things that you read in the bible aren't necessarily true." She turns the volume down.

Sean challenges her, "But you're a preacher's daughter."

"Not exactly. He's an Episcopal bishop. More progressive than most, including my mother." She looks away, thinking of what to say next and with some delay, changes the subject.

When they enter Golden Gate Park, Sean looks over at Robin, then at Ryan in the back seat. An awkward silence continues while he hunts for a parking space. Pretending to ignore Ryan, Robin looks at Sean. "So, when did you know you were gay?"

Ryan, surprised at Robin's question, is as alert as a dog hearing its name called. He leans forward, ready to listen to whatever his father might say.

With calm in his voice and deliberation, Sean looks grateful, even prepared as he answers her question. "When I was a kid, I didn't think I was gay. I had girlfriends in grade school. By high school, I was pretty insecure about sex."

Ryan listens intently, but he lets Robin conduct the interview. "You didn't have sex with guys?"

I can't believe she's asking this! Ryan thinks, eyes wide.

"No! That never occurred to me. And I was a good Catholic boy, a scared Catholic schoolboy. I was just 16 and still a virgin when Terri—Ryan's mother, who was only 14—took a fancy to me. I was game. My first shot, bam! Pregnant. Unprotected stupidity."

Ryan suddenly throws himself back in his seat and blurts out, "So, you did tell her to have an abortion?"

Sean suddenly swerves to the right and slams on the brakes. Instantly, a cab following too close honks in reprimand. It screeches and honks punitively again as it swerves around the SUV.

"It wasn't like that," Sean replies. "I was so surprised. We hardly knew each other and she sure as hell wasn't prepared to become a mother." Looking straight ahead, then glancing into the rearview mirror to look at Ryan, Sean's face creases with anxiety. "She told you that? After the shock of the news, I proposed we get married. But she said we didn't need to bother. Once I held you in my arms, I was in love with you and loved being a dad."

Robin is now looking embarrassed for being privy to all

this. Sean finally finds a parking place while Robin, biting her lower lip, says nothing. Sean and Ryan make eye contact through the car mirror, and Sean holds his gaze on Ryan for a moment.

"Some men make better parents than women. For Terri, it was about control. She didn't like the inconvenience of motherhood and still wanted to play around. And did." Sean lets his words sink in. Making no effort to leave the car, he unpacks the rest of his story, still looking straight ahead with occasional glances into the mirror. "After years of her having flings with other men, I'd had enough. But she wanted to get back at me and convinced a judge to award you to her and just give me the duty of child support."

"But she never told me…" Ryan says as he digests this information. *Daniel was right!* "Why?"

"You didn't get any letters from me because that was forbidden. I wrote to Angelo to hear how you were doing. But for you, it's like I didn't exist anymore. I'm sorry she didn't let you know anything."

Ryan's face scrunches. "What did Mom say when she found out you were gay?"

"What? That had nothing to do with it. I didn't even know I was gay then. She only knows now. Maybe she suspected back then."*

Ryan sits quietly and remembers Heinrich with his camera, sitting next to Sean at Michael Jordan's last game in Philadelphia. He also recalls the souvenir photo Heinrich gave Sean. *Were they partners?*

"That wasn't the issue. And even if I had known I was gay, I sure as hell wasn't going to give her more vitriol to use against me. Or you." Sean continues, "So after we were separated—and she wasn't going to do a joint custody thing—

she decided to file a restraining order to prevent me from even seeing you. She said I was a threat to her. Well, I was furious."

Ryan remembers his dad handing him the little laminated shamrock, then running off and disappearing into the distance. *So, this son of a bitch leaves me and makes me a bastard...*

"I think she was still fighting her own demons. I believe her father abused her and her mother blamed Terri for it. She would never tell me directly."

Ryan, still sitting motionless and looking at the back of Sean's head, waits.

Sean takes a breath to conclude his story. Looking at Robin, he adds, "Since I was prohibited from seeing my Ryan until he turned 18, there was no point in staying in Philly."

Ryan finally turns to Robin but she quickly looks away.

"I kept my child support going the whole time." Looking unsurprised yet disappointed, Sean adds, "I'm sorry, Robin. This is more than what you expected to hear. Didn't I promise lunch?"

The three get out of the SUV and walk toward the de Young Museum, taking a shortcut through the deserted open-air plaza of the Music Concourse. Ryan, with one hand shielding his eyes from the sun's glare, looks like he is scouting for someone. In the near distance, he sees a solitary figure sitting on a bench. Nudging Robin, he slows his pace and points.

"I think it's Whiskey Bill." Clearing his throat, Ryan says, "Dad?" Surprised at himself for saying *Dad*, Ryan stumbles over his next words. "There's someone I'd like you to meet. He's the guy who introduced me to Robin."

They approach the bench and see Whiskey Bill way beyond introduction—napping or nearly passed out or listening to music without the benefit of headphones. Ryan imagines

Whiskey Bill as a bronzed statue with the early Vietnam protest rock group, Country Joe and the Fish, playing in tribute to him, "I-Feel-Like-I'm-Fixin'-to-Die Rag."

Ryan approaches and nudges him but Whiskey Bill remains still. He motions for Robin and Sean to continue on to the de Young Café. Ryan is pensive as he watches Bill for a moment, then slowly shrugs his shoulders and hurries to catch up with them.

At a table near the café's entrance, Ryan and Robin can see everyone enter and Sean enjoys watching them watch. Then Sean, with a devilish grin, asks Robin, "So, when did you decide to become a lesbian?"

She laughs. "But I'm not, actually. I have always been something of a tomboy."

Even if Sean asked the impertinent question, Sean himself squirms with embarrassment.

"My haircut makes me look…well, less classically feminine. It's dangerous being homeless and on the streets—especially for girls." Retrieving her wallet from her back pocket, she produces her Oregon State driver's license. It shows off her lustrous, long brunette hair.

Ryan blurts out, "You had such beautiful—"

"That's what my mother said. She had—still has—very clear ideas about how a woman should look…" She turns aside, like a smoker not wishing to blow smoke into a friend's face, and quickly asserts, "It's not so clear about how a wife should act."

Sean and Ryan puzzle over Robin's candid comment. She quickly refocuses. "It'll grow back. Before I'm lost in Berkeley books, I wanted to see for myself what homelessness and living on the streets was like."

Ryan explains, "Robin is going to study deviant behavior.

But isn't there a word for this?"

Sean jumps in with, "*Chutzpah,* maybe?"

"Not sure about that," Robin interjects. "I want to go into law enforcement, to become a cop. I guess you could say that I see it as my calling. But first I need to get a higher education 'befitting my fine intellect,' to quote my father."

Sean laughs lightly at a daughter perfectly mimicking a father. "So, your dad approves. How 'bout your mom?"

"Let's just say she has to sort some things out."

A handsome Hispanic server deftly delivers the three entrees, whisking away the table number, 69. Only Sean notices the number and the server looks back with a subtle wink.

"Okay. So, I'm the only queer one at this table? And that used to be considered deviant." Feeling smug and sitting back in his chair, he shifts the topic, "Let me ask you, Ryan. How did you manage to get out here?"

Ryan rolls his eyes. "I don't know where to start."

"Well, you can start at the beginning, or any order you like."

After Ryan gives a brief road trip summary, and their empty cappuccino cups rest while the three sit in comfortable silence, Robin offers, "Well, there you have it. But I think father and son need some time together. I'll get Muni back home and catch up with you two later." Extending her hand as she rises from the table, she adds, "A real pleasure, Sean. You have an awesome son and you're part of the reason."

Sean stands and gives her a heartfelt hug instead, and all three leave the café.

With sunlight casting long shadows through the eucalyptus trees near the museum, it looks magical. Sean and Ryan nod to Robin as she heads for the bus stop. A black Ford Econoline van with a San Francisco Police logo on the front door quietly pulls away from near the bench where Whiskey Bill had been.

Ryan looks back to the now-empty bench. His eyes widen as tears try to form and he slowly lets his head drop. Together, Sean and Ryan walk with only the breeze through the trees and traffic noise accompanying them. Sean is not sure how to read the silence. Willing to wait, he gives Ryan a look of quiet reassurance.

Ryan looks like he has a question. *So, were you and Heinrich lovers? And what about your new guy, what's his name?* But, with an unsure shrug, he changes his mind and keeps quiet.

———□———

Walking distance from the museum is Spreckels Lake. Abuzz with radio-controlled model boats, the shallow lake is home to San Francisco's Model Yacht Club. Some are beautifully crafted yachts, some more ordinary. Sean and Ryan stop and take a seat on a park bench to admire the lake's setting. No words are necessary. They simply sit next to each other. Eventually, they notice a father and young son launching a simple sailboat.

Ryan cannot help his tears. Sean moves closer, letting Ryan bury his face in his shoulder. Then suddenly, Ryan begins pounding on his father's chest with both fists. Sean overpowers him and bear hugs him until Ryan slumps again.

"I missed you," Ryan murmurs. "I missed having a real dad instead of drug-dealing oxy addicts and a sex pervert."

Sean hesitates before asking for clarification. "You mean your mom? Terri…and what?."

"Yes, I mean her and her boyfriend at the time. He took advantage of me."

Sean falls back onto the bench, not sure if he should press

for details. Speechless and sitting motionless, he waits for Ryan to continue. Finally, he asks, "Do you need to tell me more?"

"No, not now." Ryan adds in complete deadpan, "Maybe you could help me produce a child porn movie…"

Sean is visibly offended but takes his medicine with an almost silent gulp. For a long while, they watch the boats and their respective captains and mates sail on the rippling water, a cool breeze foretelling the cooler summer evening ahead.

As evening darkens the sky, Sean pulls up in front of Robin's house. He slips the gearshift into park, slowly presses the emergency brake pedal, and turns off the ignition. Sean hesitates to end their visit. Making no effort to get out, he states the obvious. "Well, here you are. What a lovely home. More like a castle, wouldn't you say? It's even got a tower and turrets."

But Ryan ignores Sean's efforts to make light conversation or to analyze the home's architectural nuances. "Dad?"

"Yes…"

"I don't know where to go from here. It's like a joke where a kid grows up thinking he didn't have a dad and then discovers, oh yes, he did. He just didn't know it. I feel like I've been duped. And it's hard not to wanna blame you. Or Mom. Or somebody. And even Angelo was in on this?"

"I'm so sorry, son. I was prohibited from contacting you. And at the time, I didn't have money enough to hire a lawyer to fight for me, for you. Terri had your child support money but…" He looks at Ryan. "Do you mean that she never—"

"No, she never told me you sent any money. I've been used."

"At least you've made the effort to find out for yourself, to come all the way out here. I admire your drive. I wasn't sure what to expect from you—whether you'd be happy to finally see me again or if you'd want to tell me off once and for all."

"Well, actually, I wasn't sure either." Surprising Sean with an unrelated question, like a guy suddenly realizing he can't leave the house without first finding his car keys, he blurts out, "What happened to Heinrich?"

"Um…well, we moved to Chicago because he got a great job offer with the Boeing Company—he insisted I not call it simply Boeing. Anyway, Heinrich was a real friend in understanding what was going on with Terri and me, with Terri wanting to call the shots. And I didn't get that she was headed for addiction. He also knew that I was gay, even if I didn't have a clue. He let me stay at his place—maybe you remember. I couldn't impose on Mom—*my* mom." Pausing to recall dates, Sean continues, "After Heinrich and I were together almost a year—2005, I think—I was in a job I really didn't like."

Interrupting Sean's account, Ryan interjects, "He had his German camera, a Leica. He was so proud of it. I still have the shot from Michael Jordan's final game—the one of me on your shoulders."

"Oh, yes! I do too!"

Ryan thinks if either of them began to cry, who would know? It's too much emotion for one day. But he holds back his tears and instead laughs. "Okay, you done with me for one day?"

"Do I get another one?"

Ryan rolls his eyes in mock exasperation and reaches for the door handle. "Tomorrow?"

"Actually, how 'bout dinner, Sunday?"

Ryan smiles and nods, then gets out of the car and waves as Sean drives away. When his dad disappears over the hill, Ryan turns and heads for the house.

Robin swings open the front door within moments of Ryan's approach.

"You were waiting for me, weren't you?" he asks.

A tiny smile, then a sudden but gentle kiss on his cheek are her answers. His eyes open wide, and he embraces her. His lips find her mouth waiting and warm. She melds with Ryan's kiss.

Taking a quick breath, Robin whispers, "Maybe we should close the door." As she does, he steps close to her, pressing her gently against the door to continue a kiss.

"What's next?" he asks but not quite innocently.

"Dinner."

"Oh…" he slowly answers with a pouty puppy look.

"Want to help?"

"Of course."

But as Robin tries to walk to the kitchen, Ryan hovers so close, nearly clinging to her, that she stops to appreciate his affection. And for another kiss.

Once in the kitchen, Robin offers, "It's spaghetti and meatballs, puttanesca style."

"Great. Almost as popular as basic marinara at Angelo's."

"Angelo's?"

"Where I used to work. I got confirmation today that he was my secret guardian, that he couldn't let Terri find out Sean had asked him to look out after me."

"That's big. Anything else? If I may ask."

"Oh, not much." Then he laughs from deep in his gut, as if he's still digesting his day's discomforts. "What would there be to discuss? It's only been 10 years plus." *Lay off the sarcasm. She actually cares how you're doing.* He adds, "Actually, we spent a lot of time just being quiet. Remembering things."

"You know, when I first met you in the park, you were

totally exhausted. I was enchanted. And could barely keep my hands off you. I wanted to caress your face and kiss your troubles away. When you awoke and called me Daniel, I thought you were of a different persuasion. Of course, I was wrong."

"Look who's talkin'. I thought you were cute for a guy, not at all threatening—until I gave you a shove at the BART station. That turned me around—or upside down."

Robin braces herself and asks, "So, who *is* Daniel?"

"Um, well, he's a friend. Like a real friend you can talk to about anything. He accepted me even though I was from a rough part of town and not from a good family."

"Then, you've been keeping him up to date on your dad search?"

"Well, actually, we had a bit of a falling out."

"But he's your best friend."

"When I discovered he had a crush on me, I freaked. I overreacted, but I didn't know what to do. Sex has been a sensitive subject for me. And now that I've discovered my dad is one of them—well, it's all so unsettling."

"I'm guessing you are afraid of what other people will think? Of you—that you're 'one of them' too?"

Struck by her observation, Ryan begins to get up and gives her a challenging stare. Then it suddenly clicks. "Damn! You are right—absolutely right! Why should I care what other people think?"

CHAPTER 15

Ryan and Robin arrive in Berkeley and wait in Sean and Giovanni's front yard—or rather Aida's courtyard, the way it looks with her bike and toys. The princess sees them through the front window and waves, and Robin waves back. But Aida is not about to open the door with the "mad man" there.

I see she's taking no chances on me now, Ryan thinks ruefully. *And what about Giovanni?*

Sean drives up and calls out from the SUV window, "We need some groceries. Get in."

Aida opens the house door and rushes out to greet her dad. Ryan opens the SUV's backseat door and Robin helps Aida in, secures her in her booster seat, then goes around to get in next to her. Ryan climbs into the passenger's side across from his dad and sneaks a peek at Aida, who's fixated on Robin's short hair. Aida blurts out, "You're a girl?"

Sean yanks a shopping cart from the lineup in front of Whole Foods and Aida takes charge to commandeer the cart. Sean tells Ryan and Robin, "When Aida was young enough to ride in the cart, she wouldn't sit in the seat. Oh no, she'd stand facing forward like Sacagawea in that historic painting leading Lewis and Clark, pointing forward—of course, in our case—to the produce department."

Spectacular displays of California organic strawberries and other fruit capture Ryan's eye and his admiration. Ryan and

Robin hold hands as they walk through the section. Ryan notices two young men, probably a couple but not holding hands. They mistake Ryan and Robin also as a gay couple, the younger one nodding acknowledgment to Robin. Robin smiles as Ryan chokes back a laugh.

When Aida has had enough pushing the nearly full cart, she turns over the responsibility to Sean. Without hesitation, Robin takes her hand. Ryan follows behind and in moments reaches for her other hand. Aida glances up at Sean, then cautiously accepts Ryan's hand.

Leading the way, Sean notices a *Now Hiring* sign and motions with his head and a thumbs up to Ryan.

Ryan's mouth drops and his expression brightens. *You mean, I should stay out here in California?*

After checkout, everyone walks back to the SUV, Robin and Ryan with Aida between them and Sean following with a shopping cart filled with an assortment of canvas or recycled-plastic shopping bags.

A short time later, jangling keys alert Sean and Giovanni's dog, Mandy, to their return. A bearded collie—long-haired and true to her breed—enthusiastically welcomes all to her backyard domain. Sean, with arms full, fails to keep her outside as he struggles to carry the bags into the kitchen, where Giovanni is expecting them.

Sitting in its charging station, Giovanni's iPhone plays a nearly-unknown Verdi opera while Mandy bounds into the kitchen to greet everyone. Having entered Giovanni's realm, Sean makes space on the countertop but sees one of several shopping bags on the floor. In an instant, Mandy comes to inspect the unguarded groceries. As Aida attempts to restrain her, Sean simply retrieves the bag and sends Mandy outside.

Giovanni dries his hands and greets Robin with a gracious

handshake. He gives Ryan a reluctant nod, then reaches to turn down the opera music. He rummages through the grocery bags, and seeing the green onions, nods his approval to Sean.

Ryan listens to the music, then confidently suggests, "Verdi?"

Giovanni brightens. "You recognize Verdi? That's right. Sean told me you worked at an Italian grocery store. Angelo's." Giovanni then makes and holds deliberate eye contact with Ryan, testing him with a rhetorical assertion, challenging him with his own form of humor. "So, you probably know these are called scallions."

He hands them to Ryan. He also carefully hands over a butcher knife.

Ryan hesitates and studies Giovanni, who says, "Around here you can't just be ornamental. You need to make yourself useful."

Ryan remembers the butcher knife incident back home and after a moment he says, "I need to wash my hands first."

Giovanni looks thoughtful and smiles. "You come well trained."

Ryan is momentarily chagrined until Giovanni winks and mimics immigrant Italian, "It's-a gonna be okay, Ryan. Let's have a little change in the music." Giovanni goes over to his charging station and switches over to the Pet Shop Boys' "Always On My Mind." After several moments, and noticing Sean's sudden sadness, he whispers to Ryan holding deliberate eye contact, "It's true. You were always on his mind… I'm so glad you're here—at last." He switches tracks to "West End Girls."

Everyone is assigned a job to help prepare the meal. Giovanni, Sean, and Aida pick up on the rhythm of the music. Ryan slowly begins to synchronize with the music's strong beat as well. Sean, with a simple gesture, gives Robin dishes to set the dining room table. But Aida rushes over to take charge, showing Robin how to set their table, taking great delight in teaching her new pupil.

Robin lets her demonstrate proper table-setting placement. A little surprised that the young lady has been taught these things, Robin looks to Sean. Sean smiles, then nods to Ryan for him to join him in another room so they can talk while Giovanni, Aida, and Robin continue their tasks.

In the living room, Sean can see the dinner preparations through the doorway from the dining room into the kitchen. Aida comes running in to give her dad and Ryan a small dish of olives, then runs back to the kitchen. Father and son sit on the couch with a polite space between them.

Ryan blurts out, "Aida is so lucky..." He pauses.

Sean interjects, "I wanted to write. At least through Angelo. But all that was forbidden by court order... Hang on." Sean gets up from the couch and goes to his bedroom while Ryan sits uneasy, waiting. He returns with a stack of bulging envelopes, letters, and photos. He hands one to Ryan.

"Angelo took these," Ryan says as he looks at the photos. "I thought... I thought he did it because he kinda thought of me as his son."

"Well, he did. And he kept me up to date as much as he could. I had talked to a lawyer years ago, then again recently. I only hoped you would let me back into your life." Again, Sean springs up from the couch. "I have something else for you."

Returning in less time than before, he holds out a duct-taped flip phone. Ryan falls back on the couch as he opens his old phone.

"How did you..."

"I had it express-shipped from Greyhound Lost & Found. I

even got you a charger in case you didn't have one any more. So it's ready to go."

Ryan sits back, dumbfounded.

"Maybe you would like to be on our family plan—with a new phone. You can always add duct tape."

Individual salads sit at each place and a bottle of Chianti Classico sits at the head of the table, awaiting Giovanni's entrance. He brings in a large soup tureen and looks around for his guests. No one needs prompting to come to the table.

Robin tastes the soup and is most impressed. "Wonderful! What do you call this?"

"*Zuppa perduta e ritrovata*. Mother called refrigerator leftovers soup of things lost and now found."

Sean looks at Ryan with a disclaiming shrug, not sure Giovanni didn't just make this up and quickly changing the topic. "So, tell Giovanni and Aida about your trip."

"Okay… I get into San Francisco. No ID and nearly no money."

Aida can't hold back. "No idea? No money?"

"Because I was robbed."

"He has freckles like you, Daddy."

"Don't interrupt your brother," Sean smiles.

"My broder? He's not my broder." Aida jumps up from the table.

Sean hastens to tell Ryan and Robin that Aida is working with a speech therapist. In only a few moments, she returns with a framed photo of Ryan and Sean at Michael Jordan's final game in Philadelphia back in 2003.

Ryan sees the photo, looks over at his dad, and smiles—but almost looks like he might cry.

"That's when your brother, Ryan here, was just seven. He's just older now, 10—no, 11 years older." Sean nods for Ryan to continue his story.

Ryan glances at Robin, then resumes. "So, once I got to San Francisco, my luck changed. I met some good people."

Sean senses that Ryan has told enough of his story. Turning to Giovanni, he says, "Robin is going to be a freshman here in the fall. Sociology."

Giovanni sits back in his chair, smirking, as he teases Robin, "You'll be 'one of us.'" Ryan squirms in his chair even as he gets the humor.

Robin takes advantage of the distraction to ask her own question. "So, how did you lure Sean out here? Or is that x-rated?"

Sean interrupts, "No. I came out on my own. I mean, I didn't meet him until I had been out, and out here. We met at the Berkeley Art Museum when he brought an entourage of adoring students through."

Dismissing Sean's flattery, Giovanni clears his throat and modestly but confidently adds his part to the story. "We've been married since 2008, when San Francisco first allowed gays and lesbians to marry." They exchange cautious smiles. He continues, "Then we adopted Aida."

"My name is from Birdie's opera," Aida proudly adds.

Robin and Ryan glance at each other, both thinking they should know what opera that must be, then they realize it at the same time.

Giovanni leads with a question for Robin. "Tell us about yourself. You're from Portland and your father is a bishop? How'd he do that?"

Rescuing Giovanni from elaborating on his ignorance, Robin asserts, "Episcopalian. They have priests who marry—like Eastern Orthodox. In fact, I thought I was going to become a priest as well. But I developed other ideas. And why I cut my hair? It's more than just for undercover research. Anyway, that's another story, maybe rated for more mature audiences…" She winks at Aida.

Giovanni accepts that Robin has given them enough for now.

After dinner, Giovanni gets up to clear the table and asks rhetorically, "Limoncello for everyone?"

Wrinkling her nose, Aida is the one dissenting vote. Giovanni kisses her on the head as he picks up her plate. They all get up and begin gathering dishes, with Sean shepherding Aida into the kitchen.

"Let them be alone," Giovanni says to her. "You can help me and Dad. Later, I'll tell you more about your brother."

Too curious not to check his phone, Ryan wanders into the living room, sees a missed call from Dan, and reflexively calls back. He waits for Daniel's familiar greeting to complete. Pacing while he speaks, he says, "I made it, my friend. I'm here at my dad's home in Berkeley—actually his and his husband's home. They even found my lost phone. Thanks for helping me get here… I miss you. Bye." Closing the phone, Ryan sighs with relief and drops onto the couch. He doesn't notice Robin coming from the kitchen.

Putting her hands on his shoulders, then coming around the couch, she sits next to Ryan.

He says, "I just left a message for my friend, Dan. I feel like I'm in a weird new world. How am I supposed to—" He snaps his fingers. "—just like that, be all happy and accept being part of a queer family?"

She thinks for a moment, then smiles wryly. "It's a choice. Some things are a choice."

Not getting her humor, Ryan simply answers, "Maybe And what about you?"

She answers by snuggling closer to him and he surprises her with a slow, gentle kiss.

On the coffee table, Ryan's phone rings. But he doesn't jump to answer it.

After the second ring, Robin teases, "Is that your boyfriend?"

"No. You are."

Ryan picks up the phone and as he touches the *Answer* button, Daniel's sleepy voice comes over the tinny speaker. "Thank you for the call. Even if I am asleep."

Oh, damn! "That's right. Sorry. You're, uh, three hours—"

"So, you've met your dad…"

"Yes, I've met him and his fam—I mean—*my* family. I even have a little sister now. And maybe a girlfriend, Robin. She's with me right now."

"Well, are you going to introduce me?"

Ryan hands Robin his phone.

Daniel commends her, "You have great taste in men. But how ever do you put up with him? I guess he's all yours now."

Ryan has had enough. "Gimme that phone," he says as he grabs it from Robin. "Thanks for being my friend," he tells Dan. "We'll talk soon, okay? Now go back to sleep. Thanks for the call back." Ryan closes his phone and sets it on the floor. Gently kissing Robin on the lips, he leans over her for a full embrace. His head close to hers, he caresses her bristly hair and they both break out laughing.

Aida creeps into the living room. "What's so funny?"

Ryan answers, "Robin's hair. It's like mine was when I was a boy."

"You aren't a boy anymore?"

Changing the subject, Ryan redirects, "Actually, Robin was going to tell me about her tattoos. There's a story to them."

A call from the kitchen demands Aida's return to duty and she begrudgingly leaves.

Robin smiles. "Well, my story may not be appropriate for an eight-year-old anyway. Should I start at the beginning? From what my father—and mother and my aunt—have told me, plus what I have pieced together from photos, it goes like this. And with my self-taught detective training and a class on *Understanding Cinema,* I see it more as a movie—or a crime scene. So here goes…"

ROBIN

CHAPTER 16

The sounds of a city's earliest awakenings and the plaintive echo of distant train whistles announce another morning in Portland, Oregon. It is May of 1995. An intense pink sunrise, without a skyline or visible horizon, is timeless and serene until a police siren cuts through the calm. But then there's also an infant's wailing in the Trinity Cathedral deanery.* "That's me, of course."

Sunlight glares through beveled windowpanes into the soft-pink bedroom while new parents Malcolm R. Marshall and his wife, Emily—both in their mid-30s—look haggard after another sleepless night. The infant's delicate honey-colored hair matches her father's color but alas, Robin has more. The wall next to her crib displays a dot-matrix-printed banner proclaiming: *FOR UNTO US A CHILD IS BORN! ISAIAH 9:6 — YOUR FAMILY AT TRINITY WELCOMES ROBIN.* The banner's tape holding up the good-news greeting begins to fail on one side and peels away from the wall. Now only *ROBIN* remains stuck there. "My dad actually saved that thing? He thought it might foreshadow who I'd become. Hmm..."

Emily wears a rose-red chemise nightgown—suggestive of a weekend rendezvous so many months before. Although her almost shoulder-length brunette hair is more stylish than one would expect for the wife of a future bishop, her expression of weary sarcasm could be a poster title: Motherhood? Handing Robin to Malcolm, she droops into a chair and in her natural Texan drawl, says, "Remin' me now. This is gonna be worth it, right?"*

Months later, at the famous restaurant in the trendy Northwest District, Papa Haydn, Emily and her sister have desserts together. Exquisite Viennese tortes are delivered to the next table at the sidewalk seating area. But Emily is not to be dissuaded from showing off Robin in her new Rolls-Royce of a baby stroller. Adorned with her baptismal headband and an impressive white silk gardenia, Robin is momentarily asleep.

Emily's older sister, Grace Elaine, looks younger because of professional foundation and impeccable makeup airbrushed onto her face. She could be mistaken for a TV anchorwoman with her tailored suit, no-nonsense hairstyle, and her authoritative black-rimmed glasses. She smiles at Robin, happy for her sister. Then, looking at Emily, gives her a *glad it's you and not me* look.

Now twitching and squirming like a captive cat, Robin frets.

Elaine confirms, "Y'all finally got yer wish. Now ya have a little princess of your own." Glancing back at Robin, Elaine sees that the headband has come off. She cannot resist looking righteously condescending. "But apparently, I'm not the only one who thinks that head thing is a bit much."

Emily retaliates, eyes squinting. "Well, bless your heart… How's your divorce coming?"

Elaine straightens in her chair but then breathes a sigh of relief at the approaching distraction—for Emily, a passion fruit parfait and for herself, a generous slice of chocolate peanut butter mousse pie. Such caloric extravagance does not appear to affect Elaine's trim figure.

"Well," she continues, "Momma an' Daddy's marriage may have been storybook perfect—do they make them that way anymore? Outta Texas?" Tasting the pie and savoring her thoughts, she adds, "But life is good anyway… Ya know, some babies take nine months. Yours took nine years. I'm sure she'll be brilliant."

"Can you believe my aunt said that? My aunt was such a support to me, a real confidante and always ready to speak her mind."

———□———

Years later, Robin is unobtrusively observing her father as he shaves. He doesn't notice her until she nudges up next to him. And standing tall next to Malcolm, as tall as a six-year-old can, she gestures for him to put shaving cream on her face as well. She thinks, *This'll be fun.* He obliges with a chuckle, lathering up her face with his fancy brush. Malcolm lifts her so she can see herself in the mirror. But her broad smile collapses when she sees Emily's reflection, now in the mirror too, scowling in disapproval.

———□———

Three years later, in 2004, Robin is now nine. The subtle pink bedroom walls have been painted over with a deep blue. Two movie posters dominate one wall: the *Chronicles of Narnia* and *Harry Potter and the Chamber of Secrets.* Five or six of Beverly Cleary's famously popular books for children about the mischievous and rambunctious Ramona Quimby sit in disarray on her desk. Birthday gift wrap is crumpled next to *Harriet the Spy* and several *Sammy Keyes* mystery novels. A card reads, *Happy 9th, Robin! Aunty Laine.*

Breaking the calm of her bedroom comes a taunting voice over a multi-line office desk phone. "Rooob-in!" it blares. "Up and at 'em! It's your gym time!"

From deep sleep to full alert in a split second, Robin sits up like a firefighter.

Does she have to yell like that?

Robin throws off her comforter and springs to her feet, then darts into her walk-in closet. She kicks a pair of demi-pointe ballet shoes under a pile of laundry on the closet floor, grabs her aikido gear off a hook, and dresses in a flash.

Outside, Emily, now 42 with not a single strand of gray hair visible, could be a model in her fashionable yoga gear. She climbs into her husband's dark-green Range Rover. With reluctant disdain, not familiar with how to adjust the seat, she futzes with the controls. Robin rushes outside, jumps into the backseat, then leans forward and sees her mother's frustration. Jumping out of the car again, Robin comes to her mother's aid, nimbly pressing the one button needed. She then glides back to her seat in the SUV. Her confidence is reminiscent of the young Scout Finch in *To Kill a Mockingbird.*

Emily generously offers a proper thank you as well as a complaint about Malcolm blocking in her car as she pulls out of the driveway. "He can take mine if I'm not back in time for him to go."

Robin, just a little too smug, accepts her mother's appreciation. Swiping aside her long, unbrushed brunette hair, she takes the first bite of a bagel bulging with cream cheese. There is silence except for the soft hum of the car. Calm and self-assured, Robin's face says, *Whoever speaks first loses.*

Emily can't bear the quiet. "I still don't und'a-stand this aikido thing. It's just not proper for—"

"Mom! Thank you for driving me."

"And it wouldn't hurt ta put a pin in your hair."

"Well, not in martial arts. I don't want to hurt my opponent. I'll just use my hair tie." Robin carefully sets her bagel on her lap, closes her eyes, and goes into a moment of meditative quiet. When she opens her eyes a few moments later, she sees beautiful spring-blooming dogwood and magnolia trees, but then catches her mother's smoldering, fuming face in the car mirror. Emily sneezes.

The cheers of children in the gym assure Malcolm he's not too late. Dressed in an Episcopal priest's house cassock, all in black with a full, round white collar, he stands in formal contrast to the other casually dressed parents. Some are attentive, some are in cell phone conversations.

One jovial parent tries to strike up a conversation. "So, Father, are you here for confessions? Or last rites?"

Malcolm acknowledges with a civil but nearly dismissive smile, glossing over the attempt at humor. He politely asks, "Which one is yours?"

Nodding to the students now moving onto the mat, both parents are attentive to the final demonstration between Robin and Akiko, a petite Japanese American girl with her glistening black hair pulled into a simple ponytail and tied with a crimson-red ribbon.

Robin glances over at Malcolm. Absently, he wipes aside his wispy gray hair. He focuses on Robin and nods. And with his trusty little Sanyo flip phone, takes a snapshot. She smiles back with nonchalant confidence.

Akiko and Robin bow. Robin approaches Akiko too quickly, too close, and within two seconds, Akiko throws Robin to the mat.

"*Gomen nasai*," [I'm sorry] Akiko says.

They reposition themselves. Akiko smiles and Robin tries to focus, bracing herself with her weight equally distributed. Akiko makes a quick, piercing scream to distract and overpower Robin.

Akiko again sincerely says, "*Gomen nasai*."

And just as fast as before, Akiko executes a different throw and Robin is down. Stunned and hurting, Robin lies on the mat. Malcolm begins to rush over but the coach is already at her side, whispering something to her. Robin nods and slowly gets up.

Following protocol, Robin and Akiko bow to one another. As Robin limps off the mat toward Malcolm, she turns to Akiko and asks, "*Gomen nasai?*"

Like a coach, Malcolm kneels on one knee. Looking up at her, he whispers, "I'm proud of you."

Robin barely holds back her tears as they leave the gym. Malcolm reaches for her hand. She does not resist.

Robin sees her father in the mirror, then his thin-lipped smile and the twinkle in his eyes. He waits for the traffic light to change and winks with a reassuring smile. Looking away, Robin gazes out the window, not seeing anything in particular. Until…

She notices several boys at the Couch Park playground's climbing bars. Something's wrong. Like her favorite adventure-book characters, Harriet Welsch and Sammy Keyes, she is as attentive as an expert witness determined to record the action, zooming in as if with stop-motion accuracy to catch every bit of it. The tallest one, she guesses to be 13, has pushed a younger Asian boy, 10. The bully, snatching something and continuing to overpower the younger boy, tries to pull off what looks to be a new indigo parka.

Robin blares out, "Daddy! Stop!"

Malcolm slams on the brakes. The tires screech and swerving the Rover, he narrowly misses a parked car. "What? Where?"

"A boy needs our help—over there!" Not wasting a moment, and while Malcolm is still trying to pull to a stop, Robin tries to open the back door of the still-moving car. Malcolm jams the gearshift into park and begins opening his front door.

Robin is out in a flash.

"Rob—no!" Likewise rushing, Malcolm follows as fast as he can but stumbles at the curb. Straightening up, he winces and now hobbles on.

Robin charges into the group and grabs the coat from the assailant, but he punches her in the face and reclaims his prize. Robin crashes to the ground and lies next to the boy.

The leader, laughing at her, casually orders his followers, "Okay, guys. We can—" He catches sight of Malcolm running toward them and yells at them to hustle.

Robin springs up to stop him again, but before she can get more than a few feet, Malcolm tackles her. While the group scatters like cockroaches, Malcolm turns Robin over and lifts her up. He looks her in the eyes. "What ARE you doing?" His face shifts from annoyance to anger to sorrow. Blood trickles down her bruised cheekbone.

The Asian boy gasps convulsively as he tries to get up. "They tore it!"

Robin curses, "He got away. Damn it!"

Malcolm, momentarily chagrined at Robin's comment, stiffens his posture, looks at the boy, then back to Robin. "We need to help 'im." He gently wipes Robin's cheek with his bare hand, smearing blood on his shirt, and turns to the boy. "We're sorry they stole your jacket. They had no—"

But he protests, "My card!" Holding up a glossy scrap of a the Seattle Mariners baseball card, only a corner left with the "M's" logo on it, he exclaims, "It's gone. My father's gonna kill me!"

Malcolm reaches over to help him stand but the boy refuses, tosses the scrap, and runs. Calling out, Malcolm offers, "We'll take you home."

The boy ignores him as he runs off.

Father and daughter look at each other and Robin brushes her hand over her bruised eyebrow and cheek. Malcolm shakes his head in disbelief. He takes Robin by the hand and limps back to the car. Barely holding back his pride, and with a little smile, he softly says, "Wait'll Mom sees us."

Emily wears a Williams-Sonoma apron. To get Malcolm's attention for lunch, she plops three bowls onto the table for him to set, but he doesn't notice. He's focused on an article in *The New York Times*.

She is annoyed with her husband but tries to announce calmly, "Your dental office called. You missed your appointment—again." Exasperated, she asks, "What are you doing?"

"I'm wondering if aikido is right for Robin."

"*Now* you think of that? At least ballet—"

"We've already discussed—"

"How 'bout boxing? At least they wear gloves."

"It wasn't my choice—she hears a different drummer." Not ignoring Emily but letting her know what he's been thinking, Malcolm tentatively offers, "Brazilian Jiu-Jitsu. That, I believe, is more to her liking."

"And you expect them to elect you bishop?"

"I'm just trying to be a good father."

"And martial arts is the way for a bishop's daughter? I thought you wanted her to become a priest—not some kung-fu girl." She storms out of the kitchen's back door.

Malcolm settles back into his chair.

Robin enters, unconsciously rubbing her wrist and hearing Emily revving her BMW more than necessary as she leaves the driveway. Robin looks perplexed at the sound effects and asks, "Mom's in a hurry? Or mad?"

"She forgot something."

"Does that mean we have to fend for ourselves for lunch?"

A little later that afternoon, Malcolm sits at his desk scanning emails. He pauses, reading intently, then slowly presses an intercom button on his desk phone. Sounding tentative, he asks, "Robin?"

But Robin is nowhere around.

At Couch Park, where the bullies stole the jacket earlier that day, there are now adults absentmindedly observing their young children on the climbing bars. They don't notice Robin as she approaches the structure. She sees the torn baseball card and snatches it up, but casually, as if it were just a piece of litter. After tucking it into her coat pocket, Robin then notices the card's broken clear plastic case in the play bark and retrieves that as well. Lost in thought about the attack as she slowly walks toward the street, she catches sight of the rest of the card—the piece the Asian boy tossed away.

Malcolm's study door is open—his policy for letting Emily or Robin know it's okay for them to just walk in.

"Da-ad, I have a mystery for you."

Malcolm looks up from his keyboard, a little suspicious.

"You mean the mystery of angels or the mystery of the Holy Spirit? I'm just preparing—"

She thrusts forward the now plastic-encased torn card. "No. Here. I don't understand. Why do people steal other peoples' things?"

He draws a breath and speculates about what she's going to need, then gestures for Robin to come closer. Malcolm is cautiously impressed but attentive. "Oh, my… It's a Ken Griffey Jr. card." He turns to his computer and keys in a few search words, and within seconds, swings back to Robin. "The money, that's why. This card is—well, *was*—worth $300 according to one website."

Her face shows disappointment. She reclaims the evidence but is still puzzled. "Why didn't the boy let us take him home?"

"Too proud. And ashamed. He's not going to tell his family it was stolen, that he couldn't defend himself and keep it. It'll be bad enough to show up without his coat." Malcolm pauses, then hugs Robin. "But you can always come to me."

She gives him a "yes, I know" nod and presses on. "What's going to happen to the bad boy?"

Malcolm once again turns to his computer. "Good question… Does evil triumph over good? Philosophers and theologians have been arguing that one for centuries." He looks back at Robin to take a closer look at her eye. "Oh, Robbie! That's gonna be a real shiner." Looking beyond the walls of his study, he wonders, "What is the boy going to do? Maybe come back for his card—even the pieces?"

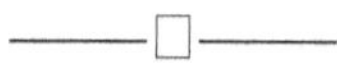

Robin, again skulking about the play area, sees none of the ruffians or the boy, so she ventures into the upscale neighborhood and heads back home. She hesitates, trying to decide which way to go.

A Portland police car stops to let her cross the intersection. The officer rolls down her window. "May we help you?"

"Yes! I'm tracking down a criminal."

Officer Shelley smiles and turns to her fellow officer, failing to suppress a laugh. She asks him something, then returns her attention to Robin. With a blonde ponytail and muted-red lipstick, she could as easily pass for a grade-school teacher. "We'll help. First, let us move this cruiser out of the way."

Robin reads the slogan on the massive car, a blue Crown Victoria Ford with white doors: *Sworn to Protect. Dedicated to Serve.*

Officer Shelley gets out of the cruiser and crouches down to Robin's level. But before she can ask her question, Robin says, "Sworn to protect? Like swearing? I thought that was bad."

"No… You saw something we need to help you with?"

"Yes. A boy, an Asian boy, had his $300 Ken Griffey card stolen." She reaches into her pocket and hands the plastic-protected, torn card to Officer Shelley.

"Nice. Oh, I see. You saw it happen? When?"

At the deanery, Officer Shelley stands at attention as Malcolm opens the door. Happy to see Robin home again but surprised to see her accompanied by the police, he shakes his head. He offers Officer Shelley entrance but she declines.

"Sharp detective girl you got there, Reverend." She shakes hands with Malcolm while Robin, head erect, proudly walks past her father into the deanery.

Malcolm blesses himself with the sign of the cross as he says, "Har—ri—et—the…" He clasps his hands. "Spy… Thank you, Officer."

Later the same afternoon, Robin sees her mom return home. She runs out to the driveway and watches Emily as she gets out of her glistening white BMW convertible—with no rain, she has the top down. Reaching into the back seat for several shopping bags, including shoe boxes from Nordstrom and Saks Fifth Avenue, she notices Robin.

"If Daddy's little priestess—" she begins, but stops when she sees Robin's black eye. "I'm so sorry, Robin. I just don't know what to do for you… My daddy wouldn't have a clue, either. He sure wouldn't have imagined a girl like you—so different from me. I'm sorry you got hurt doing the right thing for that boy. Anyway, would you help me with these things?"

Robin looks surprised by all the shopping bags. "Victoria's Secret?"

"It's retail therapy. Someday you'll und'a-stand. Maybe."

Retail therapy? Robin looks doubtful.

CHAPTER 17

Four years later — 2008

Robin is in the eighth grade at the prestigious Oregon Episcopal School.* It offers excellent college preparatory courses on a campus away from the hustle and hassle of downtown Portland. Tuition for one student per year is about the average total family income for the area.

Robin is not used to quite so many hours of sitting. She fidgets in her seat while three of her classmates at the table are mesmerized with their projects on their laptops. She looks around, gets up, opens a window, goes over to another group of students, and taps one of them on the shoulder. Several look annoyed and one looks up to the front of the room and stares at Ms. Lee for intervention. Ms. Lee, in her early 40s with streaks of silver in a pixie hairstyle, calmly removes her bright-red-framed readers. She catches Robin's glance and motions for her to come to her desk. Robin looks guilty.

"I know you don't mean to annoy your fellow students," Ms. Lee begins. "But you do. You do distract them." Pausing to consider something, she adds, "Let's meet after class. We need to find a way for you to focus better. I know you're smart." Then she quietly adds in a confidential tone, "One of my most perceptive and intuitive students."

But I'm still in trouble.

—□—

Robin's parents sit at the table with large mugs of after-dinner tea—unmatched colors and chipped but comfortable in the hand.

Emily speaks first. "You got the email too, from Ms. Lee, about her recommendin' Robin for assessment? For ADHD."

Malcolm bristles. "She's fine. I don't see Mizzz Lee's point. Robin is just a bright, high-energy girl. Lee may not be up to the task of working with so many gifted—"

"Cut the crap. You don't see it because…because you deny you have the same problem—sweetie."

Malcolm shoves his chair away from the table and charges out of the kitchen.

Emily asserts with a smile, "I see you agree with me."

———□———

A week later, Emily sits upright and tense in Dr. Kaufmann's waiting room. It's meant to feel homey—except for the typical plethora of magazines. Robin riffles through the random collection until she comes upon the magazine *Attention*. She snaps it up in one hand and salutes her mother with the other.

Malcolm is sullen. Perched on the edge of his chair across the room, he stands to greet the highly recommended doctor when he opens the door.

Very polite, with a modest demeanor and a warm smile, the doctor thanks Mrs. Marshall for calling his office. Nodding to Malcolm, he assures, "I've worked with many students at OES. I guess I don't scare them too much."

Making deliberate eye contact with Robin, he takes an empty seat next to her and Emily. His hair loss makes his head appear even larger than her father's and his goatee and round glasses make him look like a scientist from another century. He now all but ignores the parents. "Did we give you enough magazines to go through?" And seeing her choice, he chides, "Uh-oh, now you'll get all our inside secrets."

"Are you supposed to look like Dr. Freud?" Robin asks.

"Robin! This is Dr. Kaufmann," Emily reprimands.

"*Ach, ja,*" Dr. Kaufman jokes, saying "oh yes" in German. "Maybe I should get different frames."

Malcolm looks over to Emily and speaks as if Robin wasn't there. "Well, this was your idea. I hope the good doctor is used to teenagers like this one."

A couple of weeks later, the principal of Oregon Episcopal peeks into Ms. Lee's class. The students all sit quietly, including Robin, who is on a giant yoga ball—bouncing, actually. Rhythmically. Robin pauses to massage her temples. When she looks over at Ms. Lee, Ms. Lee gives Robin a quick thumbs up.

The next morning in the Trinity Cathedral vestry, Robin buttons up her cassock and dons her surplice for the Sunday celebration of the Eucharist. Processional organ music begins and she organizes the other acolytes like a border collie herding sheep, then leads them out from the vestry and into the nave of the cathedral. Robin is attentive, giving subtle head and eye movement cues to a taller, older boy whose task is simply to light the altar candles. She nods.

At the end of the service, Robin again lines up her acolytes and the very experienced organist shows off his prowess with Bach's "Toccata and Fugue in D Minor." Robin loves the piece and when she sees one of the young servers startle at the opening blast, his eyes going wide, she confides, "Bach's great toccata."

Confused, he asks, "Tostada?"

Robin holds back a laugh as she leads her group in a solemn procession. But then her eyes drift away into the distance as she hears her own music—a piece from the *Matrix* soundtrack, "Requiem for a Dream" by The Crystal Method.

The next afternoon at the Straight Blast Gym* (SBG for short)—Portland's first martial arts center, including jiu-jitsu—Robin stands strong. She's wearing her new jiu-jitsu gi, which she thinks looks like a white kimono. She tries to look bold, even as she stands close to her father. When she notices her belt is not tied like the other students' belts, she grimaces and fidgets. *How do they tie them so nice?* Refocusing, she and Malcolm observe the grappling of young students paired with one another. Their teachers, mindful of every move of those on the mat, ignore the visitors.

At a moment of calm, the playlist seems to balance the energy in the gym. Malcolm says, "I like the music."

Robin enlightens, "*Matrix.*"

"I know," Malcolm replies, then, crouching, he whispers, "You're an amazing daughter. I love you."

"I know."

CHAPTER 18

Four years later — Spring 2012

At the SBG, Robin remembers when a young woman, a blue belt, approached her and her dad when she began lessons. Now at 17, she is behind the same table assisting another father and daughter. Not buxom but lean and athletic, Robin looks at least 19, and with the right ID and lighting, could pass for 21. Wearing minimal makeup to cover an acne flare-up, she is just right for meeting new clients.

Her black-belt instructor approaches and nods his head for another assistant to take over greeting prospective students. He smiles at Robin and motions for her to meet another guest. Standing taller and more confident—now a blue belt, working toward purple—she walks with grace toward her instructor.

He introduces her to Akiko.

Robin's face transforms from socially pleasant to suppressed delight.

Robin, in perfect Japanese, says, "*Gomen nasai,*" and pauses to ensure that Akiko understood her misuse of the phrase "You showed me I had a lot more to learn."

Robin is the first to extend her hand. Akiko graciously accepts with caution.

"Oh, you've met before," the instructor says and nods toward the mat. "For old times' sake?"

But Akiko puts her hands up in concession.

That same afternoon, Emily and Elaine are returning from downtown with proof of their shopping efforts in the backseat.

The BMW's top is up because of a Portland spring drizzle. Emily hunts for a parking space in front of Elaine's condo—a red-brick, beautifully updated apartment building in the Nob Hill area. But she settles for a passenger drop-off zone. Elaine, however, is not quite ready to pass up an opportunity to give some big-sister advice.

"You worry too much, my dear. I have a suggestion." She takes in a subtle breath as if testing to see if the air is too cold. "Take her to lunch at that vegetarian restaurant she likes—you know?"

Emily nods with skeptical reservation.

"Maybe if you try to get into her world, she'll be more interested in exploring ours."

Emily gulps as if she has been asked to sample some thick, swamp-green drink.

"And if she's going to accompany you and that lovely bishop of yours all the way to the Canterbury Tales pilgrimage—"

"Now, have a little respect, *Miss Grace-E*. It's in London, not Canterbury."

"Anyway, if your Robin has any hope of following in her daddy's footsteps..."

Emily scrutinizes Elaine with that look of, *This is being recorded and anything you say may be held against you.*

"...she needs to channel her energy. I think her judo thing—"

Emily corrects her again, looking a bit surprised at herself for doing so. "Jiu-jitsu. It's Brazilian."

"Whatever. I think it's helping her. She's not the son Malcolm wanted—"

"Elaine!"

Elaine pauses. "Anyway, she's every bit as smart as anyone

else at that fancy school and Malcolm is a good dad. She has all these things goin' for her, including a caring mom." Taking a breath and wanting to assure Emily, she continues, "You've come a long way from your wayward years." She savors the memory. Taking a chance, she gently prods, "Whatever happened to that handsome hunk? The mechanic... Mm-mm-mm... But didn't he turn out to be a little *too* rough?"

Emily is not amused and refuses to go for the bait.

"Sorry. You *were* wild though. Of course, you were a teenager. Anyway, maybe you should go to one of Robin's jiu-jitsu classes or competitions. Or an open house, maybe?"

Emily calms and appears to be taking in Elaine's suggestions.

"She might even be willing to go shopping—for a prom dress," Elaine ventures. She reaches for the door handle, opening the door just enough to let her hand feel the air to see if it's still drizzling or is now raining. "Clear enough. Between you and me too..."

Emily nods with a small smile of appreciation. "There's something else," she asserts as she turns off the ignition of her car. "My life. It's so boring. I'm tired of being the perfect wife of the perfect bishop in perfect Portland..."

Elaine pulls the door closed and listens without comment as Emily's voice trails off.

"I guess I got what I asked for."

But Elaine offers a correction. "More like what Daddy asked for, wouldn't you say?"

CHAPTER 19

Robin scoots into her sporty black Mazda hatchback parked near her jiu-jitsu gym. She looks into her Marc Jacobs leather backpack and digs through it with a grimace. *Where's my notebook?* Glancing at the dashboard clock, she sees that it reads 4:35. She heaves a sigh of frustration and guns the gas pedal. The Mazda blasts out of the parking lot. Well, almost. She hits the curb at an angle and the front left wheel thuds, jolting her against the steering wheel; the horn honks in protest. "Damn!"

Not getting out or stopping to examine her car, she keeps the Mazda on the road even though the steering wheel shimmies for the half-hour drive back to her school's parking lot. She parks, gets out and slams the car door, and trudges to her homeroom.

A few dead leaves of winter remain stuck to the walkway while a lone student, zipping up his jacket against the wind, sits on a bench, waiting. Students leaving band practice walk toward the parking lot while Robin acknowledges them without stopping.

Robin, having retrieved her notebook and returning to the parking lot, notices the waiting student, Sammy Sullivan, feet fidgeting, looking toward the parking lot entrance. She stops. "Hey…transfer student?"

Sammy nods shyly. His reddish horn-rimmed glasses match his hair and his Beatles-style haircut.

Facetiously, she asks, "From Liverpool?"

"Huh?"

"So, where are you from? What year are you?"

"Um..."

She sits down next to him.

Sammy's eyes brighten and he stops fidgeting. "Re-re-red-red. Mond. M-m-micro. S-s-soft. I'm a-a-a j-jun-ior. And you?"

"I'm a senior. Do you need a ride?" *Oh, I shouldn't have offered. My car's driving kind of funky...* She waits for a moment. "What's your name?"

When a massive silver Lexus pulls up, Sammy looks disappointed to be leaving. He gets up slowly. Reluctantly grabbing his backpack in one hand, he extends his other hand to Robin as she stands. "S-s-s-sam. S-s-s-s-sulli. Yeah."

Robin nods as they shake. When he turns toward his ride, she smiles to herself and continues walking to her car. *Sweet. I like him!*

A few days later on campus, Robin hears someone calling after her. "Wha-what'd you say your-your name was?"

Following behind Robin into the Great Room and surprising her with the question, Sammy tries to look confident. Putting out his hand to reintroduce himself, he asserts, "A ca-couple days. Ago. Fri. Day. I-I-I was waiting for my-my dad." He catches his breath.

Robin shakes his hand. "Of course. You just caught me off guard. You're the junior. From Microsoft, Washington."

He laughs, still holding her hand, then suddenly realizes he should let go and blushes.

"So, you're finding your way around okay, besides finding me?"

His mouth drops and he looks like he has been caught. "I-I-didn't—"

"I'm sorry. I was teasing. I don't mean to make you more anxious. Just take your time. I know other very smart people who also stutter."

Impulsively, he pulls out his Windows Phone to distract her—or himself. "My-my. Class. I better. Go. Thanks."

Robin smiles and nods her acknowledgment. Turning to leave for her own class, she notices the *UPCOMING EVENTS* announcement on the wall-mounted monitor: *PROM 12!* She grimaces like she's just been reminded to get a flu shot.

———□———

The next morning, Emily serves up oatmeal and seats herself. Malcolm—now wearing a bishop's house cassock with violet-red piping trim—is reading his red-leather-clad iPad. Emily, thumbing through the *Willamette Week,* does not speak.

Robin slides unobtrusively into her chair. "Dad? I have a question."

"Uh-huh." Malcolm looks up, quizzical, as he searches his memory, "Another mystery?"

Robin ignores his humor. "I think the Mazda needs attention."

"Didn't we just have the 60k checkup?"

Robin glances at her mom, looking for support. But Emily is puzzled and suddenly skeptical. She bites her lip and lets Robin speak for herself.

"I think the steering isn't quite right," Robin continues.

"Well, it could be one of a few possibilities." Counting with his fingers, Malcolm continues thoughtfully, "The steering fluid is low. Or you have a flat tire." And after pausing for too long, he comes up with number three. "Or you hit a curb or pothole too fast and now it's out of alignment."

Robin is stunned. Emily gets up from the table so she can observe without interrupting the ever-patient bishop at work with his daughter. But she cannot squelch her laugh.

Malcolm, annoyed, asks Emily, "Are you in on this?"

"No, absolutely not! It's just that you are so logical." And in defense of her innocence, she adds, "I, for one, can't wait to hear what Miss Robin has to say."

Robin just mutters, "Uh-huh."

Malcolm smiles. "Now, that's a good start. Let's see what's ailing your Mazda."

Robin leaves the kitchen first. Emily silently gestures to Malcolm as though they're playing a game of charades: *How did you know?*

Like a hitchhiker, pointing with his thumb to himself, he winks. "Done it myself when I was her age."

Robin's car is at the dealership for a few days, so Emily has driving duties. In the morning, it's off to Oregon Episcopal. In the afternoon, it's waiting for Robin after school, then home to change out of her school clothes, then off to jiu-jitsu.

After a school pick-up, Emily waits as Robin jumps out of the car and runs into the house. Robin returns within minutes, now changed into her training gi and stripped of makeup. She looks at her mom with appreciation as they pull out of the driveway.

Emily appears relaxed and happy to be shuttling Robin around. Surprising Robin, she confides, "I guess I kinda miss chauffeuring you everywhere like I used to, before you could drive."

"Thanks, Mom. You've been so sweet."

"You doubt your mother's sincerity?"

When they arrive at the gym, Emily kisses her fingers, then touches them gently on Robin's cheek. "I'll pick you up after class."

Robin jumps out of the car and into the spring drizzle in front of her jiu-jitsu class. Emily begins to drive away but stops after Robin has gone inside. Thinking back to her conversation with Elaine, Emily parks the car. She first calms herself by listening to a piano and cello version of the love theme from *Cinema Paradiso.* Then, with a deep, soothing breath, she steps out of the BMW. As she braces herself for her entrance into the jiu-jitsu center, she can feel the double bass of the bluesy jazz coming from the gym. Once inside, she looks around cautiously. An attendant directs her to a section of the gym where Robin is warming up with a training partner.

A young grade-school girl, overweight and round-faced, tries to look tough in front of her assigned grappling partner. He is an eager boy the same age—not skinny but slightly built compared to the girl. They listen to Robin's directives. Clumsily, they attempt several different moves to take one another down. The boy succeeds and the girl thuds to the mat. Emily brings her hand to her mouth, looks away, and grimaces at the pained look on the girl's face.

Robin, eyes glistening, encourages the girl to try again. She whispers something into her ear and the two children re-engage and roll on the mat.

Emily looks confused but is determined to make sense of this sport. She watches almost against her will.

Robin focuses on her students and does not notice her mother. The girl makes a move and takes down the frisky boy. Robin lifts the girl's right hand like she is an Olympic winner. The girl's face is radiant as she shakes hands with her rolling partner and both children run to their respective parents.

Within moments, Robin's instructor is standing before her. "Nice job, Robin."

"Thank you."

The instructor gestures for her to spar with him. "Ready?"

"Me? Now?" Emily's mouth drops open with anxious suspense. She doesn't move a muscle.

Robin and her instructor appear to enjoy their rolling. She escapes his dominant mount. Then again when he is on top, she slips between his legs and pulls herself up, hugging him face to face, clamping both legs around his waist. Thrusting her hips up, she flips him over. With his arm straightened out between her knees and thighs in an arm bar, she exerts just enough pressure for him to submit. He quickly taps the mat three times, conceding that round.

Several parents and students calmly watch while Emily sits frozen, transfixed by the superb performance as much as her own discomfort with being there. When the match is over, Emily sighs with relief. It is only then that Robin catches sight of her mother. Robin's face, flushed from her efforts, now shows surprise and a tentative smile. "Mom…you're early."

Robin, approaching her mother as if she herself were a child caught in a forbidden room, awaits judgment. Emily doesn't know what to say—and she doesn't say anything. For several moments, Emily's hands are clasped in her lap and her head is bowed like she's in prayer. She looks up again at Robin, as uncertain and perplexed as when she first entered the gym.

"I wanted to see what you do. But I don't und'a-stand."

"Did you see the kids I was coaching?"

Emily nods. Still needing time to process what she has seen, she waits for Robin to tell her more, maybe explain something—but the intimacy she just witnessed with a handsome man like that has her confused.

Robin tells her, "I still have more coaching to do but if you want to stay, you're more than welcome."

"Thank you, but I'd best take care of my errands. I'll be

back to pick you up." Emily almost bows, awkwardly taking her leave.

Robin returns a wary smile, then turns her attention to a pair of waiting grade-school boys.

Emily gets into her car but does not drive away. She sits inside, shielding herself both from the Portland drizzle and the realities of her daughter's martial arts interests.

———□———

Days later, Robin is leaving the Great Room and passes by a monitor that scrolls school news and deadlines, including *PROM 12!* With her long hair now a more magnificent shade of mahogany, she chats with classmates. One with frizzy, flyaway hair appears annoyed and jealous. Robin throws her shoulders back in casual disregard and walks away.

In a corner is a cluster of three guys, including Sammy. Robin walks up close enough to hear what they are discussing. She waits. They stop.

Sammy smiles. "Hi, Rob-robin."

The two nerdy classmates look at her in annoyance.

Focusing on Sammy, Robin asks, "Are you going to the prom?"

"Yeah. I have a-a date."

He smiles in appreciation—or puzzlement. Not wanting to discuss it right then, Sammy turns back to his buddies. They look mildly perplexed but quickly resume their conversation.

Robin walks away, trying to contain her chagrin while the frizzy-haired girl's glare escorts her out of the room and down the hallway.

Robin sees her friend Andria in the corridor. Andria is also a senior, and an Asian American with a pageboy haircut. Robin tries to sound vaguely interested as she says, "I suppose you're going to the prom?"

"Oh, yeah. My Michael has asked me. Should be fun. What about you?" Seeing Robin's look, she adds, "You don't need a date. You can just show up solo."

"Well, I'll see. You got a new number, didn't you? Send me a text, okay?"

Andria goes to her class and Robin, turning to go to her own, notices the art exhibited on the walls: *Ravens in Legend, Literature, and Art.* One particular print, "Raven Steals the Sun," celebrates the fabled black bird with a golden orb in its beak. Wall-mounted speakers play flute music inspired by that story. She is transfixed and ignores the other students as they scurry around her to their classes.

Robin thinks about the Genesis stories she has grown up with, and smiles at the primitive explanations. But then she looks perplexed. *Could I be wrong to think there's only one explanation? After all, not one of us was there.*

It's Sunday morning service at All Saint's Cathedral. The Gothic Revival interior feels both classic and warm, perfect for the Easter season celebration. Malcolm is concluding his sermon.

"This morning I would like to tell you about a little research I did on a well-known scene. I like to call it 'Doctrine versus Practice.' We've all heard that Jesus overturned the tables of the money changers in Jerusalem. You know, *Stop making my Father's house a place of business!*"

Many parishioners nod in tentative agreement.

"But it's more complicated. Jesus was opposing the very institution of animal sacrifice—a very profitable enterprise for the temple merchants. And worst of all, he was claiming to be

God's own son. This was very upsetting to devout Jews of the day." Malcolm has their attention. "So, we have May Day coming up with Occupy Wall Street protests around the country claiming that the great money changers of our time are exploiting the 99 percenters of their hard-earned income."

Several parishioners look uneasy.

"We have a choice whether to sit by and justify our moderately comfortable lives or, like Jesus, we can be a voice for the poor and underserved we claim to care about. Be *moderate* and ignore the cry of the poor—or get out and protest the inherent greed of those who are the true threat to our great country's highest ideals. Will you join me there?"

Malcolm bows his head, pauses, and descends from the pulpit. A long silence follows.

Parishioners sit looking straight ahead until the organ gently intones Psalm 23, "The Lord is My Shepherd." Emily gives Malcolm a polite smile and slight nod.

Emily and Robin are in Chapman Square on May 1, 2012. A bigger-than-life-size bronze sculpture, *The Promised Land,* depicts a devout Christian pioneer family—including a father, mother, and son—at the end of their journey on the Oregon Trail. It is beautifully executed but controversial in its Manifest Destiny assumptions.

Emily and Robin pause briefly in front of the sculpture as a crowd of about 200 begins swarming into the park. In the distance, random voices begin to coalesce as one. The crowd chants, "Whose streets? Our streets! Whose streets? Our streets!" As they come closer, the chant changes. Falling out of unison, it becomes, "Whose park? Our park!" But the protestors seem to lack a clear direction and wander out of the park.

Robin asks rhetorically, "Where they goin'?"

Emily, almost as a plea, responds, "Not Pioneer Place."

"Let's find out."

And without waiting for an answer, Robin moves along with the crowd. Emily reluctantly follows. When they come to the first street intersection, Robin, out of habit, waits for the light to change. A Portland police sergeant engages with a small group of marchers. Robin listens.

The sergeant urges, "Just stay on the sidewalks. Keep it peaceful. Nobody gets hurt."

But the crowd does not hold back or pay attention to him. An officer on a bike is shoved to the pavement and several police officers jump into the fray to arrest the offender.

Emily hurries to catch up with Robin, visibly stressed to be mixed up in any of this.

But Robin is more enthusiastic. "Wow! They're on it!"

Emily begs, "Robin! You—we—should not be here!"

"But we should. Dad's here somewhere." Again, Robin begins to take off, but pauses. "Come on, Mom. We can still have lunch. Wasn't that your idea?"

That evening, nothing is steaming in the kitchen except Emily. Dinner is simply soup, equal parts duty and indignation.

Malcolm enters with a vaguely optimistic smile and his iPad. He offers, "Robin says it was awesome. And the police were very restrained."

"I didn't see that. To the contrary. But she seems to think this confrontation stuff is fun. If you want bread, cut it yourself."

Malcolm's eyes are big and his mouth, small. He quietly folds his iPad closed, then sets the table for two. He and Emily sit facing each other, saying nothing for several awkward moments.

Bowing his head, Malcolm simply says, "May God bless our meal and grant us a compassionate and understanding heart. In Jesus' name, we pray. Amen." Then he carefully asks Emily, "What's becoming of our daughter?"

"You're asking *me?*"

Malcolm gets up from the table, comes around to Emily's chair, and kisses her on the head. "My poor baby."

"Me? Or your Robin?"

"Come on, Em. You know, one day she is such a little girl and the next… It's like—is our Lord really calling her to be a priest?"

"Isn't there a text message from Him on your iPad?"

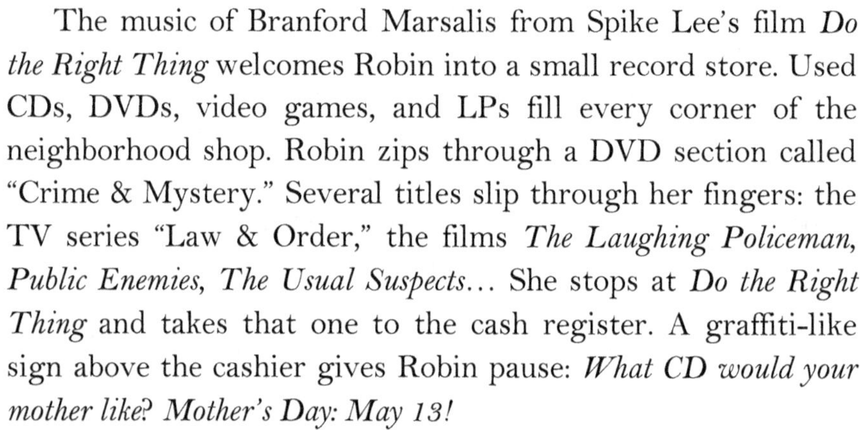

The music of Branford Marsalis from Spike Lee's film *Do the Right Thing* welcomes Robin into a small record store. Used CDs, DVDs, video games, and LPs fill every corner of the neighborhood shop. Robin zips through a DVD section called "Crime & Mystery." Several titles slip through her fingers: the TV series "Law & Order," the films *The Laughing Policeman, Public Enemies, The Usual Suspects…* She stops at *Do the Right Thing* and takes that one to the cash register. A graffiti-like sign above the cashier gives Robin pause: *What CD would your mother like? Mother's Day: May 13!*

"Do you have Barry Manilow?"

"Over there in 'Oldies Love Songs.'" Then not holding back, the clerk joshes, "I'm sorry for ya."

Robin throws her head back and laughs as she retreats to hunt for the CD.

For Mother's Day, though Emily is still awakening, Malcolm presents her with a card and a kiss on the cheek. She acknowledges with a weary smile. In moments, Robin bursts into their bedroom carrying a tray as an experienced server would, but with more flourish. A reused, self-stick red ribbon garnishes the *Ultimate Manilow CD*—and falls off.

"Oops! Breakfast is served. Croissants from *Fleur-de-lis* bakery over in the Hollywood neighborhood. They're great. And a French-press blend I created just for you." Smiling like a proud child, Robin says, "Happy Mother's Day, Mom!"

Emily props herself up to accept the sentimental show of affection. Malcolm pulls from under the bed a surprise present— a flip-top lap desk for occasions like this. "We both thought of it. It also works for reading in bed too."

Emily pushes the comforter aside and Malcolm gently snuggles the lap desk over the pink satin sheets. Emily's violet nightgown gives her a look of royalty. "But where's breakfast for y'all?" she asks.

Robin dashes out of the bedroom and thumps down the stairs. "Comin' right up!"

"I trust she's avoiding potholes and not banging into things," Emily says to Malcolm.

Malcolm coughs, shaking his head to shush an inappropriate topic, and in an exaggerated drawl teases, "Don't you be ugly now—as yer mamma would say." Then, more thoughtful, he asks, "You said you wanted to call her? It's two hours later in Fort Worth, unless Texas has opted out of daylight saving time by now. Hasn't your daddy been fixin' to be in a separate country, anyway?"

"Now is that any way ta talk about the Lone Star State—and Bishop Thorne? And yes, it's too early."

Malcolm reflects on Emily's mom. "At least she saw fit ta inta-duce us."

Emily closes her eyes and shakes her head in benign disagreement. Changing the subject, she confides, "Robin is actually kinda anxious about the upcoming prom. I know it's not really her thing. She'd rather be pinning some guy on a mat. But I believe she just might like to do a normal-girl kinda thing. What da *you* think?"

Malcolm blinks. "I…I don't know what to think. Let's not bring it up right now though."

CHAPTER 20

In The Upper School Library, Robin checks out several books, including *The Raven Steals the Light*.* She opens the book, pulls out her phone, and takes a photo of one of the illustrations.

Early that evening, Malcolm sits in his wingback chair, wearing reading glasses that make his eyes appear as oversized as his nose—or would if they were open. But he silently snoozes.

Robin quietly enters the study and stands with her arms folded like an auditor expecting an explanation for accounting discrepancies, her raven book held against her chest. "So, how did it all begin?"

Startled, Malcolm wakes up and looks at her, but seeing Robin's furtive smile, is unperturbed. "Um… You or the universe? Didn't we already cover that?"

Robin displays her book.

Unflappable, Malcolm assures, "It's all a story. You know that. Not one of us really knows. Currently, the best scientific explanation is the Big Bang theory over 13 billion years ago, give or take a few billion, when—"

"I know, I know. And those were *regular* years, not *light years*. Right?"

Malcolm closes his eyes and shakes his head as if to clear it—or dismiss the distraction..

"Anyway," Robin continues, "I found another creation story I never heard before. How can I become a priest if I don't have all the facts? Seven days. Adam and Eve. Noah and his twosomes… What's next? How are intelligent people supposed to make sense of these fables? I'd say you've been holding out on me. A lawyer can't argue a case if his client hides stuff."

"Hold on, Counsel. Let's look at the evidence."

Robin steps forward and opens the beautifully illustrated book. It features the popular Northwest Native American legend—Raven saves humans from darkness by bringing light to the world. Known for cleverness and courage, Raven steals the sun so mankind can see.

Robin stands next to her father's chair while Malcolm turns the pages. As interested as he is, he looks up at Robin and smiles, like a father might with his young daughter at bedtime. He returns his attention to the book. The first illustration is an artist's rendition of a white bird flying high into the dark sky holding a burning coal in his bill. The next shows the bird dropping the blazing orb from his beak. Malcolm turns the page to an illustration of the brilliant orb becoming the sun. Finally, smoke from the fire scorches the bird's white feathers black while the sun shines bright in the sky.

Malcolm proclaims, "And that is why Raven is black." He quickly wipes one eye so Robin doesn't notice. "Well, the raven gets better press in this story than the one we're used to in Genesis. It's beautiful. Cultures all over the world and from time immemorial have been trying to explain—well, everything. What we call 'science' is just our best effort to answer things." He pauses to reorganize his thoughts, then changes the topic. "I got an email from school that I think you'd be interested in."

Robin looks dubious.

"Teaching," Malcolm explains.

"Me? But I give my teachers such grief because I learn different—I mean *differently*."

"English! As a second language."

"You *are* kidding. Aren't you?"

She thinks, *His socks don't match!* Then blurts out, "Your socks don't match."

"Oh, no! I'll have to start the whole day all over! Okay—back on track?"

Robin tries to refocus but both start laughing until Emily comes into the study. She looks at them with raised eyebrows, expecting an explanation.

Malcolm says with conviction, "Robin has decided she wants to be Raven."

Emily smiles. "But of course."

CHAPTER 21

It is early evening in Portland's Grant Park with the popular Beverly Cleary sculpture garden for children. A life-size statue of Ramona Quimby seems to greet a small bird as it lands on her shoulder.

Meanwhile, downtown at Chapman Square, a raven stands on the pioneer's shoulder of *The Promised Land* and nearby, a young man of 25 but easily passing for younger, stands watch. When he sees the raven, he points his cell phone as if it were a handgun. Kevin is blond and wholesome in a midwestern-college-guy kind of way, wearing a forest-green Portland State Vikings jacket. He stands with confidence. He glances at his phone, then scans his surroundings, appearing to be waiting for someone—or for someone to notice his new Nike Hyperdunk USA basketball shoes in red, white, and black, designed for the upcoming London Olympics. His phone, ringer off and set to vibrate, buzzes. He answers it.

At the same time, eighteen-year-old Miguel Nariño-Lopez takes a shortcut through the square. Wearing a bright-red hooded sweatshirt from Lincoln High School, he walks with purpose. He is handsome, confident, and professional looking in his retro glasses—like an intern in a law office. But contrasting a staid law-office look is his black hair pulled back in a ponytail. Distracting more so is a jagged scar above his right cheek.

Miguel does notice Kevin sporting the newest Nikes and Kevin quickly ends his call. He smoothly slides the phone into his back pocket and steps forward in Miguel's direction. A friendly evening greeting implies a question.

Miguel responds most succinctly, "Yep. Not interested." His pace unbroken, Miguel continues through the park.

Kevin springs forward to catch up and in a straightforward way, simply asks, "Excuse me. Is this the way to the library?"

Slowing down slightly and letting Kevin catch up, Miguel softens. "Sorry. I didn't mean to be rude… Library? Which one?"

"I'm new to Portland and you look like you know your way around. There's more than one?"

"You *are* new here. Both are this way. Where are you from?"

They continue walking together, out of the park and into the street-lighted city at dusk. Miguel notices Kevin's jacket and looks a little puzzled.

Central Library is Georgian-styled, appropriately grand, and certainly worthy of being on the National Register of Historic Places. The library stands aloof as Miguel and Kevin shake hands. Miguel ascends the granite steps but Kevin remains at the sidewalk. He notices a car pulling out of a parking space right in front of the library and within mere seconds, like a hawk swooping, a green Range Rover captures the space.

Malcolm turns off the engine and Robin reluctantly gets out. Kevin instantly scans her from head to toe before she sees him. Then, noticing Kevin but without appearing to care, she tosses her head like a filly showing off to a stallion and pulls her hair from over her shoulder to her chest.

Malcolm tucks his iPad between his seat and the control console. The red-leather clad iPad looks like it is posing for a photo shoot for the well-appointed Range Rover. His skullcap is now a bishop's red-violet and he wears a silver pectoral St. Patrick cross and an Episcopal bishop's amethyst Celtic ring.

"Did you get everything, Robbie?" he says as he too gets out of the car.

From the lower library steps, Kevin smiles and gives Robin a subtle wink as she passes him—one so quick, so effortless, that Robin is not sure it really was a wink. But it was. Nearly missing a step and hesitating, she answers Malcolm, "Yes. Did you?"

Kevin answers, but to himself under his breath, "Oh, yeah…" He watches them walk up the stairs and just before entering the library, Robin quickly steals a look back. Kevin nods at her.

A placard mounted on a chrome stand points the way to the meeting room and directs volunteers: *English Now of Portland Welcomes You!** Parents and high school students cautiously find seats among the precisely arranged rows of folding chairs. Hushed conversation buzzes in the room.

Malcolm picks out a row near the front, politely deferring to Robin to find a chair of her choosing. After they are seated, Miguel enters and previews the room, surveying everything from the entrance in the back to the podium in front. He notices Robin. Straightening up, he takes a seat in the same row a few seats away from her. Without hesitation, he greets Robin and bows his head in deference to Malcolm.

Robin tries to conceal her satisfaction with another young man's attention. She sits upright, at attention, like she's in a church pew.

Two young men wearing hooded sweatshirts, their faces unidentifiable, smash the glass of a car window nearby. They approach the Range Rover and slowly glide past it on their mountain bikes. The first biker stops suddenly and waits, keeping watch. The second one also stops, dismounts, and leans his bike against the car. They do not see Kevin standing with someone in the shadows of an unused, dark library entrance.

With a miniature, high-intensity flashlight, the second one presses his face against the driver's side window and spots the iPad. Without hesitation, the thief steps back and flings a piece of porcelain from a broken spark plug at the window. It shatters. He smiles, satisfied as he reaches into the cab. But the sudden appearance of Kevin dashing down the steps prompts the accomplice to yell and the thug races away. Kevin tries to nab the thief by the hood but the teenager grabs his bike, runs alongside it for several car lengths, jumps onto it, and sprints away faster than Kevin can run.

Kevin looks at the Rover. Glass is shattered on the driver's seat and the sidewalk. He sees what they were after and thrusts his hand inside to retrieve the iPad. He tucks it under his arm and then notices that he has scraped his hand. Kevin licks his wound to stop the bleeding. Shaking his head, he mumbles, "Amateurs."

Fewer seats are available, so Miguel moves over next to Robin to make room for others, and asks, "Is this reserved? May I?"

"No. I mean, yes. I mean, sit down." She extends her hand. "Hi. So, how did you find out about this?" But before Miguel can answer, their attention is drawn to the front as the MC thumps on the microphone to test it.

A small group of four volunteer speakers is forming at the podium at the front of the room. The apparent leader, Edward, is an older, robust gentleman in a navy-blue, three-piece suit with a white shirt and a patriotic red tie. He organizes his notes. A uniformed police officer, Andres Nariño-Lopez—mid-20s, authoritative, and still wearing his hat—chats with an African American young man. The young man looks like he could be a college student, not yet 20, and wears a waiter's white shirt, black pants, and a black apron. Next to him is a petite woman of Vietnamese or other Asian descent in her 50s. Nervous, she unconsciously bobs up and down.

About two-thirds of the seats are now occupied and people are chatting quietly among themselves.

Turning to Miguel, Robin asks, "Is this supposed to be a United Nations event?" Inviting his comment, she smiles, but then notices his scar and looks quickly down.

"My brother asked me to come. He's the cop up there—in case there's trouble." He keeps a straight face to see if she gets the humor.

Robin grimaces and turns to the front of the room. Malcolm makes a few inquisitive glances over at Miguel, then checks his iPhone for messages and silences the ringer.

Edward steps up to the podium and addresses the crowd. "Welcome to English Now. Anyone not understanding me, please raise your hand," he jokes.

With lips pursed, he pauses for effect and looks around the room to see if anyone has raised an arm. He sees one overeager high school student suddenly retracting his raised arm and smiles at his attempted humor.

"Ooookay... We take communication so much for granted, we forget how difficult it is when you're foreign-born or your parents don't speak American English. On this point, let us hear from Officer Andres Nariño-Lopez from the Portland Police Bureau."

Andres, removing his cap, nods. "Thank you, Edward. It was the English Now program that helped me most in early high school. My parents are from Colombia. Now they are very busy running a successful restaurant in east Portland. But I could not have excelled in high school or gotten into Portland State without help learning English."

After the initial presentation, the young officer talks with various people, including Malcolm, Robin, and Miguel. Prospective volunteers mingle, picking up brochures on a table and chatting about why they are interested in tutoring.

A short time later, Malcolm walks beside Robin as they leave the library. Miguel allows a respectable distance slightly behind father and daughter. Looking back, he notices Kevin emerging from the shadows, tucking what looks like cash into his front pocket.

Almost at the car, Malcolm turns to Miguel, extending his hand. "Miguel, right? Very nice to meet you. Your brother did a great job. Very articulate."

Kevin swoops down the granite steps to meet them. The iPad is tucked in his jeans, hidden by his jacket.

Malcolm does not appear to notice and continues, "I appreciate your volunteering too." Then in jest adds, "Or did *he* put you up to it?"

Robin looks around, surprised. Miguel studies Kevin.

Malcolm is self-assured and pleasant, but quizzical about the interruption. "Yes?"

Kevin points to the car, "Thieves! After your iPad, maybe?"

Malcolm lurches toward his vehicle with the fob already unlocking the door. Eyes wide with alarm, he stammers, "You…you saw it?"

"Two guys on bikes. They stopped to have a look. But—"

Malcolm, winded as if hit in the stomach, looks inside and sees the damage. Turning to Kevin with a frown, he sees him holding out his iPad like a trophy, his hand freshly bleeding.

Malcolm's frown dissolves into concern for Kevin's injury.

"What did you have to do?" He shakes his head. "Thank you." He reaches for his wallet and opens it. Seeing only a couple of ones and a five, he pauses, uncomfortable and now embarrassed. "I'm sorry. I don't have enough to…to show my appreciation." Malcolm looks again in the wallet. "But here is my card. I'd really like you to stop by."

"So that's it. You're a bishop." Bowing his head, Kevin says, "I haven't met a bishop before."

"Hold'r, there, my man. What's your name?"

"Kevin. Kevin O'Connor, Pastor. I'm a Baptist—a bad one, I'm told."

Miguel corrects Kevin. "It's *Your Excellency.*"

Malcolm sees no need for pomp. "That title's Catholic. But enough formality. How 'bout a little voodoo? Voodoo Donuts?"

Robin protests, "Daaad…I'm not supposed to—you know, wheat-free, gluten-free, fun free." She redirects herself as she kicks the glass on the sidewalk with her shoe. "Shouldn't we report this?"

Miguel asserts, "Um…what are they going to do?"

Kevin nods in agreement and leans in closer to the bishop. "Careful not to scratch the leather with the glass. I'm sorry I couldn't stop them sooner."

Robin opens the door and carefully brushes the glass off the seat onto the floor. Kevin studies her for a moment while Malcolm turns to bid a good evening to both him and Miguel.

Kevin apologizes again, "Sorry your evening ends with this, Bishop."

Miguel says to Robin, "See you Tuesday, right?"

Malcolm again shakes hands with Miguel and then, with genuine warmth and appreciation, turns to Kevin. "Thank you for looking after us. Come by, okay?"

Malcolm reaches out to shake but Kevin holds up his bloodied hand and just nods modestly.

Miguel and Kevin watch Malcolm and Robin get into their car. Then they turn to one another, each now regarding the other as a player on a competing team. They watch the Rover pull away.

"Heroic introduction, Kevin," Miguel smirks. "It *really* happened that way?"

"You doubt me, my friend? So, is the fox your main squeeze?"

"Yeah. As a matter of fact, her father quite approves of me."

Kevin, turning to go, tosses out, "Cool. Well, *hasta la vista. Viva la MeXico!*"

"I'm from *here*, East Portland. My *parents* are from Colombia. Where are you from?"

"Missouri… So, you got the fancy scar in a street fight?"

"Asking questions ever get you into trouble? I was nine and my dog and I were playing way too rough. Thirty-one stitches, if you have to know."

"No offense. Your girlfriend's got taste. You're good lookin' anyway for a… Hey, you're smart, smart enough to charm a bishop's daughter."

Kevin gives Miguel a slap handshake, more hearty than necessary. Miguel shakes his head and turns away.

The Trinity administration building, as a modern structure, was designed to complement the basalt of the Gothic Revival church, almost matching the ugly gray—a design-committee creation, one would suppose. It now disgorges the Women's Guild. Emily waves goodbye with her free hand and after readjusting her load of manila folders, trudges to the deanery.

As she walks, she sees a college-age man kissing—*passionately kissing*—a young woman on the front porch of a house across the street. In silhouette, it is hard to see any details but Emily can't stop watching—until the girlfriend turns and notices her staring. Emily snaps herself to attention and continues home.

In the kitchen, Emily is still distracted. She sets the stack of folders down and they splay across the table but she ignores them. She fills a tea kettle from a filtered-water faucet next to the sink and looks for tea—the *right* tea—somewhere in the cupboard. The water overflows from the kettle onto the counter and floor. She cries but doesn't know why.

Later that same evening, Emily lies in bed. Her nightstand lamp is off. Malcolm snuggles up next to her and kisses her softly on the neck. He cannot see her eyes but it is just as well. She lets him make love to her. She lies on her back, her eyes searching the ceiling, looking far away. Closing her eyes, she continues to lie there…still, emotionless.

Down the hall, Robin prepares for sleep. The Harry Potter and Narnia posters have been replaced with a *Matrix Trilogy* poster, "Believe the Unbelievable" and one from *Titanic.* Leonardo DiCaprio catches her eye as she undresses for bed.

Turning again to the poster, she stares, remembering Kevin's wink as she ascended the library steps: *Yum. So handsome!* She switches off the light.

CHAPTER 22

On Tuesday afternoon, an ESL coordinator leaves the upscale conference room at the Bud Clark Commons. Robin and Miguel gather their guidebooks and personal belongings, and stuff them into their respective school backpacks.

Robin sighs with relief. "That was okay for a first day."

"Yep. But I needa get to work. Let me make you a cappuccino."

"Gracias. *Yo soy hombre, también.*" [Thanks. I am a man too.]

"Umm…you mean you're hungry?"

"That's what I said."

Miguel smiles warmly. "Not quite. Don't worry. Your English is better than your Spanish."

Robin looks annoyed but laughs off her mistake. "So, how do you say cappuccino in Spanish?"

Like an exasperated teacher, he gives her a playfully pompous look and refuses to answer.

Robin and Miguel exit Portland's showpiece project for addressing homelessness in the city—a beautiful modern building.

Robin wonders out loud, "So…why are you doing this?"

"Tutoring? Ultimately, I want to advocate for people like my parents. As a lawyer. I have a scholarship—actually, a full scholarship to U of O."

Robin stops in her tracks. "A real scholarship? Congratulations!"

Miguel looks back with the expectation to keep walking. "Yes.

I study hard and get good grades. Maybe I'm lucky too—my parents help me stay focused. And my brother will beat me up if I don't do at least as well as he."

Robin laughs at his humor and admits, "I can't sit still doing homework for hours at a time. No way. I like jiu-jitsu and I'm told it helps me stay on track when I do sit down to study."

As they walk past a tattoo parlor, Robin momentarily loses her train of thought. "My parents—especially my dad—are also very encouraging. They believe I'm meant to be a priest, that I have a vocation. A calling, as they say." Glancing back at the tattoo window, she continues, "I've been playing with an image for a tattoo—a raven. We make up stories to explain what we don't understand. Like how did the sun get to be in the sky? The raven brought it. It's a lovely legend and like so many of our everyday beliefs, is pure fiction."

Miguel stops, stunned. "Whoa. Everyday beliefs? Pure fiction? That's something to think about." He nods toward the tattoo parlor. "Let's take a quick peek."

"Um—okay."

Robin turns around and Miguel follows.

"Mom calls them 'taboo' parlors. I've never been in one."

Miguel smiles and shakes his head as he holds the door for Robin to enter.

A few minutes later, Robin and Miguel are back on the street. They resume their walk and pick up their pace. Miguel checks his phone for the time. "I'm due at work shortly, but there's still time for me to make you an awesome cappuccino."

Robin mulls over the notice she just saw in the tattoo parlor. "I didn't know you had to be at least 18."

"I didn't know that either. So, this gives you plenty of time to refine your design, huh?"

Coffeehouse Northwest (despite its ambitious name) is a small, locally-owned business across the street from a Starbucks. It is just right for meeting a classmate or a few friends, or working solo on a laptop. As Miguel enters, he sees his older brother at a table in the back. He is having coffee with a fellow officer, Kris—an African American with cornrow-styled hair and clear hazel eyes, maybe 23. Though engaged in conversation with one another, they are also attentive to those who enter and leave. Andres sees Miguel enter with Robin following behind.

"I remember her," he says to Kris. "The English Now meeting." He stands to greet them. "Thought you'd never get here."

"But actually, sir, I'm early," Miguel replies. To Kris, he adds, "They assigned you to this one?"

Kris rises to congratulate and shake Miguel's hand. "College scholarship offers—two, even. Yer brother's countin' on ya ta be the family lawyer." Kris steps back.

Miguel does not dismiss the compliment but wishes to move the introductions along. "Officer Nariño-Lopez, my friend, Robin. We tutor ESL." To Robin, he adds, "My brother, Andres. But you may call him Officer Nariño-Lopez."

Robin understands these formalities. "A pleasure, sir." Then, correcting Miguel, "I'm *Ms.* Marshall." And back to Andres, "But you may call me Robin."

Kris smiles at the friendly banter and gestures for Robin to join them.

Miguel, seeing their drinks and treats awaiting them, confirms, "Looks like you're both good. Well, Kris, at least." To Robin, "Cappuccino? On me. What else may I get you? We even have gluten-free scones."

"You remember! Why, yes, thank you." Robin excuses

herself for the restroom.

Miguel tells his brother, "The Episcopal bishop's daughter. I didn't know they came this hot. She's smart, trains in jiu-jitsu—"

"Little bro has a crush."

Kris teases, "Should I be takin' notes?"

Miguel abruptly turns to begin his shift.

Robin is chatting with Andres and Kris at their table when Miguel hand delivers a beautifully crafted cappuccino and a scone. Trying not to show his affection for her, Miguel turns and stumbles. But Robin is mesmerized in conversation with the cops.

"Yeah, you should do a ride-along with one of us," Andres invites Robin. "Just get your dad to sign off on the form."

Kris adds, "Your dad wouldn't object to your interest in law enforcement, would he?"

"He's all about community service. My mother is another story."

That afternoon in her bedroom, Robin studies the Portland Police Bureau website. With heightened enthusiasm, she searches several other police-related sites. The next day at school, again online, Robin continues her Google searches on police.

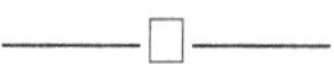

At the Trinity Cathedral deanery, Kevin stands at the front door wearing a purple University of Portland Pilots jacket. He waits for a moment, takes a deep breath, and glances at Malcolm's card. He presses the doorbell and steps back. Shivering in the cold spring breeze, he shifts his weight back and forth while he waits.

Emily looks through the security peephole. Kevin stands, momentarily side-profiled, reminding her of the young man she saw a few nights earlier kissing the girl. Bracing herself, she takes a breath and cautiously opens the door. "Yes? How may I help you?"

Well-rehearsed, Kevin assures, "The Very Reverend Marshall asked me to stop by."

Showing Emily the business card as if it were a VIP guest pass, he is relieved when she steps back and welcomes him to step inside.

"Was he expecting you at this time? He is—was—due back a while ago." Motioning to the parlor, she offers, "Do have a seat. May I get you some tea? Or coffee?"

The classic Edwardian interior with craftsman detailing, rich draperies, and sheer ivory-white curtains welcomes guests used to the finer things.

Kevin nods in appreciation. "Only if you are having any. Lovely home, Mrs. Marshall—right?"

"Oh, yes. Sorry, I didn't in-ta-duce myself. Thank you. What did you say your name was?"

"Kevin O'Connor."

"Make yourself comfortable, Kevin. Tea? Darjeeling?"

He nods as she motions for him to take off his jacket. And only now remembering his good manners, he removes his cap first, then the jacket. Kevin scans the room, especially the massive harp and grand piano. Looking with approval, he walks over to admire the vintage Steinway.

Without his noticing, Emily picks up his jacket and smells the collar, then places the jacket and cap on a nearby chair. She asks, "Do ya play?"

"Not this kind."

"Just as well. It's been months since it's been tuned."

Nodding to the harp, Kevin asks politely, "You play both?"

"When I get a chance—my responsibilities as the bishop's wife, ya know."

Emily leaves the room and Kevin briefly settles into one of two navy-blue velvet upholstered chairs. He gets up, goes over to the window, and notes the updated double-pane windows. He tries the latch and it opens. He closes it but leaves it unlocked.

Emily calls from the kitchen, "Oh, Kevin, I'm sorry. I'm out of Darjeeling. How is Earl Grey?"

Silently, now standing in the kitchen doorway, Kevin gazes at Emily as she prepares the tea. She gasps when she sees him standing there.

"The Earl would be fine. But you needn't fuss." Seating himself at Malcolm's place with comfortable familiarity, he picks up the *Willamette Week* and looks casually through the different sections.

Emily offers, "Let me get the light." She punches the knob of the old-style dimmer switch by the kitchen door. It sizzles and the overhead light flashes and flutters, then remains on. "It does that. I'm surprised it still works after all these years. Malcolm…I mean, Bishop Marshall…has it on his to-do list."

"The new Leviton or Lutron dimmers are great, especially the Lutron."

"The what? You do wiring? That's why Malcolm asked you over?"

"It's easy." Quickly glancing to the kitchen's other doorway, he modifies his cavalier confidence. "Oh, I see, it's a three-way. Well, those are more complicated."

Emily studies Kevin for a moment—for several moments, in fact, until the tea kettle sings and she takes it off the stove. She pours the boiling water into an heirloom teapot. Looking at the kitchen clock, she notes the time just as the wall phone rings. "It's about time…" she says as she reaches to pick up the receiver. "Hi, dear. You're running late?" She listens to Malcolm but watches Kevin. "Uh-huh… You were expecting a young gentleman by the name of Kevin. He's here now."

Kevin distracts himself with the newspaper's front page.

Listening and seemingly annoyed, Emily answers, "I don't think so. Let me see." She goes over to her purse, stretching the phone's coiled cord to its limit. She presses her head against her shoulder to hold the phone and at the same time, open her wallet.

Kevin jumps up to assist but Emily motions that she can manage on her own. She offers a demur smile. He sits back down on the edge of the chair.

"No, I don't." Looking over at Kevin, she says, "Maybe he would accept a check." Emily listens for a few moments, then adds, "He's also an electrician. Maybe he could fix this fritzy kitchen switch too. Okay. Thank you. Okay. Yes, I'll call them for you. Bye."

Emily hangs up the phone and returns to the stove. "Sorry about that. Our tea should be steeped by now. None of us have cash anymore. Or is it none of us *has* cash? I always wonder about those things."

Kevin is confused. "What? Oh, yes. A check would be fine."

Emily leaves the everyday chipped mugs on the shelf; these won't do. She wants to serve the tea in matching teacups. "I'll be right back."

Kevin goes over to the light switch, gives it a sniff, and wrinkles his nose in response. He checks the other switch as well.

Emily returns from the dining room with proper teacups

and two separate commercial-sized checks, folded in half. "My husband really appreciates what you did for him. I do too. And if you'd do the repair, we would be ever so grateful."

Kevin takes the checks without unfolding them, nodding in appreciation.

"You are such a gentleman. You're not from around here, are you?"

"Chicago. I came out here to go to school. Working odd jobs so I can."

"Impressive."

But he defers, "Tell me about yourself. You're originally from—Texas, I'm guessing? But you're here now. You like Portland?"

Emily, surprised at his inquiry, flushes. Like a schoolgirl at a spelling bee, momentarily stuck, she looks to the side, then back to Kevin. "How'd ya guess Texas?"

He winks.

After his tea with the bishop's wife, as he walks on the sidewalk from the deanery toward the cathedral, Kevin catches sight of a black Mazda zipping into a parking place—on the wrong side of the street. Robin, still dressed in her jiu-jitsu gear, springs out of her car and heads toward the deanery. It takes both of them a few moments to recognize one another.

Robin is first. "The library! You're *The* guy. Sure made my dad's day." She lets him take in the compliment. "I asked him if he remembered his iPad too. He's such a nice man—has a hard time believing there are real assholes in the world."

Kevin is surprised at her candor, her word choice. "You practice martial arts. Is your boyfriend your sparring partner too?"

Puzzled, Robin replies, "Um…you mean Miguel? No, no. No, we're just friends. We're ESL tutors. He's a barista. I'm on my way there now. Care to join me?"

Hesitating only a moment, Kevin shrugs. "Sure."

"You saw my dad?"

"No, your mom. They talked on the phone. Your dad is very generous. He also approved replacing that light switch in the kitchen."

"I thought you were in college. You're Catholic?"

"Um, not yet." He shrugs again.

Robin ignores his jest. "Let me throw these things inside and we can walk to my friend's coffeehouse. I won't be but a minute."

Robin walks briskly into the deanery and Kevin follows. At the stairs, she sprints two at a time. Kevin admires her graceful, athletic movement.

Busy with the after-school crowd—but surprisingly quiet, like a study hall—the upbeat coffeehouse and its music are just right for a gloomy afternoon in the Northwest. During the momentary pause between customers' drink orders, Miguel adds to his sketch of a raven in flight. Carefully placing two arrows crossed like an X in its right talon, he steps back to view his work. A young coworker, Angel, aproned and wearing a dazzling plain white T-shirt, comes over to see what he's doing, curious. Their conversations and banter are mostly in Spanish.

Angel, teasing, asks, "What's with the crow?" Taking a closer look, he puzzles, "Arrows? Like the eagle on the dollar?"

"Nooo. It's a raven. And the crossed arrows are a Native American symbol for friendship—the opposite of war."

"For us?"

Miguel dismisses Angel with a nod, motioning for him to get back to work while he himself heads for the supply room. Angel chuckles as he clears a table by the front door. While he buses the dishes, he graciously greets two patrons as they enter the café.

Kevin holds the door open for Robin and is distracted by Angel's neck tattoo—the Sacred Heart with a crown of thorns and a dagger through it. As the door closes, Kevin looks back to stare at Angel's artwork.

Robin directs Kevin to a corner table. "So, what'll it be?"

"A macchiato would be great. Can they make it Italian style?"

She retrieves her wallet and he reaches for his own, but Robin stops him. Holding her hand over his, she locks eyes with him. "My treat. It was my idea."

"You don't need to. But thank you."

Behind the counter, Miguel pours fresh, fragrant beans into the grinder. He glances up to see Robin standing there and smiles warmly. Robin returns the smile, then gives him her order. Miguel seems puzzled to hear her request for two drinks, so she nods to the corner table. Miguel looks over to see Kevin and their eyes meet. Miguel grimaces. Kevin gives him a mocking smile.

Robin notices the look on Miguel's face. "What's wrong?"

"Nothing."

"You remember Kevin from the library. He's doing some electrical work for my dad."

"I'll have your drinks right up."

Kevin keeps his eyes on Miguel even as Robin rejoins him to wait for their drinks. Kevin's eyes dart between her and Miguel. Miguel crumples his drawing and tosses it into the compost pail of coffee grounds. Angel, wiping the counter close by, watches.

Robin begins fidgeting, digging into her bag until she finds what she is looking for.

Kevin observes, "It's busy here. Good that they have a barista like Miguel. Looks like he handles it well."

Robin agrees with a quiet smile. She retrieves a punch card from her wallet. "I've already started a new one. Buy 10, get one free."

He accepts and slips it into his shirt pocket with casual indulgence.

Miguel calls out, "Order up, Marshall."

Robin looks surprised. Kevin jumps up to get the order. He presents her with the cappuccino and places the macchiato on his side of the table and sits. At first sip, he exclaims, "Awesome!"

Robin takes a deep sip from her drink but her face sours. "It's—it's off." She gets up, cup wobbling in the saucer, and approaches Miguel. "What happened? You make perfect—"

Miguel turns to listen to Robin while his hands keep working on his new order. "What's wrong?"

"It's not your perfect balance."

He stops his work, surprise showing on his forehead. Trying to remember each sequence, he looks straight at Robin. "I must've been distracted. A long pull makes a bitter drink—I'm sorry."

Robin stands there without a word. Miguel prepares another drink for her while she studies him. "You are good. Not only at your work."

Miguel avoids looking up and slides her a fresh cappuccino, quickly resuming his attention to his other orders. "I hope you like this one."

Pensive and lost in thought, Robin returns to the table.

Kevin puts aside his phone. "Not all drinks come out the way they're supposed to. It just takes practice, huh?"

"I shoulda ordered a Coke—that's Texan for Dr. Pepper, a-course."

"A what?"

"Sorry. My mother coming through."

"She's calling?"

Robin dismisses the question with a twitch of her head and slowly picks up the cappuccino. "Why'd you pick Portland?"

"School. And not as cold as Chicago. And the people are more honest."

"Honest?"

"Well, nice."

Robin nods at his Pilots jacket on the back of the chair.

Kevin playfully answers, "It was either Notre Dame or the University of Portland. Of course, I needa work to save up."

"I understand."

"Do you?"

With penetrating, slate-blue eyes, he holds a gaze, at once arresting as it is beguiling. When Robin does not look away, Kevin's knee touches hers. Unflinching, she seems to dare him. Miguel notices the contest.

"Okay," Kevin challenges. "How 'bout you? You're planning on college, right?"

Robin squirms. "Daddy thinks I'd be a great priest. And eventually, a bishop, like him. I'm going with him to London in November. It's the worldwide conference where all the Episcopal bishops gather. This one will be quite a showdown. Should the Episcopal Church ordain openly gay men and women—and allow women to become bishops too?"

"I thought Episcopalians were as liberal as Christians could be—and still be Christian."

"Baptist, you said you were? Anyway, I'll be off to London."

"Will it be your first time?"

"No. How 'bout you? You've been?"

Kevin just looks at her with a sardonic smile, hinting of scorn. "I'd best be going."

"But when do I see you again?"

"You want me to call you?" He hands her his phone.

Without hesitation, Robin calls her number and waits for it to ring softly in her blue tote. Handing Kevin his phone for him to leave a message, she grabs her bag and excuses herself for the restroom while the phone rings. As she walks in and locks the door, she pulls out her phone to see Kevin's call. But there's no caller ID. *So, how can I call him? Doesn't he trust me?* Slightly annoyed, she slips the phone back into her bag and glances into the mirror. As an afterthought, she digs into her purse, finally finding a tube of autumn-red lip gloss. She applies it deliberately but then blots it with a paper towel to nearly invisible.

Robin returns to find the corner table cleared, clean, and the chairs squared—and no Kevin. She sees him at the counter, where he thoughtfully places the espresso and cappuccino cups near Miguel.

Looking up with a piercing stare, Miguel makes direct eye contact. With deep sarcasm, he says, *"Gracias, amigo."* And then adds in contempt, *"¡No te cojes mi amiga!"* [Do not fuck my friend.]

Kevin screws up his face. "What?"

Miguel smirks, "Think about it."

Robin is disconcerted to see Kevin with Miguel. She bites her lip and hesitates. "Thank you, Miguel. See you next week."

He only nods and returns his attention to wiping down the steamer nozzle of the espresso machine.

As Robin and Kevin leave, Angel comes over to Miguel. "Looks like the rich guy cleared away the table. And your babe too."

Miguel swings around and slugs Angel in the stomach.

Angel falls back, winded. After catching his breath, he coughs out, "I—I was only teasing."

Realizing he hit his friend much harder than he intended,

Miguel apologizes. "I'm sorry. I didn't mean to hurt you."

Angel, annoyed and still hurting, reaches for the dirty cups and saucers—but stops when he sees a note on the napkin. *Loser.*

Angel exclaims, "*¡Bastardo!*" Looking out the window, he insists, "We can't let him get away with that."

Miguel looks at the napkin but resists crying. He clenches his fists. Angel eyes him and steps back. They both look around the café, realizing that they have had a full-house audience. Both quickly return to their work.

Robin drives while Kevin checks his phone for messages. She offers, "I'm happy to drop you off at your home. Really."

"Thank you again. But I'm expecting a school buddy from out of town."

"Sure. Where's he coming from?"

Glancing at his phone, distracted, he answers. "Kansas City."

"Kansas City, Kansas?"

"No. The other one. *Misery.*"

Robin does not immediately get it. The noise of rush-hour traffic and the narrow streets require her full attention, though she tries to remain calm and charming. She lets Kevin out at a corner crossing with no time for chitchat.

"I look forward to your call," she says.

Kevin steps out onto the curb. As he closes the car door, he replies, "And thank you for the coffee, Rob—"

His words are cut off by the thud of the door. Robin looks at the passenger-side mirror and sees Kevin wave.

Rob...Robbie? And lost in thought, smiling, she drives into the crowded intersection even though the light has changed to red. She inches forward, grimacing at the annoyed, smug pedestrians as they saunter through the crosswalk. She endures the reprisals of the cross-traffic cars honking. *Portland is so righteous, so annoying!*

CHAPTER 23

This morning, the kitchen is a thoroughfare for the Marshall family. As Robin is about to dash out the door, she kisses Emily on the cheek. "You're the best." And darting, she's gone. Puzzled, Emily looks at Malcolm.

Malcolm returns her gaze. "Well, you are. So there."

At school, the hallway is crowded and abuzz with students' conversations. Robin checks the monitor for upcoming events. Featured prominently is next week's prom. She looks around and sees the frizzy-haired girl chatting with Sammy. Robin pulls her phone out of her bag and sees a missed call but no caller ID. She grimaces. *Voicemail?* she wonders. She checks but there's none. "Damn!"

Crushed, she slumps away until she hears someone calling.

"Hi, Robin. Wha-what's up?"

"Not much. Hey, Sammy…you know technology. Is there a way to find out who is calling you even when there's no caller ID?"

"Oh, yeah. There's, there's a code for that. And apps too."

Robin smiles and shakes her head in silent appreciation. *He's amazing.*

In the academy parking lot, Robin sits in her car, searching websites on her iPhone. She is startled when it rings but answers without hesitation. "Hey… At school… Oh, what is your number?" A look of annoyance crosses her face, then she forces a composed response. "Okay. At home. Will that give you enough time?"

A short time later, Kevin waits outside the deanery.

Emily opens the door, surprised to see him. "Sorry, I didn't hear you ring. I was just leaving. You're here to fix the switch?"

"Actually, I'm just on my way to get them. I'm waiting for Robin."

"Robin?"

Kevin looks at the street, then back to Emily. "She's giving me a ride to the lighting supply place."

Emily puzzles, "Oh. Of course. Would you like to come inside?"

He takes out his phone to confirm the time. "I *am* a little early."

Rolling her eyes like a teenager, Emily says, "And she will be a little late." She gestures for Kevin to enter.

Kevin accepts and steps into the foyer. Looking again at his phone, he seems apprehensive and fidgets as he stands there keeping watch from the side window.

Emily reaches for her long coat from the front closet. "I do need to go, but you may wait here."

As she begins to put on her coat, Kevin takes it, as a gentleman would, and assists her.

Emily smiles, and with her Texan drawl says, "Why, thank you, Kevin." Giving him a second thank-you nod, she leaves and closes the door behind her. Down the steps and once around the corner, Emily sends Robin a text message: *Kevin is waiting. Such a gentleman. But remember, he's still a guy.*

The only sound in the empty house is the foyer's grandfather clock ticking. Kevin walks cautiously into the formal dining room. He approaches a cabinet against the far wall, slides open one of the drawers, and sees a massive set of elegant silverware. He lifts one of the knives as if to confirm its weight. Kevin steps back to look out the curtained windows, then notices in the corner a complete silver tea set. He turns over the coffee server and examines the imprint on the bottom. Kevin sets the server down and quick-steps to the window. He pulls the curtain aside and sees Robin's Mazda zoom up to the curb. With a sigh of relief, he heads for the front door.

At the parking strip, Kevin leans into Robin's view so she can unlock the car door. He wastes no time getting in and kissing her on the cheek. Her eyes widen, momentarily wordless.

Kevin teases, "Okay, Mario, gun it!"

Robin looks at him. "Mario? I thought I was Rob."

"Famous race car driver, Mario Andretti." He hands Robin a scrap of torn envelope, smiling and content with himself. "Here's the address."

Kevin straps himself in and leans back, looking straight ahead. But Robin cannot resist. She leans over and gives him a deliberate kiss.

Slowly letting his tongue taste his just kissed lips, Kevin savors the moment. "What would your mother say?" he teases.

Robin swallows hard and focuses on the task at hand. "Get there early so you won't be late—that's what she would say!" *He smells good…*

She pulls away from the curb and blasts down the street.

At the wholesale supply parking lot, the Mazda clock on the dash shows 4:44. Robin is pleased with herself. But Kevin looks anxious.

"You have plenty of time. I'll wait," Robin tells him.

He gets out and almost before the door closes, Robin is texting her friend Andria.

The front counter has one eager-to-leave employee. In his late 30s, with generous double chins and an apron meant only for a normal-sized person, Jim is not happy to see a customer at closing time. He looks up at an old-fashioned neon wall clock. Kevin does the same.

Kevin observes, "It's ahead—like 10 minutes!"

"Yep. It's hows we stay ahead of the competition. So, whatcha need?"

"A set of Lutron dimmer switches—three-way, in stone or limestone finish."

"I like a man who knows what 'e wants. What's yer account?"

"I need an account? That's right, we're wholesale."

"Yep. It's hows we stay ahead of the competition." Jim slides a old xeroxed form over the counter.

Kevin looks it over and hesitates.

"Yep. It's a pain. I'll git the switches. You do yer homework."

"You must be the owner's son."

"Yer kiddin'."

"Yep."

Not looking up to see Jim's chagrin, Kevin looks over the form, then remembers something in his pocket—the Coffeehouse Northwest punch card. He enters its address and phone number. Looking around the deserted display area, he notices on the stool next to him an electrician's tool belt bulging with all the gear a professional electrician would need on-site.

Jim returns, plops the switches on the counter, and hurries to enter the transaction on his terminal. "That's $78.45 but for you, $78.45—our closin' time special."

Kevin shrugs his shoulders in concession and hands over $80 in cash. Jim makes change and closes the cash drawer with a definitive thrust. When he leaves the sales floor for a few moments, Kevin quickly grabs the electrician's belt as naturally as if it were his own. Strapping it to his waist, and not noticing the punch card falling to the floor under the stool, Kevin tucks the excess of the long belt into one of the tool pouches.

Kevin walks out the door and Jim jams the key into the lock as he gives a perfunctory nod to Kevin. "Have a good one."

The Mazda vibrates with the gentle music of Adele's "Make You Feel My Love." Kevin approaches the vehicle so Robin can see him through the front window. Only a little startled, she turns down her song. He removes the tool belt and tosses it to the back seat along with the switches, and he gets in. Kevin looks back to the electrical supply's front door.

"You need all those tools?"

"Uh-huh." He kisses her once on the lips, looks into her eyes, and turns his cap around. Feeling more confident than with his first kiss, he closes his eyes, gently caressing her lips with his own.

A surveillance monitor at the electrical supply cycles from one camera to another, showing Robin's Mazda in the parking lot, then the darkened sales counter area, then cycles to other warehouse locations, including the back door. Jim leaves.

Robin appreciates Kevin's attention but murmurs, "Not here."

The dashboard clock displays 5:01 and Kevin stops his advances. Pressing his crotch and pushing himself back into his seat with a wry smile, he teases, "Down, boy."

Robin swallows hard and blinks her eyes as if waking from a dream.

They enter the deanery together, Robin with her school gear and Kevin with an armful of his acquisitions.

Just inside the foyer, Robin calls out, "Mom? Dad?"

While waiting for an answer, a little smile crosses Kevin's lips. He waits for Robin's lead.

Malcolm's voice echoes from somewhere in the house, "Yes,

Robbie..."

She shrugs. "I brought home your iPad angel."

Malcolm appears in the foyer and welcomes Kevin as if he were a new parishioner. Kevin reaches for the bill of his cap but blushes before removing it. Setting down his things, he reaches to shake Malcolm's hand.

"I see you're ready for anything." Malcolm studies Kevin's tool belt. *Emily did say he was an electrician.* Malcolm updates Robin, "Mom should be home any minute." And looking at his watch, adds, "I believe we should invite Kevin here to dinner, don't you think?"

Kevin's eyes widen and he looks to Robin for direction.

She asserts with a grin, "Sure. It's the Christian thing to do."

Malcolm scowls. Although Robin knows her father is not offended, Kevin looks confused.

"I'd be honored," he says. "But I need to be going, thank you. I do want to fix your kitchen light. Is tomorrow—no, is next week sometime, good? Could you show me where the circuit breakers are?"

"I'll show him," Robin says.

Malcolm steps aside for Robin to lead the way. Kevin picks up his gear and the replacement switches, nodding to Malcolm in deference as he follows Robin.

Catching a whiff of Kevin's cologne, Malcolm now watches intently as Kevin walks down the hallway. His brow wrinkles. Lost in thought, he slowly walks back to his office.

Later in the evening, Malcolm is shuffling through his desktop correspondence, intent on finding something, when Robin walks by on her way upstairs. "Oh, Robin..."

"What's up, Dad?"

"Um... I was looking for the brochure about the upcoming fall conference in London I told you about. It's here somewhere."

She smiles as he continues to search through his papers.

"But I do have a question for you besides. About Kevin."

She stops and looks away, then back again to her father.

"How old is he? He's definitely interested in you."

"Why do you say that?"

"Electricians don't wear expensive cologne to work. Not even college guys. I can see you are interested in the gentleman—and he is a hunk besides."

Robin is surprised.

"If I were a woman, I might swoon at the sight of him too."

"Daaad!" Robin remembers showing Kevin the circuit breakers in the low light of the deanery basement hallway. His kisses were intoxicating.

"I'm just observing, not objecting. I trust your good judgment. Are you still—"

"What?" She just stares at her father. "A virgin? Depends on the definition, doesn't it?"

Malcolm tries to get a breath but chokes. He tries to formulate an answer, then hears Emily approaching.

"Tea, anyone?"

Robin smiles demurely. "No, thank you, Mom. Dad was just asking if I was still a virgin." She scampers up the stairs, leaving Malcolm to stare at Emily.

He finally speaks. "Remember when we were young, when it was all forbidden?"

Emily shakes her head to dismiss the topic. "How do you get into these conversations? She's 17. You're her dad." She starts to leave the study, stops abruptly, and turns back to her husband. "Give her some credit. And me."

CHAPTER 24

The Trinity Cathedral bells announce Sunday's main Eucharistic service. Smoke from the incense in one acolyte's swinging censer swirls in the gentle, late-spring breeze, and the flames of the candles carried by two other acolytes flutter. They precede Robin as she carries the decorated processional cross in an all-parishioner procession from the Annex toward the church entrance. A Bach organ prelude can be heard through the open doors of the church as the courtly procession moves with grace until they reach the corner.

Robin notices a traveling man, a drifter in his late 30s with a backpack and sleeping bag. Scruffy and unshaven, and weathered from outdoor living or hitchhiking, he approaches without regard or respect for the service. Robin is distracted. She watches him and the parishioners' reactions to him.

"Hey, when's lunch?" he says with expectation.

With obvious annoyance and indignation, the lead deacon tries to shoo away the intruder. The deacon looks around for help. A plainclothes security guard makes an appearance at the door, looking as if he were an ordinary parishioner. The deacon catches the guard's eye and nods in the direction of the unwanted visitor. The guard reaches for his phone and steps out of view.

The drifter joins in the procession just behind Robin. "Some candles, huh? Is it your birthday, sweetie? Do I get a piece-a your cake?"

Robin swings around, stunned, then angry. But then

something clicks in her recollection of Patti Smith's "Privilege" from the *Easter* album. Robin stops the procession. She appears to be listening to the song itself as she gazes at the stranger. She stares at him and her anger dissolves. She silently mouths the words of the song.

The deacon, more distressed than ever, breaks out of the line. He says nothing as he approaches Robin, except with his eyes, and they say it all: *Just ignore him!*

The deacon shoves the traveler off the sidewalk toward the gutter.

At the cathedral entrance, Malcolm, in full vestments for Trinity Sunday with miter and crosier, stands regally in the doorway. Two police officers arrive. The older one stays in the cruiser while Andres gets out. Recognizing the drifter and trying not to smile, he greets him as a regular offender found again in the wrong place.

But when the drifter yells out, "No fuckin' pope's gonna tell me—" Andres glares at him with such authority, he stops his yelling.

Andres motions for him to get into the patrol car. The drifter knows better than to resist arrest. But he turns around, looks at Robin, and gives her the finger. Andres catches Robin's eye. She winces in embarrassment.

As the drifter gets into the patrol car, Robin thinks sardonically, *Psalm 23:6, Surely, goodness and mercy shall follow me all the days of my life.*

The Trinity Cathedral bells again announce the Sunday Eucharist service. Robin overcomes her distraction and continues the procession into the church. Like waking from a dream, she shakes her head, focusing straight ahead and holding the cross. She cannot wipe away the telltale tears. She needs to direct the acolytes and the rest of the congregation down the center aisle.

The church is filled to capacity as Bach's organ prelude concludes. Then there are several moments of silence.

———□———

That afternoon, Robin leaves her personal alb and cincture on Malcolm's office chair with a folded note. But just as she is about to leave, Malcolm enters. Her eyes cast downward, she retrieves her note and hands it to him. He reads the last part of it aloud. "I don't want to just carry a cross."

Not surprised—but disappointed, he embraces Robin with a strong, heartfelt hug.

"Did you see him? He really needs help."

Malcolm quietly agrees. "Yes."

———□———

Robin drives through downtown Portland into the Union Station passenger pick-up zone. When she sees Kevin waiting for her, the anxiety on her face dissolves. He opens the door and slides in. Eager to see him and without hesitation, she leans over to kiss him. He more than obliges. With both hands grasping her head, he kisses her gently. Then, leaning back in his seat, Kevin utters a guttural, "Mmm-hmm!"

"Where would you like to go?"

Kevin offers, "Wherever you want. I thought you had a place in mind—someplace you normally don't go?"

Thoughtful, as if given a puzzle, she pulls into another parking space. "Somewhere off limits?"

Kevin nods and waits with a self-satisfied look of expectation.

"A tattoo parlor," Robin says.

Kevin looks quizzical, then amused.

She admits, "It's illegal—if you're not 18. Not even with a parent along."

"I can fix that."

"You can?"

———☐———

In North Portland's Overlook Neighborhood, a well-maintained craftsman bungalow looks like so many of the others. In the driveway sits a gleaming black Nissan 370Z, insinuating a bachelor's home, while the dual-columned front porch gives an assuring attempt at an upscale welcome to visitors.

Robin pulls up behind the Nissan. "Your car? Wow! Okay to park behind it? I don't want to block—"

"My housemate's. He's in Chicago visiting family."

"You don't drive?"

"I do—mine's in the garage."

Robin, looking curious, replies, "Show me."

"It's just a pickup—nothing to see."

They get out of the car and Kevin leads Robin into the house instead. He heads to the back, leaving her in the front room for the moment. She notes a well-worn corduroy couch facing a state-of-the-art entertainment center in front of the drawn drapes. She hesitates, then follows Kevin. Converted from a bedroom to a make-do office with dual monitors, headphones, a digital camera, and other electronic gear, it appears to be a commercial enterprise.

Robin looks confused. "I thought you were a student."

"Well, I haven't been accepted yet. This is my housemate's stuff but he lets me use his gear. Let me see your ID. You want to be 18? No problem."

Robin is reluctant.

"It's just for getting a tattoo, right? It'll be fine," he assures her.

She retrieves her driver's license and gives it to him.

"Attagirl."

"Girl?"

Kevin gives her a dismissive smile, saying nothing.

Robin wonders, *Well, he is from the Midwest. What did you expect?*

With a Nikon video camera on a tripod, he lines up her ID and carefully focuses. He captures a shot, front and back, then another set of shots as well.

"Okaay. I'll take care of this online. But we'd better have it mailed here—unless you want your dad to see you're a year older than he thought. You have a debit card? Sorry, I'm not rolling in money."

Robin smiles cautiously. He turns to look her in the eyes. She gives him her MasterCard and he deftly enters the appropriate information into a website.

"So, what kind of tattoo do you have in mind?"

Robin pulls out the iPhone from her bag. Scrolling through her photos, she stops and sets her phone on the desk, showing him her raven drawing. But he is more interested in looking at Robin than her photos.

"I want to add something, maybe two crossed arrows in its talons—for friendship."

With only a perfunctory look at the photo, he gets up and embraces her. She hugs him but ignores his intentions. He gives her a little smile.

"Could I get a real photo of you—your face—with a decent camera?" He removes the camera from the tripod and motions for her to follow him into the hallway. "So, what can I get you?"

"Water'd be fine."

Kevin, unconvinced, asks, "Just water?"

She follows him into the front room. Kevin nods for her to have a seat while he pushes the button on the Blu-Ray player. Bruno Mars' hit song "Just the Way You Are" begins.

Robin listens, recognizing the song, waiting for the lyrics. She sits down on the rumpled, stained green couch, shifts her head, and pulls her hair from over her shoulder to her chest—preparing herself for a photo shoot with the anxiety befitting a first-time audition, yet trying to look nonchalant.

Kevin looks back at her and winks—not as subtly as his first time seeing her. He leaves the room for the kitchen, aroused, and once out of the room, discreetly shifts his personal cargo and smiles to himself.

Robin takes out her phone to check for any text messages. Seeing none, she sets it on the couch and closes her eyes. The Bruno Mars lyrics seem to be Kevin's own words. After a few moments, she opens her eyes and looks around, self-conscious and uncomfortable to be sitting there alone. She gets up and heads toward the kitchen.

Kevin is looking for glasses for the bottled water he has on the counter. He doesn't see Robin as he mouths the words to the song, And he doesn't hear her step up behind him. As the music continues, Robin glides forward, giving him a surprise yet very gentle choke hold and an elegantly smooth takedown—leveraging him below the knees over her shoulder and onto the kitchen rug for a soft roll.

He is stunned, motionless. Now on top of him, Robin smiles coyly. She slides down on him, then kisses him. Cautiously, he pushes her up to look her in the eyes.

"This is how guys fall for you?"

They take turns disrobing one another, one piece at a time—only panties and briefs remain. Kevin leads the way to a door in the hallway, leaving a trail of clothes behind them. As they continue to Kevin's basement bedroom, the music plays on, Kevin lip-syncing the lyrics at the bottom of the stairs. He leads Robin, hands on her shoulders walking backward, so he can see her face as they go through the funky cellar toward his room.

The late afternoon sunlight filters through the ground-level transom window and highlights their nude bodies as they make love. Kevin is confident yet gentle with his hands as he caresses her face and strokes her hair. He begins kissing her—her ears, neck, nipples, naval, everywhere, even to her toes. She likewise massages his neck, shoulders, and biceps.

Looking for Kevin to provide protection, she looks at him with expectation. He reaches under his bed for his Trojans.

Later, Robin's face is radiant and wide awake; Kevin's, like a little boy, faintly smiling, asleep. Without moving her head, she opens her eyes wider. Adjusting to the near darkness, she suddenly looks worried when she sees the glowing turquoise numbers on the clock radio—7:42 PM.

Gently, slowly, she tries to untangle herself from Kevin without disturbing him but he awakens. Letting his eyes focus, he lies still for a moment, then forms a kiss on his lips, but Robin is intent on getting up. She obliges his efforts to kiss her, but only on her cheek.

"I need to go, handsome. Mm-mm-mm…what gorgeous abs!"

She gives him an air kiss. Then, leaning over his nearly nude body, gives him another playful kiss on his sheet-covered erection.

"I was good, wasn't I," he says without it being a question.

"Um...yes. See you tomorrow?"

"That's right. The switches. I'll see you after school."

He begins to get up but Robin playfully pushes him down onto his bed. With one hand under the sheet, adjusting himself, he teases, "Tell me you can't wait."

She looks amused, then annoyed. *A farm boy! And I've fallen for him?*

The lingering light of the June evening reveals Robin's phone sitting on the couch with texts, missed calls, and voicemail messages. The phone vibrates with another call. Robin retrieves it, rolling her eyes with an "I'm in trouble now" look. She goes to the kitchen to get herself dressed.

As she walks out to the driveway, she notices the Nissan again. Admiring it, she shoots several shots, front, side, and back. She gets into her car, glances at herself in the rearview mirror, shakes her head as if she does not believe her disheveled image, and drives away without delay. But a few blocks away from Kevin's home, she parks and reviews her phone messages.

Once home, Robin walks in furtively and quietly closes the door behind her. She notices the silver-domed cover at her place at the table. She sneaks a peek at the meal left for her, then smiles and rushes out of the kitchen.

In her bedroom, she looks at herself in the mirror and again reacts to her frumpy appearance, first brushing her hair with hurried anxiety, then shrugging her shoulders at the sight of her blotchy mascara. She looks away to find her eye makeup remover, glances back, and jumps when she sees her mother's face staring at her in the mirror.

"Doing jiu-jitsu? You coulda called."

"Yes." She blushes. "Thanks for saving me dinner."

Emily notices her turning red and is silently smug with a

knowing look. She leaves Robin's room. Turning back, she adds, "Dad is going to be out of town through Thursday."

"Do you want me to drive him to the airport?"

"No. You're in school. I'll take him to the airport tomorrow—but Thursday, after school…" She pauses. "It'd be nice to give your daddy a goodnight kiss. There'll be no time in the mornin'."

Robin, with a sigh of relief, leaves her room, texting Andria as she does.

In the academy parking lot the next morning, Robin receives a message from Andria. Not hesitating, she returns the text with a call. "Andy! I thought you'd never get back to me. Anyway, when can I see you? I'm in love and I know I'm being stupid… Okay. Okay. I'm in the lot. I'll wait."

At the deanery the same morning, Emily greets Kevin and leads him to the kitchen. He follows, noticing her figure in a dark rose negligee.

Embarrassed, he apologizes, "I didn't mean to get you up so early."

"No, you're fine. It's about time we got this done."

As she stands there in the kitchen doorway by the switch, Emily looks at Kevin, handsome in his purple Portland Pilots jacket. Without asking and as a simple matter of course, Emily reaches to take Kevin's jacket. He obliges. She looks at his snug-fitting, gray T-shirt. Still holding his jacket, she stares at him.

He asks, "Is something wrong?"

"Oh, no. Such a fine young man—if I could just look at

you."

She drops the jacket to the floor and grasps his shoulders with both hands, as if to admire a son. But she surprises Kevin by pulling herself close to embrace him. Becoming more sensual, she slides her hands to his buttocks. Looking both ways but standing still, Kevin lets himself become aroused.

Emily drops to her knees in front of him. Looking up at him, she pauses.

He begins to unbuckle his belt.

CHAPTER 25

Parked around the corner from Coffeehouse Northwest this same morning is a silver Chevy truck with peeling paint. The front right fender shows the rust of an old collision, still waiting a year later for repair. A locked steel toolbox and spools of electrical cabling and other wiring are proof of the driver's trade. Blaring from inside the cab is the music of Johnny Cash, "I Won't Back Down."

Russ is the customer who left his toolbelt at the wholesale lighting supply. In his late 30s, he steps out of the truck with the authority of a cop but camouflages his boyish emotions with a thick beard. A stocky frame and the eyes of a hunter, squinting under the brim of a Portland Mavericks baseball cap—maybe once bright red but now faded, sweaty, and stained—give him a manly man's look. Clicking off the radio, he affirms with the title, "I Won't Back Down."

He carries only an aluminum clipboard with an invoice storage box. The coffeehouse punch card is secured by the clip. Strutting into the busy shop, he looks around but now is less sure of himself. Seeing Angel clearing a set of cappuccino cups from a small table, he inhales slowly and observes, "You'd think the least they could do is bus their own cups."

Angel, with an appreciative smile, looks up at Russ. "It's my job."

"But where's the respect?"

Angel gives Russ his full attention. "Your first time here?"

"I'm looking for a guy that might be a regular, a guy by the name of Kevin."

Angel's smile instantly dissolves. "Police?"

Russ, with a hearty snort, snickers, "Do I look like police?" He opens the hinged clipboard and shows Angel a surveillance camera's low-resolution color print with a handwritten name added: Kevin Conley.

Angel asserts, "*¡Grosero!* He's rude. I saw him only once."

"So, do you know how to get ahold of him?"

"What did he do?"

"Stole my stuff. My belt with my best tools—the son of a bitch."

"*¡Sí. Él es un bastardo!*"

Russ cautiously grins. "*Bastardo.* Yeah. So, you'll help me find *Bastardo?*"

Angel takes out his cell phone and looks for approval from Russ to get a snapshot of the document. "Come back tomorrow morning."

"Thanks, man. What's your name?"

"Angel."

"Angel? Really?"

Angel nods with a polite but almost defensive smile as he turns away. Russ closes his mouth. Simply nodding, he leaves.

CHAPTER 26

Outside of the SBG, Robin scrolls through her recent calls, scowls, and jams the phone into her pocket. She picks up her gear and stomps into the gym. After she changes into her training gi, she looks into the mirror and begins to remove her makeup—what little she used that day.

Robin spars with a male student who is at her same belt level. Several times, she lets him overtake her and she taps out each time, conceding. Robin's rolling partner is disappointed with the easy submissions. Her instructor comes over, whispers to her, then looks intently into her eyes and gives her an understanding smile. He nods for her to quit for the day. "Tomorrow, okay?"

She forces an appreciative smile, even though she is distracted by two young police officers entering the gym. Robin smiles as they approach the instructor. He leads them to the information and sign-up table and gives them brochures on jiu-jitsu. One of them looks back at Robin, noticing her watching them.

When Robin walks out to her car and checks her phone, she is surprised to see a text from Miguel to call him right away. But what about Kevin? Shrugging her shoulders, disappointed, she gets into the car. Touching the Miguel icon, she waits for an answer.

"You're not tutoring—you're at work?" she says, then pauses to listen. "What about him?" Another pause. "Okay. I'll be right over."

In Malcolm and Emily's bathroom, the shower stall's steamed-over glass reveals Kevin and Emily—Emily looking more like a 16-year-old lost in rapture. She hears the music of Fleetwood Mac's "Go Your Own Way" and remembers her high school affair might not have been the right thing to do then. But she's not going to bring that up to Kevin.

In Coffeehouse Northwest, the audio system plays Colombian guitar and percussion music. When Robin enters, she feels as though the soothing music is trying to hide something wrong. Miguel turns barista duties over to a teammate and asks Angel to pull up a third chair to a table— the same table in the corner where Robin brought Kevin the first time. Pensive and brooding, Miguel peers at the wall for a moment, then smiles sympathetically at Robin and pulls out his phone to show her the surveillance photo he got from Angel.

"But his name's O'Connor—Kevin O'Connor," Robin mumbles.

Miguel posits, "Or maybe not."

Robin jumps up from the table and storms out.

———□———

At Kevin's home, Robin pulls up to the curb. *Where's the Nissan?* She springs out of her car, charges the home, and accosts the front door. There's no answer. She stands there thinking. Looking over at the empty driveway, she then turns toward the old garage and slowly walks to it. The door is unlatched. Carefully nudging it open a little, she pokes her head inside and stares long enough for her eyes to adjust to the darkness.

A very dusty white Ford F-150, about 10 years old, could have been a utility vehicle in a former life. It shows a Missouri license plate and an equally old Confederate flag bumper sticker. And a flat tire.

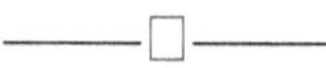

Early evening at home, Robin dashes in and up the stairs to her room. At her desk, she looks through her personal school directory. Following Sammy's advice, she again searches websites for tracking callers without caller ID. *Thank you, Sammy!* As she types, her face changes from piqued anxiety to calm resolve, like a detective investigating a reliably sourced new tip.

The phone's Tri-Tone thunk announces a text message from Unknown: *Sorry I've not responded sooner. Phone out of juice. Let's talk tomorrow.*

Robin looks up at the ceiling, then back to her screen, and searches the Apple App Store. She types a few words on her laptop and there it is—the name Seth Walker from Liberty, MO, and his phone number. Robin ponders out loud, "The blues singer? Not likely!"

Another thunk, another text—from Mom: *Won't be home for dinner. OK? Look in fridge.*

Robin leans back in her desk chair. Seeing the *Titanic* poster, she stares at Leonardo DiCaprio and Kate Winslet holding on to each other as the ship goes down.

Passing adult-only novelty stores, boarded-up buildings, the Union Gospel Mission, and a dance club called Dirty Night

Life, Kevin and Emily come at last to the Old Town Chinese Restaurant that promises good food. Kevin opens the door for Emily. She hesitates but he motions for her to go in. The bluish fluorescent lighting assures full visibility of what food is in the bowl and what a date might look like in the most unflattering light possible. The restaurant owner, an older Chinese gentleman, instantly recognizes Kevin.

"Nice to see you again. You bring mother. I am honored."

Emily's mouth drops. Kevin's eyes dart from side to side. The owner quickly realizes his error and snatches the menus from the empty table nearest them. He turns to find a more secluded table in the back.

Neither Kevin nor Emily say anything.

Robin absently walks into the dark kitchen and after hitting the light switch, sees the light flicker as usual. Wrinkling her brow, she thinks, *What the hell!*

Kevin and Emily sit at the table sharing a pot of tea. Emily pours for them both. Her phone interrupts with the distinctive church Bell Tower ringtone. Her face freezes and her hand shakes as she reaches into her purse to silence the device. After an awkward minute, the phone vibrates the arrival of a new voicemail. They sit in silence except for the ambient noise of the restaurant.

"Kevin, I...I can't tell you how wonderful you made me feel." She sets the menu on the Formica tabletop and apologizes, "But I really should be getting home."

CHAPTER 27

A little before 8:30 the next morning at the Trinity deanery door, and with no hesitation, Russ rings the doorbell. Pacing in place, he waits. Emily opens the door with her usual caution.

"Is Kevin here?" Russ asks.

"Excuse me?"

"Kevin Conley. He has my tools. Stole 'em. I have proof right here."

"Wait here, please." Staying in place and turning her head, Emily calls upstairs, "Roobin!"

Not quite dressed and buttoning her blouse, Robin descends the stairs.

"This gentleman is looking for a Kevin Conley. Some mistaken identity or—"

"Nope!" Russ interrupts. "The son of a bitch ripped off my gear. Sorry, ma'am." Reaching into his clipboard, he adds, "I have the proof right here."

Robin scowls. "Mom, it's true. I'll go get this man's toolbelt."

Emily's brows raise and her eyes widen. Robin sprints down the hallway while Russ pulls out his surveillance photo.

"I am so sorry," Emily tells him. "There must be a mistake but do step in."

In moments, Robin is standing there with Russ's belt in hand. Emily looks lost for words.

Wanting to confirm the accused's identity, Robin inquires, "What'd you say his name was? Conley?"

"Kevin Conley. You 'spect him here anytime soon?"

Mother and daughter glance at each other.

Russ shakes his head. "Looks like he's tellin' ya different things. I'd like to have a little chat with him."

Robin asks Russ, "You expect him here…like, *now?* Like this morning?"

But Emily answers, "Um…he's supposed—he's supposed to finish installing the dimmer switches."

Russ holds back a snicker and scratches his head. All three look at each other as if they have found themselves in someone else's hotel room.

Emily asks Russ, "Are you sure you want to meet him?"

"Oh, yeah."

Looking pensive, Robin chews a thumbnail and goes to the foyer window. "Well, if we are going to entertain guests, I'd better call school so they don't send out a posse." She leaves the foyer to make her call.

"Would you care for a coffee, Mister—"

"Russell. Just call me Russ. Yes, ma'am, a coffee. Black's fine."

"Do have a seat." She gestures to the parlor.

Russ looks uneasy to be in such a fine room. He glances at his watch. "Didn't mean to impose."

Emily gives him a tight smile. Looking out the foyer window, she sees a black car pull up and with a hint of sarcasm, suggests, "Maybe this is your apprentice."

Russ straightens up, takes a breath, and heads to the door. "Have to pass on the coffee."

Closing the door behind Russ, Emily shrieks. "Robin!"

Kevin closes the door of the Nissan and struts toward the deanery. When he sees Russ coming down the steps, he looks a little puzzled.

At closer range, Russ holds up the toolbelt. "Lose this?"

Kevin's mouth drops. He turns back to the car but Russ drops the toolbelt on the sidewalk and charges him. Before Kevin can reach his car, Russ grabs him by the collar. Overpowering him in muscle mass and extra weight, Russ is delighted to see the terror on Kevin's face as he squeezes Kevin's throat with his left hand. Holding him at a convenient distance, Russ is about to punch him with his right fist. He doesn't see Robin coming. She leaps onto his back, applying a rear naked chokehold, breaking his grip on Kevin. Kevin bolts away. Now off balance, Russ falls onto the lawn. Instantly, Robin mounts him high on his chest. Face flushed, eyes bulging, he is motionless.

"Don't hurt me."

Emily's eyes spring wide open, then slam shut. Bursting into tears, she jumps back into the house.

Robin assures Russ, "I won't. You won."

Russ looks confused.

"Behave now."

Russ, trying to recover, suggests, "You should be a cop."

"Yeah, I should." She jumps to her feet and moves away from Russ to a safe distance.

Kevin is already driving away.

Russ stands and puzzles, "You his girlfriend?"

"I thought I was."

Once Russ has gathered himself and his tools and is on his way, Robin goes back inside. *What a morning!* Climbing the stairs, she calls out, "Mom, I need to get to school." But she can't help hearing Emily's muffled sobs. She goes into her parents' bedroom.

"You okay, Mom?"

On the chaise lounge, Emily sits upright a little more. She

has stifled her tears—but only just moments before, and is still overwhelmed and anxious. "I'll be fine. It's more drama than I'm used to."

Robin gives her a quick hug. "Wait'll Dad hears how Kevin stole—" Slowly reconsidering, she amends, "Then again, maybe he doesn't need to know…"

———□———

While walking to class, Robin hears her phone. *Oh, no, it's Mom.*

Emily chokes on her words. "He—he's called me. He's threatenin' me."

Robin stops in her tracks. "Who is? Not Kevin!" Rushing back to her car, she tries to calm her mom. "Okay. Hang on, Mom." Inside her car, Robin puts the call on speaker and listens intently.

"I'm so ashamed. He's demanding $10,000. Or he'll expose me."

"Kevin! Expose you? For what? You mean like blackmail?"

"I'm so ashamed. I just let myself go. So handsome…and he was so willing…"

Robin stares at her phone. "What are you saying? What have you done?" She drops the phone and turns her face away. Closing her eyes, looking like she's trying to go into a meditative trance, she takes several moments, then asks, "What about Dad?"

The question hangs in the dead air.

Shifting from worry to anger, Robin simply presses the end call button. *And what about me? My own fucking mother.* Slowly, she dials Emily again. Taking a deep breath, she tries to be more composed. "Sorry, Mom. We lost each other. I have a thought… I'm only 17. And, if you get my meaning, he would have a lot to lose if it came out that... Well, you know what I'm getting at. I don't know how much, but I'll find out. Okay? Let me go."

Emily stammers, "I love you."

And Robin gives her a sweet but perfunctory, "I love you too," ending the call. *Riiight.* Within a moment, Robin texts Miguel: *IOU. Big time. Pls call me asap.*

———□———

Between classes and during her lunch break, Robin researches online. With her phone at the library desk, she scrolls back to Seth Walker. She types, *Missouri criminal records.* Robin looks at the computer screen and is silent. Her face is fixed, glowing in the blue-white light from the screen.

That afternoon, Robin walks with resolute determination into a neighborhood barbershop she's never been to before. Miguel is waiting for her. She throws her arms around him like a sister meeting her brother before leaving on a long trip— holding on to him longer than he expects.

"I'm so sorry, Miguel. I just didn't get it. You've been there for me—all along."

She quickly wipes her eyes and takes an open seat. Miguel sits next to her, takes Robin's hand, and just calmly looks forward.

In a few minutes, when it is Robin's turn, she tells the barber what she wants. He shows only mild surprise.

A short time later, Robin and Miguel walk out of the shop—Robin now with a buzz cut and a smile bigger than he's ever seen before.

"You are amazing," he tells her. "Sorry, I need to get back to work. Call me, okay?"

She nods and gets into her car. She sees Miguel in the side

view mirror shaking his head, looking at her, maybe thinking about what she had just learned and what he learned about Kevin getting his way with her. Seeing her without long hair makes perfect sense now. She nods to him as she pulls away. He gives her a small smile of acknowledgment.

Before Robin drives more than a few blocks, her phone announces another text message. She grabs the device and seeing the header, begins to read it, then slams on the brakes. *Oh, shit.*

She pulls up to a curb near the Couch Park playground— the same playground where she ran to help the Asian boy years ago. She stops and, bracing herself, grips the phone as she reads: *Dear Chase Account Holder, Due to concerns for the safety and integrity of your Chase online account we have issued this warning message.* She calls her bank, then drives to the Overlook neighborhood.

As she drives up to Kevin's home, Robin notices the driveway again without the housemate's Nissan. She parks, gets out of the Mazda, and approaches the house. Pressing the doorbell, she listens for a moment, then knocks on the door. Not waiting for an answer, she glances at the metal mailbox on the wall by the door. She hesitates only a moment, then looks through the mail, where she finds a *Sports Illustrated* and a few envelopes. One is addressed to her. Robin snatches it. She feels the envelope and tries tearing it in two but cannot, so she folds it and tucks it into her pants pocket. Leaving the porch, she pauses, then walks back to the garage and notices scraped dirt where the shed door has been opened farther than when she last saw it.

The truck is there but it's missing its license plate. She checks for the front plate, which is missing as well. She emerges back into the light, eyes squinting, then snaps her fingers. *I get it!*

Not wasting a moment, she calls Emily. "Mom! Have you talked to Kevin yet?"

"I told him blackmail wasn't goin' to work—because, because…I am going to tell Malcolm anyway. And I told him you are a minor. You know…he swore at me!"

"Um, Mom, I think we need to discuss this more… I believe your boyfriend has drained my bank account, stolen his housemate's car, and left town. I'll be home soon." Without waiting for her to respond, Robin shakes her head and ends the call. *My…own…mother!*

———□———

Robin retrieves the switches from the basement. *I can do this! How hard can it be?* The Lutron dimmer dangles from the wall by the door. Robin, with screwdriver in hand, is tightening one of the screws on the switch when Emily enters the kitchen.

The instant Emily sees Robin with her buzz cut, she shrieks. Robin jumps and sparks flash from the wall box. Robin goes over to the table and pores over the instructions and with deliberate cool, calmly asks. "What?"

Standing close to Robin, Emily looks at her shorn daughter. "Why? Why did you do it?"

Robin slaps her mother across the face with such force that Emily slams against the wall. "Why did *you* do it?" She starts to leave the room but turns back. "I know I'm not the daughter you wanted. And you're not the mother I thought I had."

Emily stares at Robin as she brings her hand to her hurting face. "What will your father say?"

Robin retorts with a tight, controlled smile, at once reassuring and challenging. "We'll find out tomorrow, won't we?" Silently, she fumes, *Ew, I did hurt her!* "I'll pick him up…

Sorry, Mom."

Emily looks lost.

———□———

At the Portland International Airport the next morning, Malcolm waits at the arriving passenger pick-up area. Robin, wearing her jiu-jitsu hoodie, drives up, jumps out to quickly kiss him, and stashes his one large suitcase into the back of the hatchback.

"So, how was the conference?" Pulling away from the pick-up zone, she heads out of the airport toward the freeway into Portland.

"It was fine. Long flights, of course. So many topics to cover. But what got me most was Gene Robinson. You know, the openly gay bishop of New Hampshire."

Malcolm buckles himself into the passenger's seat, then rummages through his carry-on and pulls out a notebook. "I have it right here: *'I think there's a terrible price to be paid when your exterior life is not an honest reflection of your interior life.'*" He looks to Robin for acknowledgment.

She says nothing but thinks, *Well, this is as good a time as any.* She slips off her hoodie and tosses her head in a single, graceful movement, moving her right hand in a habit no longer needed.

Malcolm chokes.

"Yes. I'm tired of trying to be Mom's idea of a proper young woman. How's this for—what did Gene say—an honest reflection?"

Malcolm sits there in silence as she drives onto the freeway. "You look like a twin brother," he finally says. "It'll take a little getting used to." Studying her, he adds, "You are beautiful, either way. I wish I had enough of my own hair to cut. So, what did Mom say?"

"Not much."

"Anything else happen that I need to know about?"

"Yes. I'd like to become a cop."

Malcolm can't help throwing his head back against the headrest as if Robin had suddenly accelerated.

"You're kidding, of course. You…you have such abilities to serve your community. You have empathy. You have diplomacy, a sense of humor, integrity—"

"Well, I'm trying—"

"And it's such a, a dangerous job. And for a woman—" Pausing in his torrent of objections, he sits there for a moment, then rushes to add, "You care about people and want to make things right, and you have—" He pauses again to catch his breath. "—the courage to take charge."

"Exactly."

Robin sets the dining room table for an elaborate welcome-home meal. With the dishes, napkins, and silverware all in place, Robin joins Emily in the kitchen for her culinary production. Adjusting the Lutron lighting from a warm glow to full bright, Robin gently asks a rhetorical question. "How's it look, Mom? Kevin did a nice job, right?"

Emily turns just as Malcolm enters with a cheery greeting.

"I sure missed you both. These conferences try to deal with big issues. But then we get tangled up in side topics about people's private lives—and sex, of course."

His wife and daughter do not interrupt his discourse.

"Anyway, it's nice to be back home…" And switching to his playful mimicking of Emily's Texan drawl, "Is that one of yer amazing pe-can pies now waitin' fer us all?" Malcolm looks to

Robin, doing a double-take, twitching his head in puzzlement. He smiles faintly. "Now we have to plan for the big conference coming up in November."

Robin jumps in. "Dad, I think Mom should go with you to that one. Not me."

Emily glances at Robin in surprise.

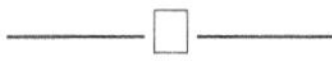

After dinner, Robin assists Emily in the final steps of cleaning up the kitchen. "Very nice dinner, Mom—like other things, best not rushed."

Still not adjusted to her daughter's new look, Emily just stares at her, wondering what to expect next.

"Don't worry, Mom. Your secret is a secret. He has a church to run. And so do you. Not everybody—not even your husband—needs to know everything. Except sometimes the police." Robin smiles with her own private knowledge as she visualizes what is happening right then. Yes, a phone call to the right person can have its intended effect.

Out the front window of the roommate's stolen Nissan, zooming by, is a Welcome to California highway sign. Visible in the rearview mirror, flashing blue lights are getting closer. Playing on the radio is the music of Johnny Cash, "The Man Comes Around." The hairs on Kevin's arms stand as he realizes that his time is up. The vehicle with a Missouri license blasts forward down the highway with a California Highway Patrol in close pursuit.

Back at the deanery kitchen, which is now sparkling clean, Robin says, "If we're all set, I'll be up in my room." Robin thinks to herself, *Well, that was a lovely meal if you only looked at the food. So why'd it feel like a meal with strangers?*

Emily tries to smile.

———□———

Robin wraps up her story. "That dinner was sure different compared to the one we just had here." Ryan and Robin sit close together, cozy on Sean and Giovani's couch. Hours have passed. The house is quiet. Sean and Giovanni, wanting to give them their privacy, have put Aida to bed and are on the patio sipping their after dinner liqueurs.

Reaching for her iPhone, Robin continues, "Let me show you some of my favorite photos. The parents were getting used to a more independent me and I was enjoying a gap year before coming to San Francisco." Robin shifts on the couch, a little uneasy. "Here I'm at the prom in a deep-blue dress Mom picked out for me. Actually, I was still getting used to the buzzcut. Miguel was—is—such a gentleman."

"Handsome guy," Ryan agrees. "I'm glad for you both. I hope it was fun. Did you behave yourself at the dance? You didn't flip him over?"

Robin answers with a gentle reprimanding nudge and swipes to the next photo. "Award ceremonies for English Now and for jiu-jitsu at SBG. I'm awarded my purple belt… Oh, here's me in a Portland police car drive-along. See my pocket notepad?" Swiping again, "Dad and me at a firearms training center. We look like we're in a recording studio with those monster ear protection muffs. He was such a good sport, being a bishop and all."

They look at a picture of Robin and Emily sitting together

in a front pew at Trinity Cathedral with Malcolm delivering a sermon. "Maybe I shouldn't have been sneaking a photo of Dad in church. I'm just so proud of him. And it seemed Mom was doing okay…but I'm not sure."

Ryan can't hide a yawn. "Sorry. I do want to see more but I'm still getting used to everything. Including having a family. And you."

TERRI

CHAPTER 28

Philadelphia, 2016

A heavy spring rain has let up, and the sun is breaking through the silver-rimmed clouds above a church in Kensington, one of Philadelphia's poorest neighborhoods. The Ascension is just one of the many Catholic churches to be closed by 2015. Now it's a year later. Poorly maintained cyclone fences enclose the once vibrant church but are evidence of a failed attempt to keep out vandals and even the homeless. Rainwater carries discarded needles, a used condom, uneaten food, and food wrappers along the gutter to the storm drain, while the sound of flowing water blends with the whooshing of steel-on-rail from the nearby Market-Frankford El.

Just a few miles away at one of Temple University's intimate auditoriums, Terri Gallagher is a guest speaker at the School of Social Work. She is maybe 10 years older than many of the students, but looks much older and very much out of place with them.

Terri is greeted with polite applause. A few cameras flash. Standing behind the podium, her cautious smile may hide her anxiety but the hands behind her back with twitching fingers tell the truth. Her natural light-chestnut hair is swept back and center-parted, and small hoop earrings help give her a professional look. But when she speaks, it is clear she has no pretenses to politics or other professions. Terri is a working-class American, not just rough around the edges. Some people, dismissive or unkind, would say she's probably just white trash.

The head of the department, Amy Hutchinson, stands nearby. She is as comfortable in her role as she is in her everyday navy-blue business suit. Several strands of gray hair give her a look of mature experience. Just like a professional speaker's coach, she gently grabs Terri's hand and whispers to her, "You're going to do great. You've succeeded in your program, even acting as secretary. I'm very proud of you, Terri. My students need to hear your struggle—and your victory."

Leaning toward the mic, accidentally bumping it and clearing her throat, Terri looks surprised. The applause suddenly subsides. They wait.

"It's an honor for me to speak with youse guys..." Looking like she said something wrong, she clears her throat again and rephrases, "I'm sorry—all you ladies and gentlemen. I don't use a mic at our meetings."

Most of the audience, consisting of graduate students and conference attendees, gives encouraging smiles. A few look like they have sat through too many PowerPoint presentations or lectures by amateurs and are relieved that this won't be one of those.

Straightening up, Terri continues, "My son waz offered a scholarship here. But I only got my GED a year ago. My Philly roots are hard to hide. Kinda like a bad hair dye job." She clears her throat again. "Anyway, Amy here heard about me, thought you could do with a nice success story." She looks down at her notes and continues with more confidence. "If you could see what I looked like two years ago..." Taking a deep breath and focusing, she closes her eyes, in effect inviting her audience of academics to follow along on her guided trip. "My counselor told me to tell my story like it's a documentary. Hope youse guys is okay with that.

"The cold white light from the street casts shadows from the blinds across my bed. The glare of my bedside clock shows 3:09 AM when the downstairs front door resists opening like it usually does. Then it closes with a thud. I'm awake now. I switch on the bedside lamp—not that I'm some sleeping beauty. I'm heavier by 70-some pounds, I looks at least 15 years older, and I'm missin' two upper-left teeth. But I'm gettin' awake for my man."

Terri does not look like the same person she's describing. And maybe that's the point she is trying to make. She continues without pause. "Mike Simonelli is strikin'ly handsome the way Mediterranean men can be, with wavy black hair and brown eyes. He's 35 and has an old scar across his neck and throat—from a street argument gone bad. Anyway, he comes inta our bedroom. Doesn't say nothing, just switches off the bedside lamp and takes off his warm-up jacket. He unbuckles his concealed-carry Smith & Wesson revolver and slips it just under his side of the bed. He takes off his navy khakis and slides into bed. His way of settling arguments hadn't changed much, and his way of making love waz rough too. I thought rough meant real. He said he'd protect me from other men. Ya see, I waz his sweetheart and I wanted to believe him. I tried to make things work for us. His nice names for me became insults. I didn't mess around with other guys. I tolerated his angry sex even if it wasn't lovemaking. It waz conquest and rape. He said I waz his bitch, his fucking bitch—sorry, Amy."

Amy doesn't flinch. She's paying attention. Terri, nonetheless, takes a breath to continue.

"Another day in the early morning, I'm hidin' behind the kitchen door and watching him in my nightgown. I have fresh bruises on my upper arms and neck. Some days his business deals didn't go so good. I felt sorry for him. But why'd he have to take it out on me? Maybe he knew I felt sorry for him. So, it waz my fault. Crazy, huh?"

One or two students jot a note while Terri presses on.

"Mike's real focused at the kitchen table. Crushing oxycodone tablets and blendin' them with another white powder on a sheet of glass, then usin' a small plastic scoop, he measures the cut powder into small baggies. He leaves the house. I sit at the table with some toast, just not hungry. I've got a cigarette in one hand—I don't smoke anymore, by the way—and an oxycodone in the other. I swish it down with a swig of beer." Terri stares into space, remembering the feeling of loss and pain, but then, coming back to the task of recounting her story, she continues.

"Mike storms in with his face black and blue on one side. I jump up to care for him. But he shoves me back, whacks me across the face with his left hand, then with his right hand, then pistol-whips me. I try to stop him. He hits me even harder and I fall to the floor. He takes all the cash from my purse and leaves again."

Several young women shift in their seats but try to maintain professional composure.

"So, I'm bleedin' pretty bad from my jaw and side of the face and nose. I'm stunned and barely conscious, but somehow I grab the cord of the wall phone and manage to dial 911." Terri takes in a deep breath, as if she were sucking in a much-needed drag on a cigarette. Then, again addressing the audience, she says, "How long would you stay in this kinda relationship? After I got discharged from the ER, I went to a temporary shelter and got asked all kinds of questions by a woman, an intake counselor. I waz a pretty sight—all bandaged up. And even though they told me I waz the victim and they were there to help me, I still felt guilty. You know, cinderblock white walls, bright lights, questions and more questions. I waz embarrassed. Youse folks call it the cycle of violence. But don't ya wonder how long does a woman have ta put up with this shh— Sorry. Well, my cycle started pretty early."

Pausing and taking in another deep breath, Terri scans the room for a moment. The audience is attentive, the younger ones, especially—unblinking eyes, everyone still. Terri looks to Amy. "You did say to tell it like it is. Am I okay here?"

Amy nods. Some in the audience squirm.

Again, closing her eyes, Terri continues, "Where waz I? Yes, my father waz alone at home with me. Or maybe my mother waz there, but not really there. Anyway, I waz just two, not even three. I'm not sure. On the second floor of our rowhouse, I'm at the top of the stairs in a yellow onesie behind an old wooden safety gate. I'm focusin' real hard and with quiet determination and pullin' with all my might, I pull the latch on the gate. It snaps up. I'm surprised but pleased with myself. I pull the gate open and just as quick, fall forward. Stumbling, tumbling, screaming, roll, bump, bump, fall—all the way down the stairs. Then on the first floor, my father races over to me. I'm crying. He picks me up, shakes me violent-like, and begins spanking me, yelling, 'You stupid girl! This'll teach ya.' The heavy diaper padding on my butt saved me. I think, maybe, but that's when I learned not to cry." Terri takes a few gulps of water before charging into her last round.

"So, let's get on to when I waz 12. I remember cuz I had sort of a birthday the week before. I waz in the cellar with my older brother in the late afternoon. He unbuckles his jeans. I don't get what's goin' on but I do what I'm told. We both hear the cellar door open jis as I'm about to be taken—you know what I mean—we're both surprised to see our father. Seeing what's goin' on, my father pulls off the amateur to show him how it's done. Maybe you people already know that Kensington now has a reputation for this kind of thing. Highest incest, prostitution, and drug addiction in our state. Anyway, I worked up the nerve to ask my mom some questions. In our front room, I approached her. She waz asleep, or passed out on the couch. An empty bottle of cheap Philadelphia whiskey waz on the coffee table. I touched her careful like on her shoulder. No response. I slumped down onto the floor at her feet, staring at the whiskey. Then I notice several white Oxycontin tablets spilled from her prescription bottle. I pretended she could hear me. Maybe it waz easier that she waz passed out anyway. I asked her if she knew—if she knew her man waz doin' it to me. I buried my head on my knees but I didn't cry."

A few students' faces show stress and puzzlement as Terri continues.

"By high school my father lost interest in me. But by then I figured I could make some money doin'…you know. But then I met Sean, Sean O'Brien. He waz 16, older 'n me by two grades. More of a challenge. Ya know, seduction can be fun—if you're the one in control. Sandy-haired and freckle-faced, Sean didn't need glasses to look nerdy. I first noticed 'im comin' out a shop with his project, a light box for seasonal something or other, he said. I waz impressed with his cheery attitude. And he had a nice box. He blushed with the attention I gave him. I liked havin' power over a guy like that. But then I began to have real feelings for him…and got pregnant. On purpose. My excuse to get away from home.

"He wanted to get married. I didn't. And by 21, I waz kinda bored with him anyway. I liked the adventure and the conquest. It waz kinda like a sport for me. I know I shoulda been faithful to Sean. After all, he waz the father of my seven-year-old. And he actually loved me. But Sean couldn't take my messin' around all the time. He thought I wasn't good enough to raise our son, Ryan. So he waz gonna move out and take my son with him. He didn't ask me to work with him about joint custody or anything. He waz just gonna pull a fast one on me. And I wasn't gonna let him get away with that. Eventually, I figured I could get child support anyway. I did get custody of Ryan—so Sean couldn't have 'im. It waz power. Me over Sean."

Terri pauses and sighs. "I come to realize, I waz jealous of him. And the way Ryan looked up to him. It really pissed me off. I never had any of that lovey stuff. If I could use my son for the money I could get—and get even with Sean—it'd be a double win for me. I now realize what a bad attitude I had about Sean and how I wasn't a good mom. I'm just tellin' ya all this so you know where a person in recovery has come from."

Terri looks relieved but exhausted. The audience looks numb. They show their appreciation slowly at first with gentle applause, then are more boldly supportive.

"Um…" Terri says hesitantly, "Any questions?"

Amy does not hesitate to raise her hand as she gets up. She walks up to the podium and stands next to Terri. "As you all know," she asserts, "every 60 seconds, 20 intimate partners become victims of violence in the U.S." Quickly scanning the room, then turning to Terri, she says, "I want to thank you most sincerely for sharing your story and your insights with us. You've been clean and sober now for over two years."

Terri nods. Her small smile is a contrast to her naturally serious look.

"Please tell the group what you do now—what you told me."

"I try to teach women how to climb—how to climb outta the sewers of their own lives. But they have ta wanna—real bad. And they have ta believe they can do it. And that it's worth it."

Amy searches the audience for questions.

A fresh-faced Asian American with stylish, white-framed glasses raises her hand.

"Yes. Name and where you're from."

"Vivian Chan. Swarthmore. My question is, um, how did you deal with Mike after your injury?"

"All the usual stuff. Hospital report—police—charges of battery—restraining order, which he ignored. Eventually, he waz convicted for dealing." Terri takes a breath, continuing with directness. "So maybe you or some of youse wonder, do I miss him somehow?"

Vivian listens intently.

"No. I come to realize, like the song, I waz 'Looking for Love in All the Wrong Places.' You could say I'm a work'n progress. There were others before him, a-course. One even— what da ya say—worked on my son when he waz only 10 or so. For many months. I don't know how many times. I didn't see it."

Vivian's eyes go wide and her brow crinkles. Amy takes a breath, cringing, but nods her head with understanding.

"At first, everything seemed cool. He waz like a dad might be—maybe more horny than I realized. My boy tried to tell me Billy touched him in his boy parts. I didn't believe nothing waz wrong. See, the molester waz also my crystal dealer."

After a long, awkward pause, Amy asks, "Could you tell us a bit more about the program you're in now?"

"Sure. I tried different meetin's: The Salvation Army. Cath'lic, 'piscopal, Luther'n. Me? With my badass attitude? I even said I don't need no stinkin' Jesus. For me, faith and willpower weren't enough. AA waz helpful—but that higher power thing? The most I could get waz that small voice inside me." She pauses to take a gulp of water. "I wasn't lookin' for God. But just maybe, God found me. At one meetin' a high school English teacher told me that for him, God waz like a hound dog. Yep. He got the idea from an opium addict's poem. I think it's called 'The Hound of Heaven.' Is that about higher power? All these religious folks. Ya gotta hand it to 'em for gittin' in the fight. If their Jesus tells 'em to do some good, I say okay. But for me, I needed a program for women stuck in addiction. Now, I know my habits seemed to help me deal with sex abuse and neglect as a little girl… Just maybe, I will find religion is also the answer I need in my life. Anyway, I volunteer at Empowering Women.* Right now, I can do the most good there. And maybe I can even get on staff there. I've also been attending classes at community college."

Spontaneous applause breaks out. But Terri wants to finish her thought.

"Next up for me is making amends with my son and his father. And learning to forgive."

Amy looks like she would like to continue the discussion, but looking at her watch, she says, "Again, thank you, Terri, for sharing your story with us this morning. And if you wouldn't mind staying for one-on-one questions, that'd be great."

Nodding, Terri moves away from the podium to the sound of genuine applause.*

CHAPTER 29

Empowering Women is a safe-haven residence for clean-and-sober women who have successfully completed a minimum of 18 months in the program. More than one tree grows in this neighborhood, but they only hint at the beautiful 2016 September colors of the Wissahickon.

Terri sits at a square Formica kitchen table in her two-person unit. With her flip phone open, she grabs her small personal phonebook, which is worn with years of use and abuse. Moving her finger to the letter *R*, she looks down. A small shudder makes her hesitate. She closes the phone and sits there. *This is so hard! But I can't go to my meeting if I don't.* Finally, she opens the phone again and keys in Ryan's phone number. After several rings, a young woman answers, slow and deep, "Hello..."

Terri looks at her phone and its displayed number. "Ryan? ... Sorry." Closing the phone, Terri is annoyed. "Figured. He must have a new number."

Terri's roommate walks in. Zari, African American, a few years older, is sturdy and imposing if she needs to be. She has short-cropped hair and a mischievous twinkle in her eye. Seeing Terri grimacing at her phone, she asks, "What you all snarly about?"

Terri simply answers her own thought, "It's been three years. And he's now in California—I'm guessin'."

"So...what's the last thing you remember sayin' to 'im?"

Terri can't hide her snarky smile. "It waz somethin' like, 'Where the hell are ya, ya good-fer-nothin' runaway?'"

"Well, that should take care-a his calling ever' night. But wasn't your boy just lookin' for his dad?"

"Yeah, yeah, yeah. And speakin' of him—I needa call him too… Makin' amends sucks."

"Right. But you don't wanna keep carrying around that load-a bricks."

"Okay. So, you make the calls for me. Tell 'em I'm clean and sober and they're 'sposed to be all happy for me, give me a medal or honorable mention—or at least send chocolates. Right?"

Zari grins, turns toward her room, then adds, "And you gonna call my old church and tell 'em I'd be happy to be treasurer again." Her eyes glisten with delight. "This time, I won't make money disappear. See if they've had a change of heart."

Zari slips into her room and quietly closes the door while Terri bobs her head in unconvincing agreement. She looks up Sean O'Brien in her old phone book. Several numbers are crossed out. Terri inhales a deep breath, then makes a note and places it for easy reference on the table. Punching in Sean's latest entry and scrunching her brow, she glances toward Zari's bedroom, then back at her note. She closes her eyes before calling and whispers a favorite saying she's learned from an AA friend. *God, grant me the serenity to accept the things I cannot change, the courage to change the things I can, and the wisdom to know the difference.*

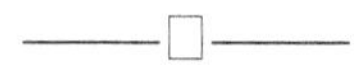

It's three hours earlier in Berkeley, California, and it's dinnertime. Clearly, this is a gourmet chef's dream kitchen with country Italian cabinetry (that also manages to hide just where the refrigerator is) and a commercial gas range with a massive hood. There are multiple sinks. A stainless steel big-dog water dish with the name *Mandy* on it, and a wall-mounted phone downgrade the look from *Architectural Digest* to maybe *Sunset*.

Now a few years older at 41, Giovanni looks even more like the Italian singer, Andrea Bocelli, than he did in his late 30s, with subtle streaks of gray highlighting his hair—so much so that he's even been asked if he was him—and he usually laughs at the compliment.

The phone rings. He calls out in his natural Italian accent, "Aida, your phone!"

Springing out from her bedroom, the eleven-year-old bounds into the living room. She plunks herself down on the red sectional couch and answers the pink princess house phone. Her glistening black hair—wavy and wild—is pulled up and banded with a purple-and-peach scarf. She speaks with genuine confidence. "Hello. This is Aida."

Terri is caught totally off guard. "What the— Is yer dad home?"

Looking puzzled and slightly put off, Aida replies, "Which one?"

"Is this Sean O'Brien's place?"

"Yes. And Giovanni Innocenti's. And me, of course—and Mandy if you count our dog."

"So is he there—Sean?"

"No. But I can take a message and—"

"I'm sure ya can. Just tell 'm Terri from Philly called."

"You must be Ryan's mom!"

"Yeah. But they don't got my new number."

Giovanni comes into the living room and looks to Aida with a quizzically wrinkled forehead. Aida turns away so she can concentrate. With a pencil poised, she listens and writes. Then she reads the numbers back. "Nice talking with you, Terri. I'll have Sean call you."

Giovanni's mouth drops open.

———□———

Terri sits motionless for a few seconds, then blurts out as she stands up at the table, "You son of a bitch, Sean!"

Zari peeks out from her bedroom door. Terri is pacing the room.

"Safe ta come out?"

"The son of a bitch is queer! Like…he has a daughter—somehow—or at least a smart-ass girl tells me one of her dads is my Sean."

"*Your* Sean? Ain't you divorced?"

"No. We waz never married."

"You saw him like over 12, 13 years ago? Married or not, he was never really yours… You jis found out you got the gay-boy prize."

"Somethin' like that. I don't get it. He liked it when…"

"Probably did. The boy was maybe tryin' to convince himself he was a regular guy."

"Well, I think it's disgusting!"

"What part?"

"The parts don't fit."

"You're talking plumbing. We all have workarounds. You should know that."

Terri's had enough, and in her version of a Black accent, says so. "What shew talkin' 'bout, girl? I still think he took me fir a ride."

Zari is visibly annoyed. "Took you for a ride? You're the one that got all the child support. You bragged about it yourself. And you don't have to make like we came up together."

Zari tries to shift away from the confrontation and approaches Terri. But Terri sees her as condescending. Irritated, fists clenched, and shaking with anger, she blurts out, "I don't need no lectures. I need…I need—*something.* At least a cigarette."

With more resolve, Zari steps closer. She puts one arm around Terri's shoulder and hugs her firmly. "What you need right now is a meetin'. You've made great progress. Let's go together."

Terri wilts into a slump.

Giovanni is preparing dinner when Sean glides in with three grocery bags. Nicely muscled, partly from his work but more from his efforts at the gym, he looks good in a polo. Keeping their ever-enthusiastic bearded collie at bay, he sets the bags down on a nearby counter.

Giovanni gives him a strong hug and an intense kiss.

Sean looks suspicious. "What'd I do to deserve special treatment?"

"Just preparing you…"

Sean folds his arms and waits.

"Aida, honey, Dad is home," Giovanni says, then quietly and quickly to Sean adds, "Aida took the message—nice job too."

"Your ex called," Aida informs him. "I told her I'd have you call her. But that's up to you, isn't it?" Looking at Giovanni, she adds, "Right?"

Sean is at once pleased and annoyed. "Okay. So, did she say anything else? Any message?"

"Nope." Thrusting her note into Sean's hand and pursing her lips, she dashes back to her room.

Sean stands motionless, thinking, while calling out to her,

"Thank you, Aida." He turns to Giovanni. "You coached her, didn't you?"

"Nope."

"So, do you have any idea what Terri wants now? More money, maybe?"

"Nope."

"Okay, okay. Let me get this over with. Then we can have a cheap Chianti or if it's anything good, we can try your Rosso di Montalcino."

Out of habit, Sean reaches for his iPhone but thinks better of it. "Best not give her my personal number, it's bad enough…" With Aida's note in hand, he calls from the kitchen's wall phone. It barely rings a second time.

Terri answers, "Yo."

"Um, is this okay? Not too late?"

"I want to say I'm sorry. I have notes to make sure I say everything. But really, I don't….I donno know where to start."

Quiet, Sean looks over at Giovanni and waits. Aida is hiding in the living room, unnoticed by either of her dads.

Sean tentatively asks, "Um…what's happened? Are you still there?"

"Yeah. I'm in a, um—a Narcotics Anonymous program. I'm at steps number eight and nine. Making amends." Clearing her throat, she adds, "You don't have to say anything right now. I just want you to know that I'm living a new life. And I want to say I'm sorry—"

"That's great. So everything is fine now because you say you're sorry?" Glaring into space, then looking at Giovanni, he rushes, "What about all the years you kept me from my son— with a goddamned court order!"

"I just needa tell ya I'm sorry. Maybe I could put something in a letter to you."

"It's been years! Like…what…13? Why now? I don't need your—"

"But I need to…to apologize. I need to make amends."

"Oh, that's wonderful."

Terri hesitates, then optimistically adds, "Um, then could I have Ryan's number?"

"No! I'm sure he doesn't want you calling. He's happy now. I can let him know you're trying to reach him. And if he wants, *he* can get in touch with *you.*"

"Thank you, Sean."

"Amends? You can start by sending me the money you wasted on your drugs instead of spending it on Ryan." Sean slams down the receiver so hard, the phone rips off the wall. Still holding the receiver like a dagger, Sean pleads to Giovanni—without words. And without words, Giovanni rushes over to him and holds him, letting him bury his head in his chest. Aida darts back to her room.

———▢———

Terri jumps up from the table and rushes for her room at the same time Zari comes out of her room. Terri pushes her aside, then grabs her coat and purse. "Don't try to stop me. I've had enough of this shit."

"I'm not yer sponsor—but I've gone through this stuff too." Her actions are all the opposite of Terri's. Blocking the door, Zari stretches out her arms to hug Terri. Resistance is futile.

Terri endures her grip. "I needa git outta here." She pulls away and leaves.

The door slamming seems so final.

Zari, downcast, goes over to her bookshelf and reaches for her much-used book of Psalms. As she reads, the Della Reese song "Walk With You" from 1998 comes to mind. She slips the

CD into her player. As she moves to the lounge chair, she stops. Listening to the song through her headphones, she hears the words about walking down road with a heavy burden. "She can't give up!" Zari yanks off the headphones, grabs her coat and bag, and dashes out the door. Zari races down the hall and into the night. She sees Terri down the block and picks up her pace to catch her. Faster than her friend, she is side by side with Terri in seconds.

———□———

Giovanni, with Aida assisting, clears the dining table and cleans up the kitchen. Sean comes over so Giovanni can give him a much-needed smooch on the cheek. Giovanni leans over to Aida, whispering, "Dad needs to go over to Ryan's."

Ryan and Robin live in an Oakland one-bedroom unit—perfect for just one. Textbooks stacked up on the coffee table and more books in the dining area along with an open laptop make it clear that these are serious college students. On the wall, there's a collection of several jiu-jitsu awards for Robin, along with framed photos of Ryan and his friends from Whole Foods, Robin and her parents at Robin's high school graduation, and Robin with Malcolm in his Episcopal bishop's cassock and collar. And more.

Robin, at 21, has an athletic physique and looks like she just finished a run and a quick shower. Her shoulder-length, natural mahogany hair is still wet. When the doorbell rings, she manages to quickly apply a subtle shade of autumn-red lip gloss.

When she opens the door, her penetrating brown eyes and generous smile welcome Sean. He steps inside and they embrace like a father and daughter.

"Your loving and ever-dutiful son is on his way," Robin

251

informs him.

"Do you know why I'm here?"

"I thought you were going to take us to dinner," she jokes. "No, I have no idea except that Ryan said you needed to drop by. I expect it's important. Good news of some sort, I hope."

"It's a point-of-view kind of thing."

"Um…okay. I'll wait. Meanwhile, San Pellegrino?"

Sean takes a seat on the couch across from a large-screen monitor. A series of photos in the Mac screensaver program scroll as Robin fetches water for Sean and herself.

Taking a seat next to him, Robin hands Sean a glass. She glances at the screen and explains, "Oh, they're the photos from this past summer. Remember when Ryan's friend, Daniel, came out with his daddy-boyfriend, Douglas?"

Sean looks thoughtful. He tries to answer but is distracted by the photos. The screensaver montage glides by like a parade in slow motion: San Francisco's ferry terminal is in the distance with Gay Pride banners as far as the eye can see leading up Market Street toward Twin Peaks. A pink triangle dominates the top of the hill. Sean admits, "Yeah—Giovanni got a little too protective of Ryan. Or you think he was, maybe, jealous?"

Robin observes, "Looks like the big boys don't want to be left out of the inclusive thing."

Major corporate sponsors like Virgin America, Budweiser, Macy's, Gap, Apple, Google, and Facebook, like credits to a movie, scroll by. Their employees and friends march in celebration. Colorful costumes range from whimsical, wild, or bordering on fetish—and some are certainly sexual.

Robin points out, "Oh, here's Daniel and Douglas."

Daniel is in Lycra, like an athlete, and Douglas is bare-chested wearing a thick leather harness.

Sean recalls, "Leather-Daddy-Doug—Giovanni's name for

'im."

There's a picture of Robin next to Ryan—and he definitely looks like a younger Sean—then another of Daniel and Douglas. Obviously, all friends, arm in arm or arms over shoulders, smiling.

Sean reflects, "Ryan's come a long way from his working-class, homophobic self."

Robin chokes in understated agreement. "Even if he's from a big city like Philly, he really didn't have exposure in his neighborhood—well, you know. And it did come as quite a surprise finding out—"

"That he now has *two* dads. So. Changing the subject. How's your dad doing with Emily's leaving? That sure came as a surprise to me."

Robin looks at Sean's half-empty glass to distract him—or avoid eye contact. But he presses on. "When I first met your folks, when you first moved to Berkeley, I was impressed with how they cared about you—in such different ways."

"Oh, they're different all right. Mom had some very conservative ideas for an Episcopal bishop's wife. Interesting how she kept her wild side under wraps."

"Ryan did tell me—after the separation announcement— that you had tried to keep Emily from telling Malcolm that she'd had an affair with someone a few years back. And you gave her some very good ad—"

Robin gets up.

But Sean presses on, "Was it someone you knew?"

"Um. Like I said, not everybody… I was trying to protect my father and his ministry."

"Sorry. Families do have their secrets."

Robin's wistful smile and awkward moments of silence are broken when they hear Ryan's key unlocking the door. Ryan bursts in. Sean springs to his feet and greets Ryan with a big hug. Ryan then gives Robin a self-conscious peck on the cheek.

"After three years, you're not up for a kiss in front of your dad?" Robin teases.

Taking off his deep-blue Warriors jacket, Curry number 30, Ryan blushes. "So, Dad. You needed to tell me something? Have a seat."

All three go back to the living area. Ryan and Sean settle in on the couch, and Robin sits in another chair. She turns off the monitor.

Without any introduction except for a big breath, Sean blurts out, "Your mother called me. She wants to call you too. Or you may call her yourself."

Ryan raises his eyebrows. "After all these years of ignoring me? Why now? I don't wanna hear from her… You came over here just to tell me that?"

"Hold on, Ry. I'm not keen on talking to her either. But you can think for yourself. I didn't want to speak for you. Well, too much. She's in a recovery program of some kind. Narcotics, I think. I thought she was just compulsive about sex. But there's more to it, I guess… She wants to say she's sorry. Something like that."

"Well, she can die with her booze and drugs. And that son of a bitch, Mike. Or did she take my advice and get rid of him?"

Sean doesn't need to hear more. There is silence for a moment, then he adds, "Well, think about it."

"What's there to think about?"

Robin's mouth drops but she restrains herself. Clearing her throat, she looks at Sean with a hint of a smile. "Would you like to stay for dinner? We've had a warm-up conversation. We could talk about both our mothers."

Ryan halts that thought, "Or not!"

"Then I best be heading home. I left Giovanni handling a very upset Aida. And a wall phone that couldn't handle the call either."

Ryan and Robin look puzzled. Not wanting any further explanation, they simply nod in agreement.

"Thank you, Dad. I'm sorry I—"

Sean smothers Ryan with an embrace. With no further words, he leaves the apartment.

Within seconds, Robin grabs Ryan and holds him at arm's length with both hands. "What did you tell Sean about my mother?"

Eyes wide, Ryan is too startled to say anything. Frozen for a few moments, he waits.

Robin releases him with a gentle shove, then grips him just as suddenly with a desperate hug.

Ryan assures her, "I didn't say anything about you. Just your quote."

Letting her hold him until she is quiet, he draws in a deep breath, then kisses her on the lips. After a few moments, when they walk back to the kitchen area, Robin says, barely holding back a laugh, "I think our mothers should meet."

"Ain't gonna happen."

CHAPTER 30

At 55, Emily is as elegantly dressed, poised, and graceful as the Pamela Ewing character in the once-popular primetime soap opera *Dallas*. Striving for the look of a fashionable 39, no one would guess that only 10 months ago she divorced Portland's very respected Episcopal bishop, Malcolm Marshall.

With her perfectly maintained mahogany-shaded hair, deep-burgundy evening dress, and lips and eye-shadow to match her delicate designer glasses, she sits as attentive as a princess awaiting a suitor. She is enchanting.

Patrick Masters sits across from her, even more attentive and focused on her completely. He says, "You're as classy and complex as my best pinot."

Patrick is handsome in a roguish way, and does not see Emily's age as a social liability. With a full head of sandy-blond hair, perfectly concealing the little gray he does have, he too looks years younger than he is. His Brioni suit is impeccable. He could be a model for Nieman Marcus—except there is none in Oregon or Washington.

Emily appreciates fine clothes on a man and compliments him. "Beautiful suit, Patrick. Nordstrom?"

"I looked but no luck. Found it at Mario's downtown."

"Mario's…very nice. They also have a stunning women's department. Pretty pricy, of course."

"Maybe I can take you there sometime."

With a slight smile, Emily nods. At the other end of the dining room, a pianist plays a jazzy, upbeat melody with enough proficiency that she nods her approval. When the waiter approaches with menus, Patrick politely dismisses that formality.

"Oh, we know what we'll have—your version of beef bourguignon."

Emily is surprised by Patrick's preemptive response. The waiter withdraws the menus.

Patrick confides to Emily, "They actually use a local pinot noir, a competitor of mine—not bad actually." He reaches under the table and presents the waiter with a bottle of pinot noir. "If you wouldn't mind. My own vineyard."

Emily muses, "I wondered what you brought to the table."

Patrick does not get her humor.

"You always bring your own wine?"

"Just on special occasions. It's our first month anniversary."

Emily puzzles.

"I like to celebrate any chance I get," Patrick says.

"And I sold my first house."

"Right…" With that, he gets up, lightly kisses her on the cheek, and strides over to the pianist. Emily sits in suspense but within a minute, he returns. "Did you miss me?"

"Terribly."

"I know you like Chopin."

The pianist attacks one of Chopin's toughest études, the "Double Thirds Étude," with the confidence of an experienced artist.

"It's one of his beatitudes," Patrick asserts.

Emily laughs. Patrick's mouth drops.

"Beatitudes? You mean, étu—"

He looks down, hurt, and backs away.

"I'm sorry. It's beautiful." She searches for words and reaches for his hand, quickly adding, "I know what you meant."

Patrick hesitates, takes his seat, and waits. And fidgets. She sits back to appreciate the commanding music with a faraway look in her eyes, a little sad. But as she closes her eyes, the pianist stops on the fifth stanza.

The restaurant's host stands over the pianist. And in a display of indignation, the pianist storms away. Patrick, irritated, jumps up and glares at the host. But Emily shakes her head for him not to interfere.

"The piano guy said no one ever asked him to play that piece here—but he'd love to." Patrick tries to control his thoughts, to calm himself, to shift the focus. "You've missed playing. You said so." But succumbing to his annoyance and nodding toward the host, "Obviously, not everybody's ready for the hard stuff." Patrick settles down again. But sulks.

When the sommelier returns, Emily looks relieved. Patrick focuses on the routine—cork sniffing, swirling, sniffing again, and tasting. The sommelier is silent with a smile that hints of a dare. Nevertheless, he awaits Patrick's approval.

Patrick assures him, "I know it's good." And to Emily, "But this is the ritual."

The sommelier's eyebrows lift and a slight smirk breaks onto his lips. Patrick nods and the sommelier pours for Emily, then Patrick.

Emily, winking at the sommelier but addressing Patrick, says, "Maybe he would like to try your pinot."

Patrick gestures to him, and moments later, returning with a glass, the wine steward allows Patrick to pour, but stops him short.

Patrick breaks out in a facetious smile. "Yes, leave some for us."

Swirling, smelling, and tasting, the sommelier smiles with controlled approval and bows in appreciation. After several precious moments, he and Patrick exchange business cards.

The steward studies the card. "Ruffian Red. Good name." He steps away as Emily and Patrick lift their glasses for a toast.

Emily puzzles, "He barely said a word."

"My pinot did the talking—and my girl." Then under his breath, he adds, "Why did you wink at him?"

Emily blushes.

Resuming their toast, Patrick affirms, "To us. Just the two of us. And us alone."

She complies, "Yes." And as she appreciates the pinot, she asks, "How did you come up with Ruffian?"

"My dad. He said I'd never amount to anything, that I was a rowdy punk bruiser, a ruffian. It's my way of insulting him. I like being a kind of ruffian." He leans closer to her. "You like it too, don't you?"

Emily shifts in her chair and appears to be thinking of what she should say. But Patrick has more.

"He kept a barber's strap in the bathroom—you know, the old-fashioned straight-blade razors?"

Emily nods with both tentative understanding and puzzlement.

"He always seemed to be on the lookout for some reason to resort to the strap." Patrick looks up and away. "I think he enjoyed beating me. And after a while, I didn't really mind. He would have a deep guttural growl, 'You take it. And you like it. And you like it. And you take it.' … Maybe it was the price I had to pay for his attention."*

Though uneasy, Emily listens with empathy. When Patrick pauses, she says. "Um, I'm so sorry. But you're such a gentleman. You should be proud of your success. And your father proud too."

"Well, he's gone…"

She leans over to pick up her purse. "Um, I'm sorry. I just need to use the ladies' room. But now at least we're having a lovely meal together. I'll be right back."

They enjoy the beef stew made famous by Julia Child…as well as a shared tiramisu—Patrick insisted.

Parked near the restaurant and just steps away from a boutique hotel, a glistening black 2014 Porsche 911 Carrera waits. At Patrick's unlock command, it blinks. Patrick likes to think it's a wink just for him. "I'll take you back to your place. Or we could spend an evening together. Here." Then he adds with his own special humor, "You don't have an open house tonight, do you?"

Not sure just how to take his sarcasm, Emily responds, "I do have clients first thing in the morning… And I didn't bring anything for—"

"That won't matter. You're all I need. Just as you are." He re-locks his Porsche.

Emily is disconcerted with the change of plans—and a little tipsy. But Patrick, already holding her arm, grabs her more firmly and sweeps her into his embrace. At first, she resists. He kisses her. Regaining her composure, she walks close to Patrick into the hotel lobby, trying to ignore the observant doorman's eyes.

Terri scrutinizes the letter she is writing at their kitchen table. Irritated with what she has written so far, she slaps down the pen. Staring straight ahead, Terri listens to a jazz station's forlorn love song.

Zari turns down the volume and objects, "You don't need none of that shit." She stares at her friend. "Ya miss 'im some?"

"No… Um, kinda—sometimes at night."

Zari sees Terri's failed efforts at writing. "You're not writing to him, are you?"

"Mike? No. To Sean… This is hard."

"I'll show you one of mine…just for inspiration, if you want."

Emily's Old Phone ringtone announces that Robin is calling. Reaching into her periwinkle-blue leather bag and pulling out her rose-gold iPhone, she takes the call as if it were a question. "Yes?"

"Mom, I was thinking about you last night. Didn't want you to think I'd forgotten your birthday. Did you get your real estate license yet?"

"Oh, yes! And I sold my first home last week. Sure takes a lot of hand-holding. But it's all good. Thank you for asking."

"Everything else okay?"

"Um. Well, I am dating now. I've found a really lovely man."

"I knew you would. Online?"

"No, actually, the old-fashioned way, in person at a wine tasting. He's so handsome. He may be the love I've—" A muffled cough interrupts her words, followed by silence.

"Mom? Hello…"

"I'm sorry. I'm talking like, like—" Clearing her throat, she confides, "I'm happy. Anyway, he's asked me to marry him—we are such soulmates, as he says."

Robin hesitates. Incredulous, she asks, "How long have you been with him?"

"Oh, I'm taking my time."

"So, how long?"

More silence.

Emily dodges the question. Reverting to her Texas drawl, "Ya know, yer father was such a gentleman in our counseling. But I just couldn't keep playing the good bishop's wife. I hope he's okay. How's he doin'?"

Robin obliges with a simple answer. "Well, he's dating someone. Like you. Not like you, but seeing someone."

Emily is surprised. "You're kiddin'."

"You don't approve?"

"Um. It's just that I didn't think he was up fer it. I jus' hope he's happy now."

Robin gives her just enough background to satisfy. "It's someone in the church. He says he wasn't looking… Anyway, I just wanted to wish you a happy birthday."

"Oh, how is, um…"

"Ryan? He's fine. He's a great student and he likes his work—his teammates are great. But I gotta run."

"Well, I look forward to meeting him again."

Robin ends her call, then suddenly adds, "But can I leave you alone with him?"

In Oakland's Whole Foods Market, Ryan surveys a depleted post-Thanksgiving pumpkin display in the produce section. Assisting him is Dion, a very dark, fine-featured African American the same age as Ryan. He has a great attitude and together, they alternate between clearing the display and answering customer questions.

Another teammate—Aya, maybe just 19, and Japanese American with turquoise-tipped hair—rushes to clock in. She greets Ryan with a friendly fist bump and an affectionate hug for Dion. His smile makes it obvious that they have a crush on each other.

Ryan asks Dion, "How's her art project coming?"

"Great. She's working with another student from State at some kind of collective."

"Cool."

"You know musicians and artists. They can't compete with high-salaried techies for rent. Anyway, there's gonna be an EDM concert there next week—local musicians, and from LA too. Aya wants me to go with her."

Ryan puzzles, "EDM?"

"Electronic dance music."

Cutting their conversation short, an overly enthusiastic PA system announcement breaks in. "One store. One team. Bagging assistance. One store. One team."*

Ryan and Dion look at each other to see who goes.

Dion volunteers with a shrug, "Oh, joy."

Ryan finishes lugging the last of the large pumpkins onto a heavy-duty cart.

CHAPTER 31

A hand-addressed letter sits like a dead weight on the coffee table. Sean picks it up with dread, then falls with resignation onto the couch.

From the kitchen, Aida calls out, "Daaad?"

But Giovanni stops her. "No. Your dad needs private time."

Sean settles himself and carefully opens the Hallmark card. It has a bouquet of flowers on the front and inside, and enclosed is a wide-ruled sheet of notebook paper. As if Sean can hear her, but not the Terri he was used to years ago, he reads:

Dear Sean,

Thank you for calling me back a few days ago. I am writing this letter because I need to tell you something I never told you or nobody before. When I went into treatment, it took AA and Narcotics Anonymous for me to come clean with this.

Sean leans back, blinks his eyes, and takes a breath.

When I was 12, my brother and father raped me. The first time was in the cellar of our house. It went on for years. That's how I learned to use sex to make some money.

Sean's jaw drops and his eyes try to refocus on the letter.

This is not an excuse. I am sorry for how I have treated you. And Ryan. I don't know what to tell him. I don't keep secrets no more. I was never good enough for you and I don't expect no one to understand me or forgive me. I just need to ask anyway.

He looks away for a moment, then finishes reading the letter.

I'm sorry I hurt you and Ryan. And maybe it don't mean much comin' from me, but I appreciate and love you both.
— Terri

Sean sits there, stunned, thinking, lips moving to form words, but nothing comes out. The ever-happy bearded collie comes bounding into the room. Sean absently accepts her greeting with a pat on the head but then turns to her. "What would you do, Mandy?" He waits. "Yeah, I know." When he gets up, Mandy follows.

Giovanni is whispering to Aida in hushed tones when he sees Sean enter. Giovanni cocks his head like Mandy might when waiting for her master. But Sean says nothing.

Trying to be upbeat, Giovanni asks, "So, how's life in Philly?"

Sean makes a whimpering noise. Holding the letter, not willing to let it go, and not saying anything.

Giovanni tells Aida, "Looks like iPad time for you."

"Yeah, yeah, yeah… Call me when it's safe to come out. But I *am* hungry." Aida gives Sean a smile of encouragement and a quick squeeze of his free hand.

Sean thrusts Terri's letter into Giovanni's hands. "Read it yourself. Please."

Halfway through, Giovanni stops for a moment. When he finishes reading, he slowly hands the letter back to Sean. Giovanni bows his head into his hands, trying to think of an answer. Instead of giving Sean one, he simply embraces him in silence.

A call comes from Aida's bedroom. "One, two, three, four." And opening her bedroom door, she adds, "So, here I come—ready or not."

Both Sean and Giovanni take a breath and Giovanni asks Sean, "So, you're calling her now?"

"Of course."

Aida stands half hidden at the archway to the kitchen. "So what did your ex have to say?"

Giovanni glares at her. Sean folds the letter tight, looks to Giovanni, then to Aida, and finally speaks. Aida is undaunted as she stares at his clenched fist.

"She really wants to talk to me. She's in an alcohol and drug recovery program. They're supposed to reach out to people they have hurt. I need to acknowledge that."

Aida has heard more than she understands. Silent and now sheepish, she glances aside.

Sean grabs his phone off the counter and excuses himself to their bedroom.

———□———

Terri sits back on the couch listening to an old Walkman CD player with headphones. Her cell phone vibrates on the coffee table. Seeing it jiggle, she grabs it, looks at the number, hesitates, then answers. "Yes. This is Terri. Sean?"

"I had no idea. You never—I don't know what to say."

"You don't have ta… I'm still sorting through shit—I just wanted to let you—let you know I'm workin' on makin' changes, makin' my life mean something."

"So what was I to you—just a…a conquest?"

"At first. But no! You were—*are*—one of the few men who

wasn't trying to exploit me." Terri squirms on the couch, changing positions, and sits up.

"Okay..."

Terri hesitates. "Have ya had a chance to talk with Ryan?"

"Um, yeah. But not since I got your letter. I just opened it minutes ago."

"So after all these years, are you okay being—"

"Gay? Yes. We've been married, um, eight years. Six years with our adopted daughter. She's 11 now."

"Pretty perky too."

"You got that right." Hesitating for an awkward moment, he adds, "I look forward to you meeting her someday."

"That would be nice. But it'd be awful expensive to get out there. So…is there something I should say to Ryan?"

"I don't know. You lived with him for 17 years. I've only— Sorry, you asked an honest question. He doesn't care much what either one of us says." Clearing his throat, he adds, "For him it's more what we do. What's done is done. Your letter was very thoughtful and—"

Terri cuts in, "Thanks. That means a lot to me, coming from you."

"Okay. We'll stay in touch."

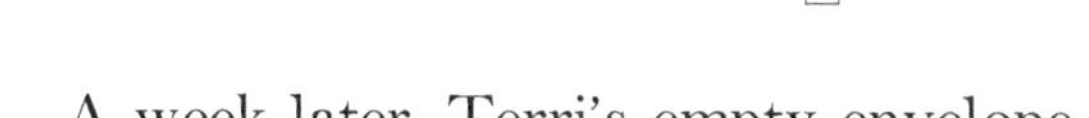

A week later, Terri's empty envelope still sits on the coffee table. Sean, empty-handed and with a blank expression, plops onto the couch. Giovanni comes in and sits next to him. After a few moments, he looks up at Sean, waiting for him to say what's on his mind.

"I guess I'll have to bring Ry up to date, don't ya think?"

Giovanni smiles. "I guess so. But dinner is ready regardless."

———☐———

Terri sits back on her couch, trying to relax, trying to listen to her music. She listens intently, not noticing Zari enter the room. Zari moves into Terri's line of vision and waves a hand. Terri takes off the headphones while the song continues playing.

"Sorry. I borrowed your Gershwin CD—I'm such a sucker for 'The Man I Love.'"

"Not still waitin' for Prince Charmin' I hope."

Terri reassures her, "Not quite. But—"

"You know who I really like is Nina Simone. She helps me make sense of all this shit."

"Yeah, well, I miss a man. Don't you? This thing about no romantic relationships—I miss the good times."

Zari gives her a heard-it-all-before look. "Yeah."

Terri rubs her knees together in mock sexual pleasure and obvious defiance. Zari swats her on the shoulder in reprimand as an older sister might. So Terri goes another step.

"Well, then it's time for a little oxy and a few drinks on the side. Whaddya say, girl? We gotta have some fun."

Zari closes her eyes, presses her lips, and shakes her head. Going over to her collection of Nina Simone CDs, she finds "Be My Husband."

After listening to a couple minutes, Terri takes off the headphones and demands, "Does being a wife mean ya needa be a sex slave and a house servant too? Even if he beats her? Well, Nina objects and so do I."

———☐———

It's a cold but sunny day—perfect for a Sunday afternoon open house in the hills of Northwest Portland. One of the substantial and almost ostentatious craftsman homes in the Forest Park neighborhood, the front door displays a fresh, fragrant magnolia and eucalyptus wreath. Emily rings the doorbell as a routine courtesy, and expecting no answer, allows herself a sweeping entrance into the contemporary home. It is perfect for entertaining. A concert grand piano in the living room is welcoming—or intimidating, depending on who's entering. *That woman was so lucky to have her own Steinway. I'm happy they let it be part of the staging.* Emily quickly glances at her watch and returns to her car to retrieve the homemade cookies and gourmet cheese and crackers she has brought. She heads for the kitchen—a designer's dream layout.

She slips her perfectly manicured fingers under the wrapper of the cookie tray. *For me? Why, yes, thank you.* She indulges in one of the lusciously-thick, chocolate-chip cookies. In reverie, Emily wanders through the home. Again looking at her watch, she fidgets with her realtor lapel pin and finds her way back into the living room. Before sitting down at the piano, she tests several keys with both hands, then plays a few chords. *Well-tuned!*

Looking in the bench for what sheet music might be there, she sees a "Very Best of Nina Simone" songbook. Tucked inside is a printout of "Wild Is the Wind." Taking a deep breath, Emily places it on the piano's music desk and begins playing the delicate, plaintive melody line. Enchanted with the haunting sound of the first several bars and focusing on the lyrics, Emily does not notice the man behind her.

He clasps both hands over her eyes. Startled, she shrieks. He grabs her by the waist, lifts her off the bench, and enfolds her in an attempted passionate kiss. She wrestles with him to stop.

"But I love you. And you need me," he says.

"Patrick! Don't surprise me like that. You frightened me. But…actually, I *was* thinking about you. I was thinking how you are a new life for me, like spring…"

"I'm sorry. I, I just wanted to see you. I don't like being without you."

Regaining her composure, she puts her head lightly on his chest. "But this is an open house. I expect there'll be people here in minutes. Can we meet this evening? Unless I get an offer…"

Patrick's lip protrudes in a sulky pout. He thinks for a moment, then says, "I know you miss your piano. But do you miss loser-boy bishop?"

Emily creases her forehead in disbelief.

"Well, you said he was great in the pulpit, just not very good in bed."

Emily begins to walk toward the kitchen but turns. "Patrick! Thank you for dropping by. Sorry I screamed." Smiling to make up to him, she adds, "May I call you later?"

Without comment but visibly annoyed, he leaves.

Back in the kitchen, Emily removes the Saran wrap from the snacks.

CHAPTER 32

Ryan and Dion uncover the potato displays in preparation for the day. Their hands seem unable to stop working as they enjoy their banter.

Dion, trying to sound upbeat, says, "You still comin' with me to Aya's thing?"

"Not sure. Robin wants to do somethin' else. She's not into electronic dance whatever—EDM? Is that what it's called?"

"Yeah. Me neither. But it's for Aya."

"I'll see what—"

Dion makes a low guttural groan, but to be clear adds, "That means no."

"Hey! Don't bully me or guilt me into this." Ryan attempts a brotherly hug. "Okay?"

Dion backs away. "I need my wingman. She wants me around but she'll be hangin' with her artist buddies."

"Okay, my friend. I'll charm my sweet Robin. Somehow. You owe me."

Dion looks relieved.

Ryan reluctantly asks, "So, where's this place?"

"Just a couple blocks from the Fruitvale Station."

"Like the movie, *Fruitvale?* But nobody gets killed, right?"

"Yep." And adding with taunting facetiousness, "Besides, you'll have me there to protect you."

"Me?"

"Well, it *is* Oakland."

"I live in Oakland too. We'll have Robin to protect us. She's itchin' to become a cop."

Dion shifts his tone, almost defensive. "That's what I'm afraid of. You people might be more at risk being see with me."

"Okay, okay. So we'll meet you there after work. I'm on the closing shift."

Dion confirms, "It's a warehouse off International Boulevard on 31st. Graffiti on the outside. And music you'll probably hear when you get off the bus. It's that avant-garde electronic shit without much soul but a heavy-duty beat."

"Sure you want me there?"

House music throbs in the otherwise quiet industrial neighborhood. Mexican-inspired mural art and graffiti on the two-story building make it obvious it's an artists' collective with its name hand-painted in bold block letters, *GHOST SHIP*. Dion and Aya, wearing a sleeveless dress, wait outside near the doorman. They look down the street toward the Fruitvale Station.

Aya complains, "If we're going to wait out here in the cold, I'll need my jacket. You're used to working in a cooler. I don' know how you do it." She shivers, nods to the doorman, and dashes back inside. A moment later, a text from Ryan shows up:

11:09 PM Friday December 2
See you in a few

Dion looks both ways on 31st, sighs, and shrugs. People are milling about and a few new patrons arrive, paying the $15 to the doorman. He says, "Enjoy." Then to Dion, "Waitin's the worst."

"Yep. But I think I see 'em."

Ryan and Robin pick up their pace when they see Dion. He greets Robin with a hug.

"Glad you could make it. I wanted you to meet Aya." Dion hands over a 20 and a 10 to the doorman.

Ryan gives an appreciative glance and mutters under his breath, "I hope this is worth it."

Dion raises his eyebrows but says nothing.

Ryan asks, "So, where's Aya?"

"Went to get her jacket. But we can go in."

Like entering an eccentric neighbor's home, they walk among a strange and quirky collection of art pieces, old upright pianos, and secondhand store furniture. Charming, maybe, but bizarre. And hard to see in the dimly lit interior. Dion leads the way, turning this way and that until he finds the stairs to the upper level.

Calling out over the music, Dion assures them, "Aya should be up on the second level."

Robin and Ryan, holding hands, are hesitant but begin to follow Dion up the stairs. But they are not real stairs. They're made from scrap wood.

Ryan thinks, *Made from pallets? Like the cheap ones delivered to Whole Foods? Clever though.*

Halfway up the "stairway" is a landing and a restroom. Dion continues up. Several steps behind Dion, Robin and Ryan stop when the restroom door opens. It's Aya.

"You made it! You both did! I'm so happy. Did you see Dion outside?"

"Yes," Ryan says, nodding to the second level. "But he's looking for you now."

Suddenly, they hear someone yell in alarm, "Is that a fire?"

Smoke is now billowing from somewhere on the first floor, spreading fast. The power goes out and the music stops. There is an orange glow, and a crackling sound, like kindling catching fire, spreading upward.

Robin yells to Aya and Ryan, "We need to get out! NOW!"

Panicked people—dozens of them—grope their way through the blackness toward the staircase. Robin and Aya are pulled along with the others down the makeshift staircase. But Ryan calls into the smoke, "Dion! This way, Dion!" Ryan sees the rickety steps to the second floor catching fire. He dashes down.

The doorman just outside the entrance yells into the blazing warehouse. "The door is this way! The door is this way!" he yells over and over.

Sounds of sirens from approaching firetrucks compete with his calls.

Choking from the smoke, he croaks out, "Dion! Can you see me? Down here. Dion, Jump!"

Dion, barely able to see, jumps toward Ryan's voice. He knocks Ryan over, then grabs his friend and they crawl in the direction of the doorman's voice. Dion is ahead of Ryan.

It's 11:35 PM. Flames leap from the windows as firefighters prepare to douse the inferno. Robin leaves Aya at a safe distance and rushes back to the entrance. *Where's Ryan?* she thinks, panicked.

The warehouse belches smoke and people. Robin yells into the blackness. Dion comes crawling, then stumbling out. But no Ryan. She coughs out, "Where is he?"

"He…he…" Dion croaks, pointing.

Robin yells his name again into the smoke. Then, taking a deep breath and holding it, she stumbles over other patrons who are crawling out. She lunges in. Moments later, coughing, she drags Ryan out by both arms. He is face down, collapsed and unconscious. She rolls him over. His forehead has a gash and is bleeding. Without hesitation, she checks his pulse, then begins chest compressions. She yells to Aya, "Kleenex—

something for his head!"

Aya retrieves a packet of tissues from her pocket and begins to hand them to Robin but she tells Aya, "You do it! His head. And keep it tilted back."

Robin continues compressions, then gives Ryan a mouth-to-mouth rescue breath. Seeing his chest rise, she gives him another lungful.

Ryan suddenly coughs and heaves. Aya, trying to hold her hand on his wound, looks at Robin, who takes over holding the compress on his head. "Good," Robin says. "How's Dion?"

Aya rushes to embrace Dion, who is on the ground trying to sit up. He looks like he is about to throw up.

The doorman continues his calls—even when no one else comes out. Several firefighters in full turnout with respirator masks and SCBA tanks motion for him to move aside.

EMTs and paramedics hurry through the crowd outside to check the panicked or dazed survivors. One EMT comes over to Ryan. "You all made it out okay?"

Robin speaks for him and her small group. "Yes, but—" She gestures with her head to Ryan and Dion.

Dion holds on to Aya while she sobs quietly. He croaks, "Yeah." He is surprised by his own voice and shortness of breath. His eyes are bleary. He rubs them and sputters, "We… made…" is all he can manage.

Ryan, still on the pavement, moves his head but starts coughing again. Robin quickly defers to a paramedic to take over his care.

Thick black smoke and flames roar from the windows, and flames shoot through the roof. Dousing efforts to quell the blaze create more smoke. About 30 people in small groups huddle together texting, making calls, and waiting, stunned and watching in silence. Or crying.*

Like an airport boarding area, the Highland Hospital waiting room is large and modern. It is crowded with Friday night mishaps and injuries but only a few from the Ghost Ship fire. The collective anxiety seems to have used up all the room's oxygen. Robin and Aya sit close to one another. Both are on their phones.

Robin calls Sean and leaves a message. "Sorry to be calling so late. Ryan and I are at Highland Hospital. There was a fire at the concert. Ryan has smoke inhalation—I don't know how bad. I'm okay, I think. But they do need to run a couple tests on me. So if you could come…" Finally taking a breath, she thinks to add, "I'm in the waiting room. He's already in Emergency."

Aya speaks into her phone, "We're classmates at State. But I don't know if she made it out. I'm waiting for some test results before they let me go… Yes, in the waiting room… But right now, I gotta go." Cutting off her call, she turns to Robin, trying not to cough, and leans her head on Robin's shoulder. After a few moments, Aya whispers, "Dion actually went deeper into the fire looking for me."

Robin holds her tight.

Later that night in the emergency department's triage area, Ryan and Dion are in adjacent bays, curtains drawn. Blood is taken. They are sedated and endotracheal tubes have been installed to provide oxygen through the mouth. Both are unconscious. The nurse on duty reassures Robin and Aya that they need to be kept "asleep" for their own protection.

"We don't want these young men pulling out their tubes. That'd create even more problems. They're going to be out of commission for a couple of days."

Robin and Aya are stunned. They just look at each other, wondering what to do next.

Robin, Aya, and Sean are at the hospital early the next morning to watch over the boys as they sleep. On the second day, the hospitalist assures them that they might see some stirrings but they should not expect to have real conversations with the patients. A nod of the head will be about it.

When it is finally allowed, Robin rests her hand on Ryan's shoulder. Aya is bowed over Dion and Sean stands at the foot of Ryan's bed. When he sees Ryan open his eyes, he speaks to both patients without expecting answers.

"The doctors have briefed us all. You and Dion have had some serious lung damage. They're not sure how bad, so they need to leave the oxygen tubes in place. They're doing blood tests again right now."

Dion's eyes try to focus. Ryan looks confused. Maybe he didn't even hear Sean's words.

Sean, turning to Dion, continues, "And you didn't break anything when you jumped. Lucky man."

Dion nods, but just barely.

"You're supposed to rest. I'm just glad you—all four of you—made it out. Many didn't." Sean pats Ryan's foot. When Ryan's eyes begin to well up with tears, Sean moves from the foot of the bed to his side. Robin is already making room for him. And as awkward as it is with all the monitoring equipment, Sean hugs Ryan. "I'll be in the waiting room and will check back a little later. Okay?"

CHAPTER 33

It's a very early morning for Terri. She couldn't sleep any longer, so why not get up? With coffee in hand, she reaches for her phone on the way to the couch. Zari, usually up anyway, stays at the kitchen table reading the *Philadelphia Tribune*.

When the phone comes on, it shows a voicemail from Sean. Terri listens with the speaker on but at low volume.

"I know it's early. I've been at the hospital all night here in Oakland. For Ryan."

Terri slowly sinks deeper into the couch.

"I'm fine but he was in a major fire last night—you'll read about it. Anyway, he's got lung damage, they think. I thought you'd want to know. Call me when you can."

Terri groans and Zari looks over at her. "Waz up, Ter?"

"My son. He's in the hospital. Some kinda fire. Sean wants me to call."

"Your son?"

Without hesitation, Terri hits *Call Back* and within a few rings, a groggy Sean answers.

"Yeah. Thanks for gettin' back. I thought you'd wanna know that our boy—he's in ICU. If we're lucky, he'll recover without too much lung damage. We don't know yet. It's too early. He breathed in some heavy-duty fumes saving his friend from work. The friend's in the same shape."

"I'll come out. I want him to know…I tried. I loved him. As best I could. I need to make amends. Somehow."

Sean clears his throat. "You don't need to do that. We can let him know you care and you called."

"That's not good enough. Remember what you said? He don't care what ya say, it's what ya do. I needa tell 'im myself. In person."

"Let's talk a little later."

"He don' needa know I'm comin' and gettin' all concerned. Okay?"

"Okay."

Finished with the call, Terri looks straight ahead, like down a long corridor. "How 'm I gonna 'ford this? What've I said?" She swallows hard.

"Well, I couldn't help hearin' an' all. What you sayin' is you're flying ta California ta see yer boy. No regardin' the cost."

Frozen still, Terri begins to take in one breath at a time.

"I don' mean-a be rough on ya. Let's think about this."

———□———

The Highland Hospital waiting room is occupied by only a few friends or family members reading or making quiet phone calls. Robin, exhausted from a sleepless night, slouches over, looks at the time on her phone, takes a breath, then makes a call.

"Dad?" But crumpling into tears before she gets any further, she smothers the phone on her lap, takes another breath, and continues. "Sorry. There was a fire—" She pauses while her dad speaks. "Yes. Ghost Ship. In Oakland."

"I'm okay but Ryan isn't. He's in ICU here at Highland Hospital. I'm waiting to see him before I go home for a nap." Looking slightly more relaxed as she talks, she adds, "He tried to—no, he *did* save his friend's life by staying in the fire long enough to help him get out but it was too long—enough to hurt his lungs."

Malcolm blurts out, "There's so much crazy news, including Trump claiming voter fraud."

She tries to listen but doesn't want to get caught up into her father's distress. She breaks in. "Good for you, Dad. He's not my president either... Of course, leave it to Portland to protest, huh?" Looking a bit revived to be finishing her call, Robin says, "I'll call later—after I get some rest. Sean's going to take me home." She listens to her dad, then assures him, "You always have. I love you too." Ending the call, she squeezes her eyes closed with an attempt at a smile.

Robin gets up and plods over to the admissions window, where the receptionist gives her a "not yet" smile.

Later that morning, after rounds, Robin looks into Ryan's room. She approaches the nurse with a question forming on her lips but the nurse gives Robin a shushing gesture and whispers something to her. Robin nods, smiles politely, and leaves.

———□———

Robin is asleep with the blinds closed, but restless. Her phone, charging nearby, starts chiming. Robin bolts upright and grabs it. "Mom? Sorry. I've been sleeping—sort of. So you know." Touching the speaker button, then resting the phone on the nightstand, she perches on the edge of the bed.

"Your dad called me. He can't come to be with you. But I can."

Robin grimaces.

"He's committed up to his ears preparing for Trump protests. You know him. The conscience of the community."

"I know. And I agree. Trump is powered by greed." Robin chokes.

Emily, avoiding any political talk, asks in halted words, "Are...you...okay? The fire! I want to come down to see you—

and that sweet boy of yours. I'd like to be some help for y'all."

"Sweet boy? I guess he is. Yes… He's going to be okay, they tell me. You really don't need to."

"I am your mom."

"But my place isn't nice enough."

"I'll stay somewhere in Berkeley."

Robin raises her hands in concession. "Okay."

Zari hammers away on an old desktop computer while Terri sits anxiously on a folding chair, watching as Zari searches airline websites.

"Well, you jis watch. See what I can put together for ya." But the monitor suddenly freezes with the infamous blue screen of death. Zari grumbles, hits the monitor's off switch, and the screen's data zaps into a phosphorescent dot.

It's Ryan's second night at the hospital. His bedside monitor still tracks his vital signs. Sean quietly slips into Ryan's area but seeing him asleep, tiptoes back out. As he paces near the doorway, Sean notices Ryan stir. Only half awake, Ryan nods at his dad. Because of the intubation tube in Ryan's mouth, Sean can't quite see if he is smiling. He rushes to Ryan's bedside.

"Good to see you, son. We're all cheering for you. Even your mom."

Ryan's forehead wrinkles.

"She   she wants to come see you."

Ryan shakes his head in defiant protest. He reaches for his face and tries to pull the tube out of his mouth. Wincing in pain, he repeats his disapproval with restrained movement—but no less emphatic.

—————□—————

Zari reaches for her cell phone, finds an airline number, and calls. After listening to various prompts, she hands over the phone to Terri.

"It's old school—but you want a real human to hear ya. You be wanting to get to Oakland ta see yer son in the hospital. It ain't no holiday. And you can't spend more money than I can help you with."

Terri's appreciation for Zari's help shows in her eyes.

"You're gonna be on hold."

Terri sits in Zari's folding chair, waiting on the phone for what seems like forever. Then an agent takes her information and Terri reads out Zari's credit card information.

A short time later, Terri is packing clothes and toiletries into a modest thrift-store suitcase. She wishes out loud to Zari, "If I could just be there without all this effort and expense... But thank you so much, Zar."

Zari hugs Terri at their apartment door and hands her an old iPod with earbuds. With a reassuring smile and another hug, she tells Terri to listen to Mandisa—for inspiration on her journey.

This is Terri's first time flying. She can't anticipate all the routine steps of the trip: the early morning trek to Philadelphia International Airport; feeling overwhelmed, anxious, and confused; not knowing where to stand or where to go but trying to look in control; the crowds and long lines for TSA clearance. And of course, the five-plus hours in flight. But she gets through it, determined to see her son. She jams the earbuds into each ear like stoppers, fidgets, and switches her suitcase from one hand to the other. Her flight arrives in Los Angeles by 9:00 AM California time, where she will need to wait for four hours for the flight to Oakland.

Terri looks like she's been up all night. Her hair, normally swept back over her ears, has fallen. Her fatigue is obvious and she wears no makeup. She calls Sean's home number but gets his voicemail greeting. With a sigh, she leaves a message.

"Hi, Sean. I'm almost there—well, I'm in LA waiting for my flight to Oakland. I should git in at like 2:00. Then I'll go to the hospital. Bye."

Terri slumps into a waiting-area chair with her little suitcase by her side. She even manages a conversation with a child psychologist—a pleasant relief! Later that afternoon, Terri is in another waiting area—this time, the one on the ICU floor at Highland Hospital. It's like a quiet living room. Maybe too quiet. It's intended to be comforting for friends and family.

Terri paces, then finally sits. Hair now combed and some makeup applied, she finds Zari's iPod and puts in the earbuds. She presses the play button and closes her eyes. When Sean enters the room, Terri does not see him.

He just watches her. Quietly, he walks closer. Terri opens her eyes. Startled, she snaps her head up, stands, and swipes the earbuds out of her ears. She holds out her hand but Sean ignores it and hugs her instead. Unfamiliar with his embrace, she twitches after a moment. But smiles.

He smiles back. "I'm amazed. You're here."

"Me too. I got a good-priced ticket. Had to wait a couple days for it. But I'm here."

"I am impressed. But…actually, I tried to call you. Before you left Philly. I only got your message from LA a few minutes ago."

Sean drags a chair over, in effect inviting Terri to sit down again.

"So, when can I see 'im?"

"Um…well…that's why I tried to call you." Sean picks at a tooth and tries to think how to say it, but then just blurts out, "He doesn't want to see you."

Terri's face falls. Crushed, she asserts, "I was gonna surprise 'im. You told 'im I was comin'?"

"I thought he would actually be happy—happy that you cared enough to make the trip out here."

"He won't see me?"

"He can't talk. He's still got a breathing tube down his throat. He just shook his head no, no, no."

Terri looks lost.

"The ICU nurse told me they would be removing Ryan's intubation tube and replacing it with an oxygen mask soon. His throat will be pretty tender and he should not talk much. We're supposed to let him rest."

Bewildered, Terri leans back in her chair and looks at the ceiling.

"Let's get some fresh air," Sean suggests. "I think we both could use a walk. There's a wildlife preserve along San Francisco Bay."

Hours later, the lead nurse gives Sean an encouraging nod of approval to approach Ryan's bed. Without the endotracheal tube, Ryan's eyes look brighter, happier, and the clear plastic oxygen mask makes it easier to see his attempt at a smile.

Trying to lighten the mood with a little humor, Sean jests, "Well, this is a sure way to have one-sided conversations, isn't it?"

Nodding in agreement, and surprising Sean, Ryan slides the mask to one side for just a moment to sneak out a sentence in a crackly voice. "What day is it?"

Looking anxious, Sean breathes deeply as if he's the patient being asked an orientation question. "Sunday. Sunday afternoon. Robin will be here too." Hesitating, like testing a stove's burner, he adds, "And your mom."

Ryan rips away his mask and croaks, "You're kidding! I don't want to see her."

Sean leans in so he can keep Ryan's anger between the two of them.

His throat still raw and hurting, Ryan squeaks out, "She left me alone a lot as a kid. Why's she doing this Florence Nightingale stunt?" He props himself up some more and coughs out, "She can leave me alone now." Exhausted, he sinks back onto the pillow and continues his choked tirade. "One of her men fucked me like I was his girl—whenever he could."

Sean is stunned. His mouth drops. He's speechless as he remembers Ryan telling him at Spreckels Lake something about this guy.

Ryan now takes several breaths of oxygen from the mask and continues, "I was 10. I tried to tell Terri…" Gasping and grimacing, he continues, "…but she wouldn't believe me. Billy was her man, her source." Taking another dose of oxygen, Ryan chokes out, "And YOU weren't there." He slams the mask back on and dismisses Sean. "Go 'way."

Sean tries to respond but thinks better of it. He slowly steps aside. Head down, he backs out the door and slowly creeps down the hallway to the family waiting area.

Terri sits on the couch in the same position she was in when Sean left. She remains motionless and quiet, and avoids looking at Sean.

Sean waits, but needing a straight answer, calmly demands, "What did Billy do? To Ryan? He was only 10."

Terri looks up at Sean with a blank look on her face. Then,

trying to remember, she slowly says, "Um…he was my oxy dealer. He lived with me. Ryan liked him. He gave him attention like a—a dad."

Sean fumes, "This guy of yours—he was fucking our son!"

"No. Uh…I didn't think so. I didn't believe Ryan."

Sean barely restrains himself from striking her.

"It didn't make no sense to me…at the time." She shrugs. "I don't know."

Sean backs away from Terri as if to leave, then slowly turns. "Where are you staying? How long are you out here?"

"Don't worry 'bout me. Let me just be here for now."

"Ryan's got a lot of resentment. Not just against you. But me too. Robin has been a good influence. She'll be here in a few minutes."

Terri is unresponsive.

Sean continues his monologue. "She came here from Portland with plans to become—" He shakes his head. "—a cop of all things. Definitely not your average girl."

Terri looks up. "That her coming?"

Down the corridor, two women approach—obvious as mother and daughter in height and hairstyles. When Robin sees Sean, she steps ahead of her mother. She flings her arms around him and they embrace—strong but brief. Robin steps aside so Sean can introduce Terri to Emily.

"Ryan's mom, Terri Gallagher—all the way out from Philadelphia. Just got here."

Terri stands to greet Emily.

"And coming from Portland, Robin's mom, Emily Marshall. I mean, Thorne. Sorry." Sean adds.

Both mothers nod to each other.

Robin is uneasy with introductions. Shifting her stance and looking over at Terri, she guesses, "You must be exhausted. So, have you seen—"

Sean interrupts her with a gentle elbow nudge and smiles with an apologetic grimace at Emily. "I think we should visit just one, maybe two at a time."

Emily is surprised at Sean's preemptive comment and glances at Terri for some reaction. Emily waits a moment, then offers, "Maybe you two should go in and leave us moms to chat."

Terri tries to smile.

"We'll wait out here," Emily adds.

Motioning for Emily to take the more comfortable lounge chair, Terri returns to her seat. Both women wait for Robin and Sean to be out of earshot. They also look uneasy with each other. Emily, stylish in a Ralph Lauren outfit, looks appropriate for showing a multimillion-dollar home. In contrast, Terri looks out of place. Maybe wearing scrubs over her Goodwill outfit would help.

Emily asks a gently rhetorical question. "What've we gotten ourselves into?"

Terri, in her straightforward candor, agrees. "Fer sure. Ain't no party, huh? And we're s'posed to make pleasant talk while 'r kids 'r recovering."

Emily breathes a sigh, not of relief but for a quick charge of air. "Robin has a classmate who lived in that warehouse thing."

"Yes," Terri says. Looking at Emily's lapel pin, she puzzles, "What's the *R* for?"

"Oh, I'm a realtor. I sell homes in the Portland area."

"Sean tells me you're divorced. Just recent like?"

Emily hesitates. "Over a year now. Been dating. I think I've found the love of my life." She pulls out her iPhone to show Terri Patrick's face on the lock-screen photo. "He didn't want me to come here by myself."

Terri puzzles over Emily's comment but observes, "He's

good lookin' fer sure."

"He says the other women he's known just didn't come up to his standards. But I do. He's so romantic. He says we're soulmates."

"You're totally in love."

Emily is beginning to blush but can't help herself. "I've never had anyone tell me what my deepest desires…before I even…" She stops. "I shouldn't be tattlin' on myself." Wishing to shift focus, she shares, "Robin said we were supposed to meet. We have things in common."

"Ya don't say. I've never been in love with a gentleman like yours. I'm glad I'm single now, just trying to reconnect with my son. It's been three—"

Emily's phone dings with a new text message. Paying attention to Terri, she ignores it.

Terri admits, "He's holding on to past hurts. I was not a good mother. I'm guessin' he's not ready to—" She stops and nods toward Emily's phone. "Do you need to answer that?"

Emily looks at the message, then holds up her phone to show Terri the emoticons of hearts and flowers signed *Patrick*. "He sends me notes almost every hour."

"I bet he's eager to get you married."

"How'd you know?" Wanting to shift the conversation, Emily asks, "So, tell me—besides being a concerned mom—what is it you do?"

"I was a security guard before I went into my recovery program."

Emily pulls back as if standing at an intersection and getting a whiff of sewer gases. "Sorry."

Terri shrugs her shoulders and cheerfully counts off with her fingers, "You know, the usual. Drugs. Alcohol. Denial. Domestic abuse. Lose job." Looking at her open hand, she adds sadly, "Hit bottom. But that's how we make our recovery. Now I help—"

Emily's phone dings again with another message. Emily looks relieved, welcoming the distraction. She reads the message from Patrick with rapt attention. *You made it to the hospital! Tell Robin she'll be ok. She's a big girl now. Lucky to have you.*

Robin and Sean return to the family waiting area.

Sean tries to be upbeat and announces, "The patient is improving."

Robin adds, "He's a little more coherent. His teammate from Whole Foods should go home tomorrow."

Emily looks at Robin. "Patrick just now sends you his best. Here, you read it for yourself. So, is it our turn to see the boys?"

Robin reads the text but ignores Emily's question. "Big girl? I'm glad he's confident I'll be okay. We're still learning who didn't make it out." She furrows her brow. "He knows we just got here… Do you have *Find My Friends* turned on?"

Apprehensive, Sean nods for Emily to visit Ryan. He glances at Terri, defeated.

Robin, refocusing on Sean, suggests, "Maybe my mom could pop in and say hello, not stay too long." Robin reaches for Emily's arm as if escorting a guest, and accompanies her down the hall.

Once they are down the hall, Terri comments to Sean about Robin, "She's so polite."

"Her training," he replies.

Terri squints her eyes as she observes, "This Patrick—he's sure fixated."

"A real gentleman according to Emily—in the wine business. Her ex is an Episcopal bishop."

"Um, so looks like you'll have yourself a bishop's daughter?"

Before Robin and Emily reach Ryan's room, Robin leans toward her mother to whisper as they walk, even though no one is close enough to overhear. "You know, Terri's come all this way to see her son—to reconcile with him. She's been through a lot and is living on a shoestring. It'd be ever so thoughtful if you'd invite her to stay with you."

Emily stops dead in her tracks. She looks like a mother stepping into a disaster of a kitchen after kids have made cookies.

"Sean offered to pay for her to stay somewhere but she's too proud," Robin continues. Then she teases lightly, "Just two moms getting a rare chance to connect."

"Maybe you should have stayed on track to become a priest, the way you like to meddle in people's lives." Emily takes a deep breath to charge into what she really wants to say. "Tell me you've thought better about becoming a cop. Some of those bullies in blue are thugs in disguise. And you really don't wanna to be in some criminal's gunsight."

Careful not to sound too defensive, Robin proclaims, "Officers of the law serve their communities in all different ways. I want to help people do the right thing. Like Dad."

As they resume their walk to Ryan's room, Emily shakes her head.

———□———

Terri and Sean sit in awkward silence until Terri clicks open her suitcase and digs through it, looking for something. From the bottom, she pulls out a postcard and a piece of paper. She unfolds the printout calendar from June 2013 and hands it over to Sean.

"He didn't tell me he was leaving. But he did leave this note."

She sits back and lets Sean read.

Thanks for the card.
Going to travel while I can.
Take care of yourself.
Dump Mike. You deserve better.
R.

Leaning forward and in a soft voice, Terri asks, "Will you please give him this and thank him for me? I appreciate him. He told me I deserved better. And I did dump Mike. And I'm keepin' in recovery."

Sean gets up. "And the postcard?"

She holds out the card for Sean to see. On it is a photo of a San Francisco cable car with a Rice-A-Roni advertisement on it. "No. I keep this one. We ate a lot of Rice-A-Roni. I hoped we would take a ride..."

Sean's shoulders sink. He begins to leave to deliver Terri's note but Terri touches his arm. "There's more I'd like to say but—" She retrieves her earbuds and the iPod. "You've heard the saying *don't let the sun go down on your anger,* right? Here's River City Extension. Have a listen."

Cueing up the song, she gives one side to him while she listens with the other—like children on a school bus listening to one shared headset. After Sean has heard enough, he nods and gently removes his earbud. With no further words, he slips away with Ryan's note in hand while Terri continues to listen to her music. She pulls out her well-worn Narcotics Anonymous handbook.

Later, while Ryan rests, Terri, Sean, Robin, and Emily get something to eat from the hospital's cafeteria—an awkward mini meal with the primary discussion being the Ghost Ship fire. What is not discussed are their respective relationships with Ryan and his refusal to see his mom. Emily has graciously invited Terri to stay with her—not citing Robin's gentle pressure to do so.

CHAPTER 34

I t's early evening but Oakland's city lights are on full display in the hotel room. Emily and Terri have a view that includes the Tribune Tower.

"We have a Tribune in Philly too," Terri says. Turning to the wall opposite the queen beds, she is impressed by the big-screen TV. "Look at the size of that screen! Oh, and there's a refrigerator and a microwave."

Emily smiles kindly and heads to the bathroom.

Terri continues to look around the upscale room. In addition to the pair of cozy-looking queen beds, there is a tall table lamp plus a desk and an office chair perfect for business travelers. Terri's suitcase looks out of place compared to Emily's. She tries to slip it under the bed but it won't fit. She notices a chest of drawers.

Emily calls out, "Doin' okay, Terri? I'll be out in a minute."

"Oh, yes. I'm good." *Well, I'm tryin' to be good!* She opens the bottom drawer and dumps in her clothes. *I need to hide this thing!* Seeing another door and thinking it must be a closet—though wondering why a closet would need a lock—she opens it and is surprised to see another door within. She wonders, *Is this to another room?* She jiggles the knob but the door remains locked.

Emily's phone dings with a new text message.

"Sounds like you got another message from lover boy," Terri announces.

Terri opens another door, this time a closet, and stashes her suitcase there. Emily emerges from the bathroom in a lovely violet nightgown and matching robe.

"Beautiful," Terri compliments her.

"Oh, I've had these for years. But thanks. Your turn."

As Emily reaches for her phone, the hotel phone rings. She first glances at the text and exclaims, "He says, *I'm here. Surprise!*" She looks at the ringing phone.

"Aren't ya gonna answer it?"

Emily is frozen.

Terri thinks, *Is he stalking her?*

The room phone stops ringing. A few moments later, a text message appears on Emily's phone. It reads, *I know you're here. I love you.* And has a two-hearts emoticon.

"But does he know I'm here too?" Terri asks.

Emily only shakes her head. The room phone rings.

"I better get goin'. I don't want to be in the way," Terri says.

"Yes… No." Emily shakes her head. "Why is he doing this? We didn't plan this."

"He likes to look after you. Maybe even track your every move? Does he ever frighten you?"

There is a knock at the door and Emily turns to Terri with a pleading look on her face.

Terri nods. "I'll see who's there."

Emily rushes into the bathroom and closes the door as Terri peers through the peephole.

"Hotel guy. Looks like a cop," Terri reports.

He knocks again and Terri asserts, "One moment…" She turns toward the bathroom door. "Emily, come out."

Emily opens the door for the young security guard. His name badge says *TORRES*. He looks more like an airline steward with shoulder epaulets on a long-sleeve white shirt, and wears an official cap. He is more cute than handsome—

Filipino American with a trim mustache and goatee. He's nervous as Emily escorts him in.

"I don't want to disturb you, but according to the front desk—oh, by the way, my name is Gary— there's a gentleman waiting. Your fiancé? He says he booked the room just for you. And when you checked in, you added Ms. Gallagher."

"I understand." Turning to Terri, Emily adds, "I wasn't expecting him. Let me get you another room."

"You're sure? I mean, you're okay having Patrick come up?"

"Oh, yes. He's soo—um, passionate." She smiles at Gary. "Before you go, might we arrange this from here? Gary. Could you tell my fiancé I'm not quite ready. I'll call the front desk to arrange things." She turns to Terri. "That okay by you?"

Terri nods a slow consent. "Thank you, you're so thoughtful."

As Terri retrieves her suitcase and clothes from the bottom drawer, Emily calls the front desk.

Gary tells Terri, "You'll need to sign in and pick up a key."

As they leave, Terri reassures Emily, "Call me if ya need."

Emily smiles absently as Terri closes the door.

In the hallway, Terri considers, *She doesn't have my number but the front desk will know where I am.*

Terri commends Gary, "Good job. I'm impressed you folks do this security thing. You never know."

He nods in appreciation.

As they approach the elevator, she adds, "Best if we're not seen together. I'll catch the next one."

He pauses, thinking, then agrees. "I understand."

The front-desk clerk steps aside from the terminal so the night manager, Sergio, can see the account on the screen. At 33, Sergio looks like a soccer player ready for a much anticipated date, handsome with a natural smile. But he is serious now.

Patrick paces like a caged animal until he cannot hold back. And louder than necessary, he booms, "Finally, somebody with a little authority! You can let me into my goddamn room. I'm in your system."

Sergio looks up from the terminal like a puppy puzzling over his angry human, and in a lyrical voice, assures, "Yes, I guess you are here. And here's your name too, on a credit card to hold the room."

Gary glides around to the back of the counter and waits for Sergio. Sergio is savoring the moment while Terri steps out of the elevator and listens at a distance. Patrick does not notice.

Sergio continues, self-assured, "But someone else—I'm not at liberty to say who—actually is on the account to pay for the room."

Patrick's eyes dilate as he glares at Sergio and Gary. The observant front-desk clerk jumps back as Patrick slams the counter with his fist.

"You sonsabitches!"

Sergio calmly discovers, "Oh, let's see. It also has an additional note. *He first acts like a gentleman but quickly gets threatening and aggressive if he doesn't get his way. Notify security.*" Sergio flashes a sweet smile before quickly adding, "But I can override this. Would you like an upgrade?" Sergio waits.

Patrick, momentarily puzzled, calms and puffs up his chest.

Sergio continues, "I can upgrade you to our special 911 service. It only takes a few minutes."

Patrick is stunned.

Gary whispers something to Sergio.

Without changing his polite demeanor, Sergio turns to Patrick, and in the same tone announces, "But the lady will see you in a few minutes. She will call—"

Interrupting Sergio's performance, the assistant clerk answers the phone and in a moment, nods her head in approval—not to Patrick but to Sergio.

Patrick turns in a huff to leave.

"Would you like to know the room?" Sergio asks.

For the few moments it takes Sergio to complete the transaction, Patrick notices a woman with an old suitcase in hand now standing behind him. Giving her the once-over, he says to Sergio, "How'd she get in?"

Terri pretends not to hear and waits her turn. When Patrick has left, she steps forward.

After Patrick is on the elevator, Sergio speaks. "I am truly sorry. You don't know him, do you?"

"No. But my friend youse guys protected? She gets to have him for the night. She called down to get me another room."

Sergio gives Terri a sly, sardonic smile. "You didn't want to stay in one room together?" Not needing an answer, he keys into a different screen. "I just need your ID. I only have one room at the discounted rate—actually, right next to your friend. If you wouldn't mind. She's paid for you."

Terri graciously accepts.

Her room is similar to the larger one she and Emily shared, but with only one bed. Terri enters timidly. Setting her suitcase on the floor, she plops down onto the bed and sighs with an exhausted, "Ahh..." The clock radio reads 9:50 PM and she mutters to herself, "What a day."

She picks up her phone and scrolls to Zari's name. *But wait...none of these clocks are on Philly time. It's too late to call. No wonder I'm zonked.* Noticing the low battery level on her device, she hunts in her suitcase to find the charger. That's as much energy as she can expend. She just closes her eyes, the lights still on, and falls asleep. Almost.

Noises and fragments of muffled words come from Emily's room. Terri sits up. She strains her ears, hearing only part of what's being said and trying to understand what she can't quite make out. Surmising that it must be Patrick, she hears, "I've been worried about … can't leave me. Do … hear what I'm saying? You're … phone too much."

She hears the muffled sound of a hand slap, then, "Patrick. Please. I love…"

Then the sounds of a struggle and a thud to the floor.

"…keep…quiet…"

Then hand-muted yells.

Terri springs off her bed. Eyes wide, looking from side to side, she carefully turns the door lock to the adjacent room and opens it to hear better. She hears slaps punctuating each word: "Don't…you…leave…me…"

Then the only sounds are Patrick's rough lovemaking grunts, swear words, and obscenities.

Terri touches the room-dividing door she failed to re-lock earlier. Like a child afraid to touch a stovetop burner, she quietly cracks the door open. The lamp from her room sheds just enough light on Emily's face that Terri can see a leather-strapped mouth gag is keeping her quiet. But Emily's eyes blink.

Emily sees only a woman's silhouette in the door. But just as fast, Terri pulls her door closed. She rushes to her bedside lamp and rips its cord out of the wall socket. Then, looking uncertain, she runs out into the hallway. Looking for the exit signs, then sprinting down six flights of stairs, Terri reaches the lobby floor, breathless.

At the front desk, Sergio and Gary are chatting. Both look up as Terri runs toward them.

Surprised, Sergio asks, "Ms. Gallagher?"

"He's beating her. Call the—"

Before Sergio can reach for the phone, Gary dashes for the elevator.

Sergio confirms with Terri, "You're sure?"

She glares at him with confident conviction.

"Okay. I'm calling. I'll need more info. Please stay here."

Gary presses his ear against the door to Emily's room. Hearing nothing, he pauses, thinking. He glances at his watch and waits, then turns and walks to the stairwell. He calls on his two-way radio, "All quiet. Either a false alarm…or we're too late."

"Stay there. They're coming," Sergio radios back.

Gary returns to Emily's room and stands by the door, listening again. He paces, then waits. Two Oakland police officers quietly approach. The older African American male officer, AJ Williams, in his early 40s, nods at Gary in recognition. The younger, ponytailed Latina officer, Angela Martinez, follows him.

Gary quietly knocks on the door. Then again more loudly. "Hotel security."

They hear sounds of rustling in the room.

After a few moments, with controlled reassurance, Patrick says, "Be right there."

Patrick cracks open the door with the security latch in place, nearly nude, looking like a swimmer still wet from the pool. He defies their entrance at first, but when he realizes he needs to defuse the situation by letting them in, he unlatches the door.

AJ sizes him up without a word. Angela ignores Patrick's physique, focusing intently on his eyes. Patrick scowls at Gary.

"So, what's this interruption about? Gentlemen."

Angela's eyes squint.

AJ states without accusation, "There's been a complaint. One or more guests are concerned about goin's-on in this room. If you wouldn't mind letting us have a look."

AJ leans forward and Patrick steps back. Grudgingly.

Sitting up in bed with the bedside table lamp on, Emily sits with a hardback book on her lap. She quips, "Is this supposed to be room service?"

Gary offers, "I'm so sorry, Ms. Thorne. We had a noise complaint."

Angela steps forward without hesitation, approaching Emily's side of the bed and extending her hand to Emily. Likewise, Emily raises her hand in greeting, poised, like royalty.

Angela introduces herself. "Officer Martinez. Stay comfortable. I'm sorry for the intrusion."

Gary flushes. AJ is stoic and steady—his eyes glancing between Angela and Emily's interaction. Patrick fidgets.

Angela proceeds, "Is there anything we should—" She pauses and turns to the men in an attempt at privacy. "Excuse us, gentlemen."

Emily assures her, "No. I'm fine. I'm sorry if we caused anyone concern. I guess we were—you know…"

Angela, noting the hardback, inquires, "You like to read the bible—after sex?"

Emily stares her down. Then, as Angela turns to leave, she notices something gleaming not quite under the bed. *Handcuffs?* Angela addresses AJ. "If you gentlemen could step into the hallway for a minute, I need to have a few words with Ms. Thorne."

AJ gives her a nearly imperceptible, knowing nod. Patrick

snorts his disapproval.

Patrick sneers, "May I have a bathrobe, Officer?"

"Sure," AJ replies, but instead, he hands him a coat hanging in the closet. The three men leave the room.

Angela asks Emily, "Where you from?"

"Portland, Oregon."

"Okay. You don't need to respond to anything I have to say." Sitting down on the other bed, she continues, "I just want to tell you that we get calls every day for domestic abuse. You may think he's just playing—"

Emily squirms.

"When you get back home, you should look into this. And ask yourself, why is he doing this?"

With that, Angela leans over, picks up the handcuffs, and gently drops them onto the open bible. "Don't get hurt. Okay?" Touching her own neck, she adds, "Ice will help."

Angela steps into the hallway and closes the door behind her gently, acting like nothing happened.

A few minutes later, Patrick comes back in, proud. "Police ever come visit you and the old bishop for havin' too much fun?"

Emily just glares at him. Depositing the cuffs onto his pillow, she then slides the bible into the nightstand drawer and turns off the lamp.

Patrick gets into bed and Emily gets out of bed. "I need ice."

Terri and the front-desk clerk are sipping tea in quiet conversation in a small conference room next to the hotel's registration desk. The clerk rises and offers her chair to the senior police officer when they arrive.

AJ speaks first. "Thank you for staying with Ms. Gallagher.

And thank you, Ms. Gallagher, for calling. You did right. I'm Officer Williams. This here is Officer Martinez." Gesturing for her to take over, he says, "Angela?"

"We've seen it all before," Angela begins.

Terri's head sways just a little and her eyes cloud over. "So have I."

Sergio and Gary stand at attention outside the room. Just as the officers are wrapping up their interview with Terri, Sergio enters the room but waits for AJ's nod. AJ and Angela rise.

Sergio quietly announces, "We've found you a different room, different floor. Gary will accompany you. Try to get some rest now, okay? You are safe here."

Terri can't help herself. Angela comes over to her and Terri hides her face against her shoulder.

Late in the night, Terri's phone dings with a new text message. She barely lifts her eyelids, then closes her eyes again. When she comes out of her sleepy fog, she looks around, disoriented, and looks at her phone again. She calls Zari and gets her voicemail, so she leaves a message.

"Morning, Zari. Or afternoon. When you git this, I might be in a meetin'. Amazing. There's one just a couple-a blocks away. I sure need one… I'm still really tired. I think I bumped your number last night when I plugged in my dead phone. Sorry if I waked ya. Anyway, thanks for the text."

Terri only now notices a red light silently flashing on the room phone on the other side of her bed. Sliding over to that side, she studies the instructions for retrieving the message and follows them. She listens and her shoulders droop. She opens the drapes to a bright morning and greets the day with a deep breath.

The front desk is busy with guests checking out. Terri approaches a smiling clerk and states, "Morning. You have a note for me from Emily, Emily Thorne, I think. I'm Terri Gallagher."

Terri accepts the note. As she walks back to the elevator, she reads it, stunned. On the way to her floor, she thinks about what to do.

After straightening out her unmade bed, Terri sits down with her phone, dials, and waits for an answer. She looks at Emily's note sitting on the bed next to her. When Sean answers, she says, "So how ya doin', Sean? Quite a night here." She pauses while Sean speaks, then repeats, "Robin can't reach Emily?" She picks up the note and reads it again. "Emily checked out—said for me ta call ya... I dunno. With Patrick, I'm guessin'... What? Stay with youse guys? Um...okay. Do you also provide a police escort? ... Just kidding. I'll explain later. See ya at two."

In front of the hotel, at the passenger pick-up zone, Terri, looking as professional as possible, waits. An Oakland bus glides by with a public service announcement from La Casa de las Madres, showing a woman removing duct tape from her mouth. The copy reads, *You Have The Right To A Healthy & Safe Relationship*. Terri gasps and braces herself.

Sean's SUV Pathfinder swerves into the zone. Robin jumps out and gives Terri a hug—and her seat.

Terri asks, "That fire's sure in the news. Do you know anyone who actually lived there?"

Robin shakes her head. "Not sure yet."

Sean answers, "I think the count is up to 36. But identities are not yet known—or not yet released."

Robin has a faraway look in her eyes as Sean pulls away

from the passenger zone, not looking at either Sean or Terri.

But Terri needs to change the subject. "Well, there's somethin' else goin' on I think we needa bring up. Your mom."

Robin asserts, "I think she's left her phone off."

But Terri counters, "Maybe. But I think there's somethin' goin' on you two should know about."

Sean glances over to Terri. "Like what?"

"Like the police comin' to check on Emily last night."

"What?" Sean looks from side to side. "I can't drive and concentrate on what you're saying." Finding an open place to park, he jerks the Pathfinder into a free parking space.

Terri cautiously begins, "I'm not sure I should be tellin' a daughter about her own mother's adventures. But I think yer old enough. And you should know."

Robin leans forward, focused.

"I believe her lover boy Patrick—"

Robin interrupts, "What are you saying?"

"I called the police. Because of what I heard. And saw. I believe she is falling into something with Patrick."

"Well, he has been tracking her…"

"We should go back to the hotel. I'll fill you in on what I can, and you can talk to others there."

Turning to Robin, Sean asks, "Okay if we delay seeing Ryan?"

Robin agrees as she puts both hands on her face, touching, almost like she is praying.

Back at the hotel, the lobby is busy with new check-ins. Behind the counter is the same clerk who gave Terri the note. Recognizing Terri, but looking puzzled, she nods in greeting but turns to Sergio to intercede.

"Thank youse guys for yer help last night. We think Emily's missin'—she came here to help her daughter deal with the warehouse fire. But I'm suspectin' something's wrong."

Sergio agrees. "Ahh, yeah. I can see that—yeah. Gary is going to be clocking in momentarily. Meanwhile, if you could wait over there." He motions toward the end of the counter.

Terri speculates, "Maybe there's a report—since the police were called?"

Robin's eyes blink but she bites her tongue.

Sergio asks Sean, "You're together, right?"

Sean smiles wearily, looking anxious, glancing between his ex and his prospective daughter-in-law. The three endure the overly cheerful background music and the quiet hustle-bustle of the lobby.

Sean breaks their awkward silence. "Terri, could you fill us in on what you—"

Gary cautiously steps up next to Sergio. And before Terri can answer, she defers to Sergio.

Nodding to Terri, Sergio apologizes. "Excuse me. May I introduce our night security, Mr. Torres."

Without hesitation, Robin gives Gary a hearty handshake. Sean, likewise, greets the security guard, but with polite restraint.

Gary speaks in a hushed voice, "Let's meet in a quieter place."

Sergio leads the way to the conference room and hands Gary a set of papers. As Gary takes a seat at the head of the table and invites the others to sit, he quickly reads over the documents.

"Yep. That's pretty much it. But it doesn't say what Terri heard and saw for herself. So why don't we start with—"

Robin's phone rings. "So sorry," she mumbles. As she begins to silence it, she recognizes it as a local number. "I think it may be the hospital. I'd better take it." She answers, then says, "Mom? You're at the hospital?"

Sean gestures for Robin to switch to speaker mode so they can all hear. She does.

"So, where have you been? Are you okay? It's not like you to have your phone off."

"He's taken it from me."

Robin's eyes tighten and her shoulders straighten up like she's in jiu-jitsu, ready for a takedown. Gary seems thoughtful as he strokes his goatee, looking like he wants to speak, but keeps quiet. Sean observes all of this.

Robin confirms, "Patrick?"

"I can't talk now—here—but when you come, I will."

"Where's he now? Does he know where you are?"

"I dunno. Please come."

"Okay. Stay right where you are. You're on the ICU floor? We won't be long—within the hour. Love you, Mom." Pressing the off button, she sets the phone down on the table like evidence before a jury.

Gary cautiously asks, "Um...where were we?"

Sean answers with his opinion. "I think Terri knows what's going on with Emily."

Terri gasps and acknowledges Sean's vote of confidence.

CHAPTER 35

Down the hall from the nurses' station on the ICU floor, Emily waits in the family waiting room. With designer luggage at her side, bent over, and alone on the couch, she looks lost.

Sean whispers to Robin, "Cate Blanchett in the final scene of Woody Allen's movie."

"*Blue Jasmine*. Okay, Sean—let's not get melodramatic."

When they approach, Emily looks up. Beaming to see Robin, she nearly runs to greet her. As they hug, Emily takes several short breaths.

Sean slows his pace and keeps a respectful distance. He takes the opportunity to make a call to Giovanni's voicemail. "Geo, my man. Looks like we do have a houseguest tonight. Could you make old-style Philly cheesesteaks? Just us and Terri. Well, maybe Robin and her mom too—for dinner but I don't know where Emily's going to stay."

Sean slowly walks into the family waiting area and greets Emily. "Glad you're here. Terri's given us her perspective."

"Where is she? I need to thank her."

"She's in the car. She wanted to wait there—not here."

"Robin is so smart. She's going to clear my phone—somehow, without me having it—but keep my contacts in the cloud? Is that where they're supposed to be?" Trying to discreetly wipe the telltale tears from the corners of her eyes, she shrugs. "Have I been in a cloud? I guess just to be on the safe side. But Patrick doesn't mean any harm."

Robin reacts but ignores Emily's comment for the moment.

She is intent on keying in code numbers into her phone. "Okay. Here's where you enter your password," she tells Emily.

Sean adds, "So, maybe tomorrow, a replacement phone? At least Patrick won't be able to find you here in Oakland."

Robin, finished with her task, now has that look of delayed enlightenment. "But if he was tracking you… Does he have a criminal record of some sort?"

Sean and Emily look at each other and back to Robin.

"Don't we need to see Ryan first?" Robin asks.

Emily seems not to have heard Robin. "Yes, my Robin is very good at investigative research." Emily blushes despite her attempt to compliment her daughter.

Robin acknowledges, "There's an app for just about everything. If you could jot down all the contact information you remember about Patrick… We should check with the nurses. They may have already moved the guys off intensive care."

Ryan is sitting up in bed and chatting with Dion without his oxygen mask. Dion is dressed and ready to go home. Besides fresh clothes, Dion's mom brought his favorite dessert—sweet potato pie.

Ryan pronounces, like judging a contest for best pie, "Better than pumpkin!"

Robin says, "So, you're outta here. Where's your family?"

"They're waitin' for me. I just needa tell my boy Ryan…" He goes around the bed and gives Ryan a hug that crushes him. "…that I love you, man. Thanks. Next time, you pick the party."

Robin hugs Dion and he whispers to her, "And thanks to you, we've still got Ryan."

Sean and Emily look like guests in a receiving line but are

not sure what to say, so they just smile.

Robin asks Ryan point blank, "So, what about you?"

"Tomorrow. If I'm good."

Robin and Sean take turns kissing and hugging Ryan. Emily reaches for Ryan's hand, holding it with warm regard. After a few minutes, the three leave, with Robin turning around to give Ryan an air kiss.

———□———

Terri, still waiting in the front seat of Sean's SUV, wakes up from a cat nap, alert and attentive. She jumps out of the car as Robin, Sean, and Emily approach. Relieved and happy to see Emily, Terri greets her with a hug, like a sister. But quickly self-conscious, she steps back.

Emily, however, pulls her back into a warm embrace. "Thank you so much, Terri. I had a vision—a dream, I guess—that an angel appeared to me in that hotel room when I was gagged and cuffed. An angel with light shining behind her came through a door between our rooms to save me. Crazy, huh?"

"Uh-huh…"

Terri embraces Emily once again.

Robin takes charge. "Okay, girls. We have three things to take care of."

Emily, refusing Terri's offer to trade her front seat, gets into the back seat with Robin. Before Sean can start the car, Robin, with her thumb up, counting, begins, "First we need to know where Patrick is."

Emily offers, "Right this minute, I don't know. But after we checked out of the hotel, he drove me to another one nearby." Barely catching her breath, she confesses, "While he was in the bathroom, I made my escape with my suitcase. But he had taken my phone. I told him I needed to be with Robin. It's just that he's so jealous."

Robin assures Emily, "With your phone, he can see everyone you've called. Unless he wrote down those numbers before I erased your phone, you're good."

Terri, thinking aloud, adds, "What about when you're back in Portland? You're in real estate—that's very public."

Robin is on her phone. No one says anything for a few moments while Robin keys in answers from Emily's note.

Sean muses with a sly reference to recent political news. "It's like waiting for election returns. Do we get to lock up anyone?"

Terri is fast with her opinion. "Not funny."

All remain silent again until Robin announces, "No criminal record... But restraining orders are civil and he just might show up..."

Emily sits solemnly, like a widow at a funeral.

Robin has something. "Here. Yep. Earlier this year." Handing Emily the phone, she says, "Maybe you wanna read this yourself."

Emily glances through the posting, then hands the phone back to Robin and turns away in deep chagrin.

Sean tries to brighten the mood. "Well, that was second on the list."

Robin announces the third. "Eat."

"We could treat Emily to a Giovanni dinner." Sean winks at Terri. "It's Philly night in honor of Terri."

Emily smiles enough to signal a possible return to the living. Sean makes a quick survey of his passengers and reaches for his phone.

Giovanni's voice comes over the car's sound system. "How's my hunky husband?"

"Giovanni! I'm in the car with Terri and Robin. And her mom... We're in the hospital parking lot." Sean looks to Robin with a guilty smile, then confesses to his passengers, "We do keep track of each other."

Giovanni is confused. "Are you talking to me?"

Terri's phone now rings. Fumbling for it, she answers.

Sean continues talking to Giovanni.

Robin's phone also rings and she answers Ryan, "What? I love you too."

It is a pandemonium of unintelligible conversations with Emily sitting forlorn, without a phone. After just a few moments, everyone ends their calls.

Sean consoles Emily, "You might enjoy a few days off the grid."

A faint smile, appropriate for receiving a consolation prize, shows up on her face—until Robin's phone rings again.

Robin cautions, "It's an out-of-area call. Mom, is this Patrick?"

Emily freezes. Robin barely holds back from taking the call. Letting it ring through to voicemail, they wait. Sean studies each woman's face. When Robin's phone signals a new message, she asks Emily for permission to play it.

"Why not? Everyone seems to know everything anyway."

Robin's face tenses but she refrains from comment as she presses play and holds up the phone. Patrick's voice greets their ears.

"Robin, dear, would you tell my Emily I don't know what happened. Why'd she run off? We were going to have a nice few days together after seeing you. I was so looking forward to meeting you too… Please tell her when she comes back Thursday morning, I'll pick her up at the airport. I have all her flight information."

Emily nods in numbed agreement. But Terri shakes her head in animated disagreement. Robin looks at Sean. He knows better than to say anything. His silent snarl of disapproval is obvious enough.

Terri speaks in a hushed tone. "Emily, you and I needa talk. Privately."

Sean starts the SUV and pulls away. Giving Emily a wink, he says, "I think y'all will enjoy Giovanni's dinner."

———□———

Aida is hauling a pink pillow and a baby-blue blanket from her room and stacking them neatly on the living room couch. She addresses Terri, "Papa thinks you would like to have your own room. I don't mind. And Dad said you two need to talk private-like."

Emily's brow twitches. They follow in procession to Aida's room, which is pink. Definitely a little girl's room. But there is a set of designer-color paint chips on Aida's desk. "I don't mind the color but Papa and Dad actually argue over the meaning of colors like mauve and periwinkle. Whatever."

Terri declares, "I never looked pretty in pink."

"And I was required to wear it," Emily says ruefully.

"Well, you ladies can discuss this. Or more important things," Aida says. She leaves her room and closes the door behind her.

Terri sits at the foot of the bed. "Mauve?"

Emily, a good arm's length away, without appearing rude, closes her eyes and shakes her head. She can't help observing, "She reminds me of my Robin when she was this age." But she needs to shift focus. "I'm not so sure now about Patrick."

Terri wants Emily to consider what may be ahead. "Maybe this guy is a real Romeo or a guy into scary shit or... You was freaking out, gagged and cuffed."

"But Patrick loves me. He's not going to hurt me. He's

teaching me to trust and—"

"Emily! No. He's settin' you up for more. It's part of the game: domination and control. Cut you off from friends and family and takin' away your phone is just a sample of what's next."

Like a girl in church praying, Emily puts her hands together and remains quiet.

"You may think I'm jis poor white trash and ain't got no idea how I kin help you."

Emily, stunned and indignant, leans away from Terri. "You have no idea what I think."

"But I do. You think you can't live without this one man's attention. No matter what. That if you don't comply, you'll lose him. And you'll be nothing."

"But…he loves me."

"Well, maybe you deserve better. You wanna be kept like private property, his personal plaything? Do you needa be beaten black 'n blue and rushed off ta the ER?"

Emily just stares, speechless.

"You needa do yer own research on domestic abuse. It's not just about poor girls like me. Or women only, for that matter. Look for the signs."

The doorbell chimes and Mandy barks.

Speaking over the barking, Terri continues, "I'm jes sayin' look for the signs. Before it's too late. There needa be two proud mothers at our kids' weddin'."

When the front door opens, Mandy stops barking.

Robin can be heard in the living room. "How's my little sister?"

Emily and Terri are silent. They hear Aida announce, "They're here! They're in my room having a big-girl talk."

A few minutes later, Robin lightly knocks on the bedroom

door. "Mom?" Entering without hesitation, Robin hugs her mother, then Terri. She closes the door but stays standing. "Okay, I did a more thorough background check on him. You really don't want to get any deeper into him than you are. Three restraining orders, with child abuse in one of 'em."

Terri presses her lips tight and looks at Robin.

"Listen to Terri. And others like her who've been down this path."

Commotion from the kitchen and the aroma of dinner distract the three women. Robin opens the door to leave and to let Emily and Terri have time with each other. She nods in respect to each, with a special nod of encouragement at Terri.

Like a well-managed restaurant with synchronized kitchen and dining-room duties, each person has specific responsibilities. Aida and Robin set the table, Giovanni finishes assembling the Philly cheesesteaks, and Sean puts out beer and sparkling apple juice. In no time, everyone is seated at the dining table while Giovanni presents the cheesesteaks with a flourish normally reserved for gourmet steaks.

"The rib-eye is from happy, grass-fed steers and the cheese is authentic Italian—from provolone cows."

Not getting Giovanni's humor, Aida adds her own. "Not chocolate-milk cows?"

Sean jumps up from the table to serve the beverages. Each has a favorite. Aida and Terri have sparkling apple juice and Emily chooses the same. Giovanni, Sean, and Robin have a locally brewed IPA.

Seated at the head of the table, Giovanni toasts, "To Ryan's recovery! And to Robin, for her courage."

Hesitating, but saying it anyway, Emily adds, "For all of us— recovery!"

Terri adds, "And to friendship."

——□——

The next day, Robin stands next to Ryan's bed, arms folded, challenging Ryan with a cheerfulness that puzzles him. "You would have totally loved the Philly cheesesteaks Giovanni prepared last night."

"And without me?"

"For Terri. She stepped up to defend my mother. Her boyfriend turns out to have a record of stalking and domestic abuse."

"Your mom—what is it about her choice in men?"

"Hey! You're forgetting one of those men was my father."

"Right. Except her dad chose Malcolm for her—lucky for you. And what about her seducing your own boyfriend?"

"Okay, okay…"

"I'm glad I wasn't at the dinner. Two highly defective mothers at one table."

Robin's mouth drops, her face scrunches in disgust, and she steps back from Ryan's bed. "I've forgiven my mother for her indiscretions—okay, her betrayal and her adultery. It's for me, so I can be over it. It's not because I now approve of her actions. She was a fuck-up as a mother—maybe like yours."

"Well, that's very noble of you." He thrusts out his left hand for her to see the old scars. "I told you it was an accident. It wasn't. My mother held my hand on the hot stove to teach me a lesson for trying to cook myself lunch. I was eight. Another time she tried it again for taking quarters from her purse. She wouldn't give me money to buy school lunch. But I wouldn't let her." Building momentum, he continues. "By the time I was 10, she was really into oxycodone. And one of the sleazy men found me too sweet to leave alone. He had me like I was his secret girl—whenever he could. It hurt. It doesn't matter now. The last one was Mike. He bullied me, kept calling me queer, even once lunged at me with a butcher knife. There were more, but you get the point."

Robin is speechless for several moments. "You never told me. I am so sorry. Why didn't you tell me any of this?"

The hospital noises fill the silence. Robin notices tears forming but dares not touch Ryan at this moment. "Does your dad know any of this?

"Some." Ryan is quiet.

"You've been carrying all this for so many years. No wonder you resent her. Is this why you're in psych?"

Ryan looks off into the distance.

Robin continues, "Remember that saying about resentment? It's the poison you drink thinking it will kill the other person."

Ryan shifts in his bed.

"So right now, should I resent you for not letting me help you dump the burdens of your past? Maybe it's time." Not waiting for an answer, Robin reaches into her bag. "Before I forget, your mom has kept this ever since you first came to San Francisco. I was there with you when you bought it."

Handing over Terri's postcard of the iconic cable car, she adds, "You said, 'I don't want her to wonder where I ended up— not that she cares.' But you did care. I was impressed. I was impressed that you would do the right thing."

She walks out the door, barely turning around, almost dismissive. "Later."

In Robin and Ryan's apartment, Emily sits on the couch reading through one of Ryan's textbooks on family counseling. Also sitting on the coffee table is Maurice Sendak's famous *Where the Wild Things Are*. When Robin comes in, Emily discreetly sets the textbook aside and picks up the local real estate magazine on her lap.

Robin asks playfully, "Family practice or real estate? They kind of overlap, don't they? … And children's fantasy overlaps with adult reality, too, don't you think?"

Emily nods but doesn't want to consider such topics. "May I use your phone? I'd like to call Malcolm. I'd like him to pick me up from the airport. But on a different flight."

Robin goes over to Emily, sets her phone on the coffee table, and gives her mom an uninhibited embrace.

Emily quietly sobs, "Please don't tell him about Patrick. I need to look into my relationship—"

"And…" Robin gently challenges, "a restraining order. Right?"

Emily looks away, sad.

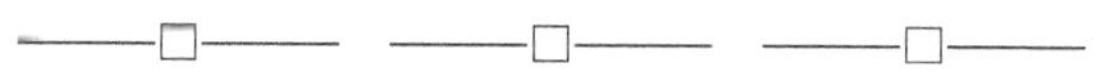

Sean treats Terri to a cappuccino in his living room.

"I don't drink froufrou coffee," she says, "but this is good. You always did have nice taste—especially in women."

His phone rings even as he tries not to laugh. "Yes, my son? Are the nurses finally ready to take their eyes off you? … Great. … Yes, she's right here. … I'm sure she'd like to come."

Finished with the call, Sean looks pleased but puzzled. "He also said we all need to take a ride on the Powell-Hyde cable car—like on the postcard?" Sean searches Terri's face. "He remembers the card? You kept that."

"No. I gave it to Robin. Why hold on to a hope ya can't have?"

Then she smiles

CREDITS

The 1967 Summer of Love was a truly crazy but exciting time to be in The City, especially for college-age students. Momentum was building for protests against the Vietnam War, not just in San Francisco but worldwide. Then in the fall of '68 the Black Student Union and the Third World Liberation Front brought further attention to the needs of people of color to get equal opportunities and college educations. A few teachers, honoring the five month-long college strike, meet with students off campus. So much history was playing out most boldly on the streets, yet somehow, I did manage to fulfill all my requirements to graduate in 1969.

Then a mere 42 years later, I'm sitting in the same classroom of the School of Cinema. Now more focused, I worked in earnest to craft my first feature-length screenplay. It was accepted by the faculty to represent the school in the hope of winning the Humanitas prize.

Once in the program, I just kept writing. It seemed that my characters just told me what they needed to do and what they wanted to say. I would follow them on their adventures, including submitting my work to many screenwriting contests. The Moondance Competition awarded me a prize for what is now "Terri's Story."

An actual incident on San Francisco's vintage F-Market & Wharves streetcar became the basis for three screenplays and ultimately this novel. One afternoon, coming home from State, I lost a my wallet when the old trolley lurched forward. I did not notice then that it had fallen out and was hidden under the seat in front of me. Inside that wallet I had a note to please call me if found.

What a surprise, within two days I did receive a call. The young man who found it was from the East Coast in search of his father. His returning my wallet became the inspiration for this entire story. Yes, I have tried to reach him, to thank him, but to no avail.

BEHIND THE SCENES

Pure fiction and every word is true—that is what I strive to offer. And to that end, I wish to acknowledge the people who helped me bring my characters to life and to resonate with the realities ordinary people face every day.

My editor, Cris Wanzer, has spared you the inconvenience of confirming the correct American spelling of words. More important than that, she has also improved my clarity in transforming the film scripts into the novel now in your hands. Ironically in film school, I was reprimanded for sounding too much like a novelist! Also, Cris was not afraid to challenge me to clarify my characters' motives and actions—even tracking details just as an experienced travel guide makes sure that everyone's luggage gets on board the bus. And off.

Professor Joseph McBride at San Francisco State University, film historian and critic, especially focused on the legends of Hollywood, was an inspiration for all the screenplays including the conversion of the trilogy into a novel. He encourages all his aspiring writers to recognize the diversity in America and to have their work reflect that. Professors Scott Boswell and Julian Hoxter, also at SFSU's School of Cinema, helped me structure the storylines in the original film scripts and keep the characters authentic and their plot progress compelling.

To that end, much of the dialogue comes from real conversations overheard or dialogue I heard growing up. Emily certainly channeled my mother, Rita Curtis. Her advice to my sisters on how to be alluring to young men still stings.

Likewise, my brother Martin, thirteen years my junior, has given me insights of a younger brother. His experience growing up was not the same as mine and therefore a wonderful resource.

What about the challenges of parents going through separation and fighting for child custody? Why not consult a court-appointed clinical psychologist with over 13 years in family dispute cases? With an insider's view of people tangled up in domestic trauma, Charles Roth, PhD, my husband, was most helpful in the development of Terri Gallagher's character. I had such a hard time understanding how a woman could be so terrible as a mom.

The Redwood Writer's 2020 Anthology, *Sunset Sunrise*, edited by Crissi Langwell, included my opening chapter—but not without important feedback. The judges reminded me that readers need to empathize with Terri. Then my first beta reader for the entire novel, Elaine Vickery, said we needed to cheer for her, to have hope for her recovery. She needed to have more humanity.

In addition to Redwood Writers and Elaine, Beverly Ford gave me invaluable reassurance in her thoughtfully reading my rough draft.

Researching domestic abuse was daunting. In addition to the many women with whom I shared Terri's story, I found an amazing resource. San Francisco's La Casa de las Madres— once I was allowed into the highly secured facility for women seeking shelter from abuse—was most informative. With printed resources, including TED Talks, I have since learned that domestic abuse and sexual abuse, are far more pervasive in our society than I originally thought.

CHAPTER 1

* The opening setting is Kensington—think Sylvester Stallone's *Rocky*. The neighborhood my husband grew up in the 1950s now has the unfortunate ranking in the entire state of Pennsylvania for highest levels of poverty, drug addiction, domestic violence, and incest. How are we to climb or crawl out of these circumstances? *Lost & Found* is my exploration into that. It is also a success story for families of all kinds.

CHAPTER 3

* Scrapple is a mélange of pork scraps of head, heart, and liver, plus trimmings, corn meal and spices. "Waste not, want not." Right? It is considered an ethnic food originating from the Pennsylvania Dutch. Vegetarians relax. It's not available everywhere.

CHAPTER 4

* Margaret is inspired by what my mother would have said and done if she were Sean's mom—a "spitting image" as she herself would have said. Growing up, we would see the *Maryknoll* magazine proclaiming the heroic efforts of that American Catholic religious order serving in foreign missions. Mom contributed to them every month from her college years to her passing.

* My brother, Lieutenant Colonel Joseph R. Moran, USA, Retired, assisted me in his experience as a career officer and his understanding of many things military. He helped me honor Sean's father and grandfather—and of course, all the men and women who have served.

* Yes, Childhelp is a real entity—1-800-4-A-CHILD, https://www.childhelp.org/. They do good work in spite of some parents' efforts to outsmart the system to get what they want. Sean may not have tried hard enough to prevail over Terri. It's complicated.

CHAPTER 10

* In all my research and in conversations with friends, I get a mix of views on just what is the best way to identify people. *Black* or *black* or *Afro-American* or *African American* without the hyphen… We know *negro* and *colored* are quite dated. And what about people of Asian or Filipino descent? Latino, Latina, Latinx. And while we're at it, what about the LGBTQ+ alphabet string to be inclusive? So the point of this note is to say that I believe we need to appreciate the great stew of American mixed races, religions, cultures, and more. We do not need to become a homogenized mass. We can appreciate how different we look and accept our unique heritages. We just need to respect one another.

* This lady on the bus is as close as I can create a character based upon a dear friend, Beverly Sallee Ophoff. She has been so influential in my life and so many people around the world, I just had to include her in this story. Check out her books: *Sunday Morning: A Step by Step Journey to Wholeness*. Also: *A Woman's Guide to Bootstrapping a Business* and *Hitting the Highest Notes*. On Goodreads or Amazon.

CHAPTER 11

* The character Ryan is the fictional name for the honest and thoughtful young man from Baltimore. He introduced me to a real character, here known as Whiskey Bill. Whiskey was required to live at the Seneca Hotel and not on the streets—or in

the parks. He was a good storyteller and claimed to have been close to Grace Slick of the Jefferson Airplane. Though I find that hard to believe, it did inspire me to include "White Rabbit" for the bus ride.

CHAPTER 14

* Only in the last couple decades has the alphabet string LGBTQ+ come into common usage. When I myself was coming to terms with my sexuality, I attended the Gay Fathers Association in Seattle, https://wp.gfas.org/. I believe Sean's story resonates with men coming to terms with their orientation. They may not yet understand or may not be in a psychologically safe enough place to admit they are gay. Times change. A little.

CHAPTER 16

* Trinity Episcopal Cathedral is a lovely community of Christian believers who do aspire to put into practice the teachings of Christ. However, Malcolm and Emily and Robin are entirely my own creations. They are not based on any members past or present.

* Our regional and ethnic accents are wonderful and as I appreciate and respect them, I have sought out confirmation and correction for what you hear in this novel. Thanks to Jacalyn Kinney for help with Emily and Grace.

CHAPTER 17

* Oregon Episcopal School is a very real school and, like the Trinity Cathedral, it's characters are my own.

* Likewise, SBG, the gym where Robin learns jiu-jitsu, is real. When I began developing Robin's character—or was she

calling the shots?—I took my original descriptions of jiu-jitsu moves to the local martial arts school in San Francisco's Japantown. When the owner of Bay Jiu-Jitsu, Stephan Goyne, said I could join the other adults even if I was seventy-whatever, I accepted. So glad I did. He has created a very welcoming environment. Even the members respect and adjust to each other's skill level. That way nobody gets hurt.

CHAPTER 20

* *The Raven Steals the Light* is a 1996 reissue of a timeless collection of Haida myths by Bill Reid and Robert Bringhurst with a new preface by Claude Lévi-Strauss. Of course, there are additional beautifully illustrated books and calendars on Raven.

CHAPTER 21

* English Now is my own name representing the extensive list of organizations offering ESL. The Multnomah County Library: https://multcolib.org/learn-english and Portland ESL Network is another: https://portlandesl.com/

CHAPTER 28

* My sisters deserve thanks here: Kathy for taking me to her AA meetings and sharing her decades-long sobriety; Georgia for recounting stories about her church-sponsored work with alcohol, drug, and unsheltered people in downtown Spokane, Washington. Empowering Women is my own name for a composite of organizations that provide different shelter and support options for women in Philadelphia.

CHAPTER 30

* Luis Ochoa is a tattoo artist and fellow teammate at Oliver's Market—yes, I work a few hours a week there. He gave me the

lines, "You take it. And you like it…" His use of the phrase was only in playful jest, never a setup for abuse. Special thanks to Caren in Wellness and Coleen in Gourmet Cheese for reading segments of the story. Also customers, Michelle Ferguson and Barbara Brennan for their thoughtful review of my characters.

* Whole Foods Market, in San Francisco's Potrero Hill neighborhood where I worked, inspired several characters for my story. Special thanks go to Aya, Brian, Dion, Gonzalo, J.C., Karen, and dear friends Cathy and Stephanie.

CHAPTER 32

* Joe Braden was my apartment building manager when I returned to San Francisco State to pick up where I left off my screenwriting pursuits. He read my script version and declared that Robin most certainly would not flee the burning warehouse without returning to rescue her Ryan. So obvious for her character! Thank you, Joe.

And while seeking authenticity in reporting the disturbing news, I combed through the coverage by local TV stations and newspapers. I especially appreciate my neighbor, Alex Eberle. As a paramedic, he confirmed some of the basics in fire rescue work and the resulting damage done to patients with smoke inhalation.

—————

And you my reader:
Thank you so much for reading or listening to my debut novel. I sincerely appreciate your feedback. We have work to do to

repair our families and inspire deeper respect for one another in our society.

If you would like to delve deeper into these topics, or are in a book club or organization that works with these issues, please visit my website for *Questions for Discussion.*

curt@jcurtismoran.com
www.jcurtismoran.com

www.ingramcontent.com/pod-product-compliance
Lightning Source LLC
Chambersburg PA
CBHW070744160726
48004CB00001B/43

9 798987 622933